D1146729

NUFFIELD DESIGN & TECHNOLOGY

STUDENT'S
BOOK

Longman

Edinburgh Gate

Pearson Education Limited
Edinburgh Gate
Harlow
Essex
CM20 2JE
England

ISBN 0582 41114 9

First published 1995
Revised edition 2000
Fifth impression 2004
Designed and produced by Gecko Ltd, Bicester, Oxon OX6 0JT.
Printed in Singapore (FOP)

The Publisher's policy is to use paper manufactured from sustainable forests.

Project directors

Executive director Dr David Barlex (Brunel University)

Contributors

Dr David Barlex, Brunel University
Catherine Budgett-Meakin, Intermediate Technology Group
Jo Compton, Institute of Education, University of London
Keith Everett, Education Consultant
David Fair, Education Consultant
Nick Given, Exeter University
Ann Hampton, Intermediate Technology Group
Margaret Jepson, John Moores University, Liverpool
Neil McLean, BECTA
Mike Martin, Intermediate Technology Group
Jane Murray, Somerset LEA
Julie Messenger, Sawtry Community College
Jon Parker, Northampton Advisory and Inspection Service
James Pitt, York University
John Plater, Old Palace School, Croydon
Val Rea, Intermediate Technology Group
Marion Rutland, Roehampton Institute
Eileen Taylor, Sefton LEA
Irene Tilley, Education Consultant
Torben Steeg, Manchester University

Early developments

Ian Fletcher, Warwickshire LEA
Ann Hepher, Kingston LEA
School of Education, University of Bath
South West Region School Technology Forum
North West Region of TVEI
Nottingham Technology Education Development Group, Nottingham Trent University
Nuffield Chelsea Curriculum Trust
United Biscuits Leicestershire Development Group

The Nuffield Design and Technology Project gratefully acknowledges the support of the following commercial concerns in developing the published materials:

GEC Education Liaison

Zeneca Pharmaceuticals (formerly ICI Pharmaceuticals)

Tesco Training & Education Department

United Biscuits UK Ltd

Picture researcher Louise Edgeworth

Indexer Richard Raper, Indexing Specialists

Safety advisor Colin Whitfield

Illustrations by Gecko Ltd, Barry Atkins, Nathan Barlex, Gill Bishop, Harvey Collins, Joe Little, John Plumb, Archie Plumb, Chris Rothero, Martin Sanders, Tony Wilkins

Contents

Acknowledgements

We are grateful to the following for permission to reproduce photographs and other copyright material:
(T = top, B = bottom, L = left, R = right, C = centre, A = above)

Andes Press Agency 7BR, 47BL, 50TL; Authentics 247; Aviemore Photographic 191T; Barnabys Picture Library 209BC & 209BR(Ruth Turner); Biophoto Associates 15AC; John Birdsall 4T, 15BC, 15B, 47TL, 103B, 162TL, 162BC, 162BR, 164, 171T, 179T, 179CL, 179BR; Blundell Harling Ltd 209TR; Bridgeman Art Library 4CL(Victoria & Albert Museum, London), 4CR(Private Collection), 4BR(Private Collection); British Motor Industry Heritage Trust/Rover Group 25; Neill Bruce Photographic 7T; J.Allan Cash 194T, 194BL, 199C, 207B; Chris Coggins 35-38(screen frames); Collections 46(Anthea Sieveking); Colorsport 191TC, 194CL, 194CR; Cotton Council International 117CL; Crafts Council 103TL(Martin Chetwin), 103TR(J.Cleverly), 130TR(S.Bosence), 136BL(Anne Sicher); Creda Ltd 72T, 72C; Paddy Cutts 9, 34B, 41C, 42B, 47TR, 50BL, 76T, 192T, 193TR, 195B, 196T, 199T, 199B, 202T, 202C, 203, 205, 206, 209TL, 209TC, 209CL, 209BL, 216T(inset), 216T, 216CL, 216CR, 216BR, 218; Charlotte Deane 191BL, 200T; Dowdeswell Engineering Co Ltd 193B; Duracell UK-MDPR 216BL; Economatics (Education) Ltd 34T, 238BL; Caterina Fadda 246(Bill Osment); Ford Motor Company Ltd 41B; Werner Forman 130TL, 130CL; Gillette Group UK Ltd 39; Nick Given 207T; Halfords Ltd 195T; Robert Harding Picture Library 4BL, 62, 130CR, 136BR, 209CR(IPC Magazines); Michael Holford 191TR; Holt Studios International 117TC; Hotpoint 238TL; ICCE Photolibrary 16(Sue Boulton), 65(Sue Boulton), 76C(Mark Boulton), 76B(Mark Boulton), 191BR(Mark Boulton); Jaguar 74T; Neville Kuypers Associates 149, 150, 158, 173; Lego UK Ltd 34C; Longman Photographic Unit 8, 22, 30, 60T, 68, 74B, 79, 80, 81, 92, 93, 97, 99, 101, 102, 117B, 122, 124, 129, 147, 148, 159, 161, 162TR, 162BL, 162CR, 165, 171B, 178, 179CR, 179BL, 181-184, 186T, 192C, 192B, 201B; Mansell Collection 15T; McDonald's Restaurants Ltd 7BL; Milepost 92$\frac{1}{2}$ 200B; Northern Foods 185T; PPL Ltd 194BR; Pictor International 6T; Pifco Ltd 202B; John Plater 63; Potterton Myson Ltd 43T; Science Photo Library 226L(Malcolm Fielding, the BOC Group plc), 238TR(Sheila Terry); Harry Smith Collection 201T; Sony UK Ltd 196B; Lara Sparey 113-116; Stanley Automatic Doors 226R; Still Pictures 78TL(Mark Edwards), 78TR(John Maier), 78BL(Mark Edwards), 78BR(Nigel Dickinson), 117TL(Paul Harrison); Stone 117TR(Arnulf Husmo); TEP 85, 87, 88, 89, 90; TESCO 185B, 186C, 186B; Technical Blinds 242; Techsoft UK Ltd 93BL; Shirley Thompson 193TL; John Walmsley 3, 6B, 10T, 41T, 44, 47BR, 60B, 120, 121, 151, 152, 153, 154, 238BR, 243T, 243B; Wind Energy Group 72B(Margaret Haynes); The Stock Market Photo Agency 2, 10B, 40, 50TR, 50BR, 117C, 117CR, 226C.

We are grateful to the following organisations for their assistance in setting up photographs:
Harlow Technical College 92(except T), 97, 99T, CL, CR & BL, 102; Supercast 92T.

Using this book

When you do design and technology at school you have to design and make things for people to use. This can be tricky and there will be times when you...

- are puzzled;
- can't work out what's important;
- don't know how to do something;
- need some information;
- can't decide what will work.

That's when you need this *Student's Book*. It contains lots of information that is useful for design and technology.

To help you understand and use this information it is linked to short practical activities called Resource Tasks. The reference numbers for the tasks are given in boxes like this:

Resource Task
SRT 1

1

1 Strategies

Working methods for designing

Each design and make task you do will be made up of lots of smaller tasks. You will need to use different methods or **strategies** for each of these.

Your teacher may help you to learn some of these strategies by setting you Resource Tasks that give you practice.

▲ *There are lots of needs and preferences here.*

Identifying needs and likes

What to look for

In designing something it is important to find out the users' needs and what they like (their preferences). Look at these three important areas:

- **The place** – Is it small or large, crowded or empty, noisy or quiet, well-lit or gloomy, pleasant, comfortable?

- **The people** – Is there a wide range of ages, cultures, sizes and appearance and different genders, or are they all similar?

What are they doing? Are they having difficulties? What can you tell from their faces?

- **The existing products and systems** – Are they easy to use? Do they work well? Could they be improved?

Tools for recording

You can record your findings in many different ways:

Notes – You only need a note pad and a pencil. Write up your notes in more detail soon afterwards.

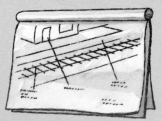

Sketches – A quick sketch is often better than a lot of writing. Write short notes on your sketch to explain the important points.

Audiotapes – Before you start using a pocket tape recorder check that it works, is adjusted to your voice level and that other noises do not drown out your voice. Carry spare batteries and tapes. Producing a transcript (written copy) can take a long time.

Photographs – This is a good way to record a situation. First you need to learn how to use the camera. Keep brief notes on

each shot you take and use them as captions for the photographs.

Videotapes – The equipment for video recording is expensive and you will need training to use it. Many people behave differently if they realize they are being filmed, so you have to be discreet. The tape may need editing, with a commentary. This can take a long time.

Resource Task
SRT 3, RMRT 1

Interviewing

Sometimes the only way to find out about something is to ask someone who knows. You will need to conduct an interview. Here is some useful advice:

- Dress tidily and be polite.
- Ask for permission if you want to tape record the interview.
- Have a list of questions ready plus a pencil and pad to jot down answers.
- Some people like to see the questions beforehand to prepare their answers.
- Do all you can to put the person at ease. Smile, be friendly and, if possible, hold the interview in a room where you can both sit down and feel comfortable.
- Make sure that the person understands the question and give her the chance to ask if she is not sure.
- Say 'Thank you' at the end of the interview.

▲ *Conducting an interview.*

Looking in books and magazines

Other people may already have written about your subject in books or magazines.

In libraries books are organized into subjects using the Dewey decimal numbering system. You can look up the numbers for a subject. The books will be arranged on the shelves according to these numbers.

You may have to choose between several different books. Use the contents pages to find out what each is about, and read the introduction to find out its level. You may be able to borrow it. If it is for reference only, you can make notes or take photocopies of important pages.

Specialist magazines, on sale at large newsagents, report on the latest developments in technology and the technical aspects of sports or hobbies.

▲ *The choice of information sources can sometimes be bewildering!*

Resource Tasks
SRT 4, RMRT 3

3

...Identifying needs and likes

Analysing needs

Designers and technologists must understand people's needs so as to be able to meet them. The **PIES** checklist helps us to think about needs. Each letter stands for a different type of need.

P We all need food, water and air to breathe. We need to keep warm and be protected from the weather. We need regular exercise. These are **physical** needs.

I We need to learn new things and to be stimulated. We use games, books, television and radio, and so on, to meet these **intellectual** needs.

E We all need to feel safe. We need to feel that people care about us, and to have ways of expressing our feelings. These are **emotional** needs.

S Most of us like to spend time with our friends, talking and doing things together. These are **social** needs.

▲ *The PIES checklist will help you identify these people's needs.*

Exploring style

People of different cultures have different views on what is visually pleasing, and even within the same culture people often disagree. Fashion and changing style influence what people like. It is important to be aware of these differences when you are designing. The area of design concerned with how a product looks is called **aesthetics**.

These pieces of furniture come from a variety of times and cultures. ▶

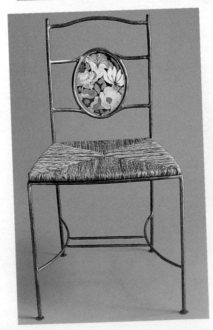

Resource Tasks
SRT 5, 17, 41, RMRT 2

4

Appealing to our senses

What makes something beautiful? Not everyone agrees – it depends on our individual taste and on our culture. But all designers, including you, need to be aware of some basic principles. A beautiful product is pleasant to look at and pleasant to use. This is true both for something small, like a cup or kettle or personal stereo, and for something large, such as a building. Designers work with a number of visual elements shown in the panel below.

So designers have all these elements at their disposal – line, shape, form, space, light, texture, colour and size. The secret of good design is to arrange these elements into a single, harmonious whole.

- **Line** is the most basic element. Lines can create shape, pattern and movement.

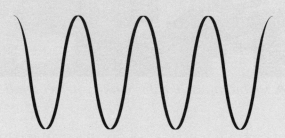

- **Shapes** give objects character. They can be positive or negative. You should use the word **shape** to describe two-dimensional objects.

- Designers use the word **form** when talking about three-dimensional objects. Some objects are based on geometrical forms, others have more organic forms. The form of the object determines the **space** occupied by the object.

- Designers also work with **light**. They need to think how light is reflected from an object. Some parts will be lighter or darker than others.

- The **texture** of an object, whether it is rough or smooth, hard or soft, also affects this. Texture applies both to the look of an object, and to the way it feels.

- The **colour** of an object is very important. Colour, more than any other quality, has an emotional or psychological impact on people.

- Finally, designers need to think about the **size** or **scale** of an object – about how it relates to the people who will be using the object.

Resource Tasks

SRT 19, RMRT 2

You can understand this by thinking about music. A good piece of music is not just a wild collection of unconnected sounds. There is a basic structure involving melody, rhythm and harmony. In a vocal piece, the words and form of the music combine to make a pleasant or exciting composition. It is the same with a product. If the shapes, colours, textures and other qualities are thrown together without an underlying structure, the end result is chaotic and unpleasant. So, like a composer, the designer uses certain principles to orchestrate the visual elements.

If everything about a product is the same it can look monotonous. So the designer introduces **variety**. The designer also thinks about **rhythm**, sometimes using repeat forms or shapes to create a feeling of expectancy. Certain parts of the design might be more important than others; so the designer might give these greater **dominance** or **emphasis**. Finally the designer needs to consider **proportion**. These are all different ways of organising the basic visual elements listed on page 5. The overall goal is to design a beautiful object in which all the different elements come together as one, harmonious whole.

▲ *Do buildings like this make you feel small?*

▲ *Two products for playing tapes but very different aesthetics!*

...Identifying needs and likes

Looking at colour

Colour is important in our lives. It can make us feel excitement and happiness or relaxation and sadness. Designers use this knowledge when designing products.

▲ *Red gives this car an exciting appearance.*

You can set up colour preference tests (using colour cards and a questionnaire) quite easily to give you an idea of how people react to certain colours. But you also need to think about how and where the colour is to be used: even if blue is someone's favourite colour, they might not be too happy if you gave them blue food!

◄ *A colour wheel shows a complete range of colours to help you make choices.*

Colour is important in helping us to identify the flavour of food. We can easily be fooled when the familiar colours of foods are altered or disguised. For example, people find it difficult to identify the flavours of soft drinks when they are blindfolded.

Colour influences people's behaviour. Red can make us feel warm and comfortable, but can also make us feel restless after a while.

▲ *Colour often gives a clue about the flavour of a drink.*

▲ *A colour scheme may encourage you to remain seated or to get up once the meal is over.*

Resource Task

SRT 18

Advertisers and manufacturers use colour to shock or gain our attention. They have also discovered that we associate certain colours with certain types of product.

You would expect to find different types of product in different colour packages. ▶

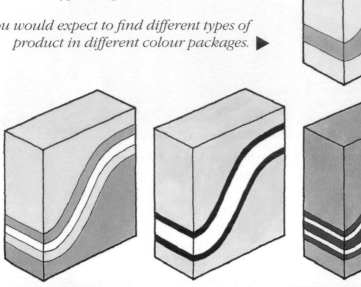

Image boards

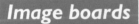

One way of thinking about the people for whom you are designing is to set up an image board. This is a collection of pictures – cut-outs from magazines or newspapers, quick sketches, specially taken photographs – to do with the people. Pictures of the people themselves, where they live, where they work or go to school, what they do in their leisure time, the food they eat, the clothes they wear, where they shop – these can all go on the image board, which will help you understand the people's life-style and what might appeal to them.

Resource Tasks
SRT 8, 15

Design briefs

Understanding a design brief

When you are designing, you will start by exploring a situation where there is a need or want. If you decide that there is a practical problem that you can solve, you will need a **design brief**. This summarizes the aim of a design project and states briefly the kind of thing that is needed. Here is an example.

The messy desk top in the picture above presents an opportunity for design. There is a need for some way of keeping the desk top tidy. The design brief might be:

> ❝ Find a way to keep drawing equipment tidy on a desk top. ❞

There are many possible solutions to this design brief. The picture on the right shows some of them, ranging from simple containers to more complicated racking systems, and even a computer-aided drawing system. This is an **open brief** and allows the designer a large degree of freedom to experiment with design proposals. An open brief does not say what the solution to the problem is going to be.

▲ *Ways of keeping a desk tidy.*

Sometimes a design brief narrows the likely outcome. For example, the design brief for the same situation as above could have been:

> ❝ Design and make a pencil box. ❞

Although it is still possible to produce a variety of different solutions from the brief, the kind of product that is to be made is more limited. This is a **closed brief**.

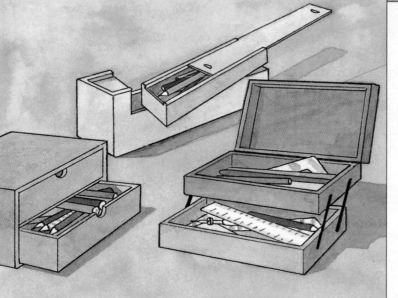

▲ *Different designs for a pencil box.*

Writing a design brief

When writing a brief, choose the words that you use carefully. It is best not to make your design brief too detailed. For example, instead of writing the brief 'Design and make a pencil box', use a more general term like 'container' or 'desk tidy'. This offers you a much wider choice of solutions, and you may find a more interesting way of solving the problem of clutter on a desk than making a pencil box!

Other good words to use in design briefs are 'device', 'item', 'system' and 'could'. For example:

- Design and make a device to help a young child learn to tell the time.

- Design and make a storage system that could be used in a nursery.

- Design and make a container for snack food.

Here are some situations for design, and design briefs that have been written in response to them.

| **Resource Task** |
| SRT I |

Specifying the product

Writing a performance specification

On starting a design and make task you will need to develop the design brief into a **performance specification**.

This should always:

- describe what the product has to do.

It might also state:

- what the product should look like;
- that the product should work in a particular way – use a particular material or energy source, perhaps;
- any legal or environmental requirements the product should meet.

You can use a specification to check your design ideas as they develop. In this way you avoid designing something that does not meet the requirements. You will also need to check the finished product against it.

Examples of some products and their specifications are shown on these two pages.

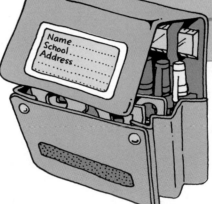

SPECIFICATION
SCHOOL EQUIPMENT BAG

What it has to do:
- hold pens, pencils, rubber, ruler and stencils
- stay shut when closed but be easy to open
- be tough enough to withstand everyday use
- be small enough to go in a rucksack
- be easy to carry about on its own

What it has to look like:
- be brightly coloured
- have a modern look and indicate who it belongs to

Other requirements:
- use biodegradable materials as far as possible

SPECIFICATION
PIECE OF JEWELLERY

What it has to do:
- be suitable for everyday wear
- remind people about endangered species

What it has to look like:
- be based on animal or plant form

Other requirements:
- be part of a range of similar items for teenagers sold in a chain store
- use natural materials as far as possible

Other considerations

You will need to take into account other things as you develop your design ideas. You should ask yourself:

- How much time do I have for designing and making?
- What tools and equipment are available?
- What materials and components are available?
- How much money do I have to spend?

Using a performance specification

Once you have some design ideas, review them against the specification. Ask:

- Will it do the job?
- Will it look right?
- Will it work?
- Is it a practical suggestion?

Answering such questions will ensure that your designing gets off to a good start.

As you develop your design ideas, it is important to ask yourself these questions again, to avoid losing sight of what the product has to do.

Once you have made your product you need to evaluate it. Evaluating it against the performance specification is one way to do this but there are other important evaluation techniques (see pages 47–50).

SPECIFICATION
HEALTHY EATING FOOD PRODUCT

What it has to do:
- provide the main meal of the day as a 'single-cook' dish
- be suitable for someone on a low fat, high-fibre diet
- be suitable for microwave cooking
- introduce consumers to spicy foods

What it has to look like:
- be strongly coloured
- contain recognizable foods

Other requirements:
- be part of a series of food products from Mexico

SPECIFICATION
INTRUDER ALARM

What it has to do:
- detect break-ins through doors or windows
- sound a loud alarm
- show on a display panel where the break-in happened

What it has to look like:
- its presence should be obvious and not hidden
- its visible parts should look modern
- the display panel should be easy to read

Other requirements:
- it should be impossible to deactivate it from outside the building

Revising the specification

Sometimes you will have an exciting design idea which does not meet the specification. It is very tempting to change the specification so that it fits the new idea. This can lead to serious problems unless everyone involved with the design is consulted and agrees to the changes.

Resource Tasks
SRT 2, 6

Generating design ideas

Brainstorming

Brainstorming is a good way for a group of people to generate (create) lots of ideas quickly. This is how to do it.

1 **State the problem or need.** Write down the problem on a large sheet of paper or a chalkboard. Be sure to record the problem and not what you think the solution might be.

2 **Write down every idea suggested.** One member of the group can write down everything, even if the ideas or words seem silly at first. Use words, phrases or pictures to capture the ideas. As suggestions are recorded, they will spark off more ideas.

3 **Concentrate on quantity.** Produce as many ideas as possible. This gives you lots to choose from when it comes to picking the best.

▲ *Sorting out the ideas.*

4 **Don't make judgements.** If you say someone's idea is stupid, it may stop them producing more.

5 **Allow a set time for the session.** The first part of a brainstorming session usually produces the more obvious ideas and thoughts, so allow enough time for some unusual ideas to emerge.

6 **Sorting out the ideas.** The ideas collected now have to be sorted out. Repeated ideas should be removed. Some will be impossible to use: they might be too difficult, cost too much or take too much time. This will leave a set of new ideas that can be used as starting points for design and technology.

Knowing when and how to use brainstorming

Brainstorming does not work for problems that have only one solution, such as the size of the population of France or the sales of television sets. You would look these up in a book or on a database. Brainstorming does not work well if one member of the group knows a lot more than the others about the subject of the problem.

Brainstorming only works if:

- people don't butt in;
- the ideas are short;
- people don't criticize one another's ideas;
- the ideas are imaginative;
- the group members use the earlier ideas to spark off more ideas.

Bubble charts

Before you can start work on any design brief you need to ask: *what? where? when? who?* and *why?* The answers will give you a better understanding of the problem. It is also a good way of generating ideas for design solutions. One way of recording your answers to these questions is to draw a bubble chart.

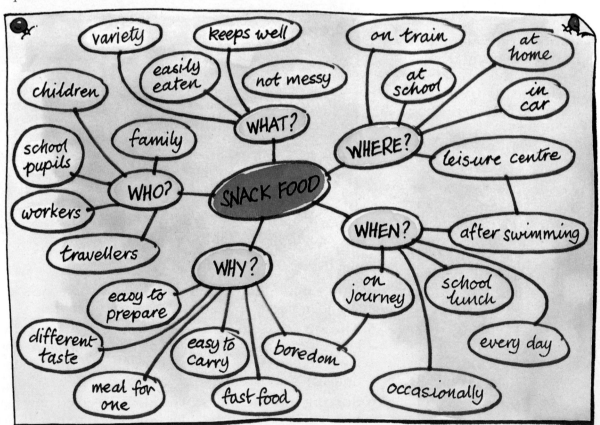

Start by writing a key word or even a design brief statement in a bubble in the centre of the page. Then use the questions to generate more words and ideas. You can combine this with brainstorming to come up with ideas.

▲ *A bubble chart helps you to understand the problem.*

Resource Task

SRT 11

… *Generating design ideas*

Observational drawing

The world around us has been a rich source of ideas and inspiration for many designers and inventors. Leonardo da Vinci made sketches of subjects from nature which inspired his wonderful ideas and inventions.

   The example below shows how close study through drawing has resulted in designs for jewellery with a pattern.

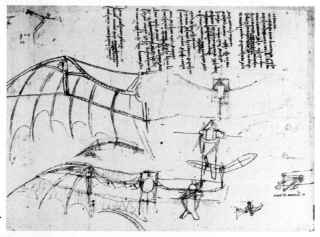

Leonardo da Vinci developed designs for aircraft wings by observing and drawing birds' wings. ▶

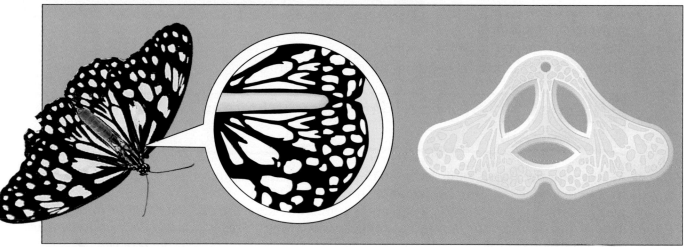

▲ *This brooch design is based on a butterfly although it doesn't look like one.*

Making connections

Design ideas are rarely completely new. Often the idea may have been suggested by something in nature, or by connecting two different ideas in a new way. For example, if you needed to provide portable shelter for a hill-walker, you might look at natural or man-made forms of protection: umbrella, snail shell, bus shelter, seed pod, eyelid, dustbin liner. Each of these suggests a different way of solving the problem for the hill-walker. Each provides an interesting starting point for further development.

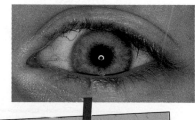

Resource Tasks
SRT 12, 13, 16

▲ *Connecting ideas can help generate new designs.*

Attribute analysis

Designers and technologists use a technique called **attribute analysis** to help them produce new designs for familiar objects.

A group of pupils used attribute analysis to design a pen which a garden centre might give away to visitors. This is how they did it:

1 They wrote down all the different words they could think of to describe the pen.

2 Then they looked at each word to see what it represented, as in the photograph.

The body of the pen is made from plastic – a **material**. The pen is a tube – a **shape**.

The pen is rigid and this is to do with the material's **properties**.

It is light and this is to do with its **weight**.

It is cheap and this describes **cost**.

3 They used these ideas as headings for a table like this:

Material	Shape	Properties	Weight	Cost

4 As a group, the pupils brainstormed entries for each column. In the 'material' column, for instance, they wrote down plastic, metal, glass, pottery, wood and stone. They kept the idea of a garden centre in mind to suggest some ideas. This is their completed table:

An attribute analysis table for producing new designs of pen. ▼

Material	Shape	Properties	Weight	Cost
plastic metal glass pottery wood stone	tube cube leaf spiral	rigid soft flexible	light heavy	cheap expensive

5 By looking across their table in different ways they produced different ideas. One was for a metal, spiral-shaped, flexible, heavy, expensive pen. They decided to make a wooden, leaf-shaped pen that was rigid, light and cheap as the gift for the garden centre. What would you decide?

You can use attribute analysis to help you think about the design of any product.

Resource Tasks
SRT 14, 40

Modelling – how it can help

When you come up with a design idea, you are the only one who knows anything about it. While it is just an idea you cannot test it, see what it will look like or know that it will work. Modelling helps you to convert the idea into a form that you can think about more easily and show to other people to get their opinions.

How can I get my idea clear?

No, that one will go round the other way!

Look – like this.

Sometimes you can model your idea by talking about it. At other times you will need to model it on paper using sketches and notes. Often, as you do this modelling you will realize that there are things about your idea that are not clear enough yet. So it has to be rethought out for you to come up with a better description or clearer sketch.

You may need to work in three dimensions to get a really clear picture of your design.

Some models will help you to see how it will look, while others will help you to see how it might work.

You can use computers to model your design ideas too. For example, some software can help with electronic circuit design.

TYRANNOBURGER REX

Pages 18–38 describe the different methods of modelling that you can use to help you when you are designing.

You can use modelling in three ways:

● to clarify and develop your design ideas;

● to evaluate your design ideas;

● to show your design ideas to other people.

I've got it now – just needed that extra link.

17

Modelling product appearance on paper

Sketches as well as talking help define design ideas. Most designers model their ideas by sketching them, adding notes as they go to make things clearer.

These quick drawings are called **annotated sketches**. Although they are rough, they are very useful to you and other members of the design team because they help you think about your ideas.

Simple shapes and guidelines

Use faint pencil guidelines when drawing simple shapes.

If the object you are sketching is symmetrical (both halves the same), a lightly drawn centre-line can act as a useful guide. For irregular shapes, mark out the main features so that you can position everything correctly.

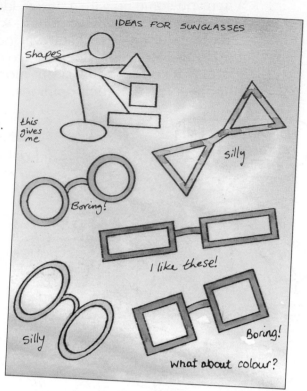

Keep all your sketched lines faint until you are sure that you have drawn the correct shape. Then go over the outlines to make the shape stand out from any guidelines.

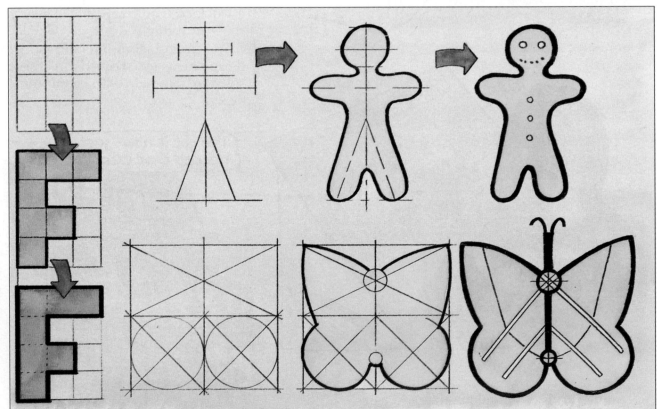

Resource Task

SRT 21

...Modelling product appearance on paper

Grids

Grid papers are useful for mapping or planning arrangements of shapes. You can sketch garden plans, room layouts and circuit boards more easily and accurately on squared grid paper.

Grids are also good for developing interesting patterns. You can plot more complex shapes, and use different types of grid paper to experiment with pattern. With a grid, you can repeat a pattern accurately and regularly.

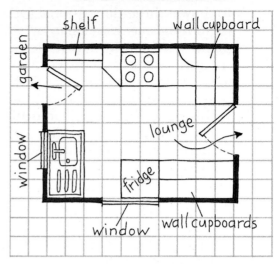

▲ *Planning a room layout on grid paper.*

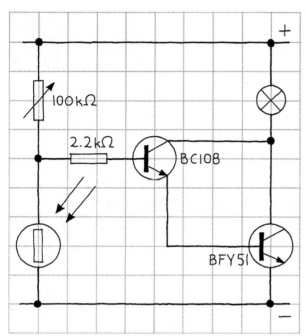

▲ *A circuit board layout.*

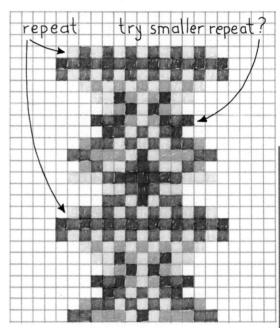

▲ *Using a grid to experiment with repeat patterns.*

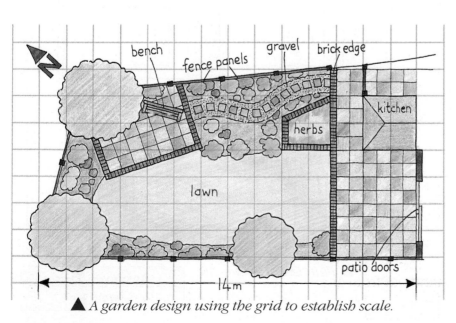

▲ *A garden design using the grid to establish scale.*

Resource Task
SRT 22

19

Quick 3D views

To draw a three-dimensional (3D) view of something start with a flat, two-dimensional (2D) shape – say, a front or side view of the object. Draw in parallel lines from the corners or edges of the shape at an angle of about 45°. Joining up these lines will give you a 3D form.

This view of an object, an **oblique view**, is an easy way of drawing circular or curved forms because oblique views are always based on 'flat' front or side views.

You can use the squares on grid paper as a guide when drawing the basic shape and the parallel lines. If you don't want the grid lines to appear on your finished sketch, draw on a piece of thin paper laid over the grid and fixed down with tape or clips.

Simple shapes made 3D. ▶

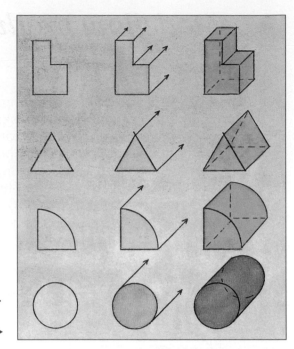

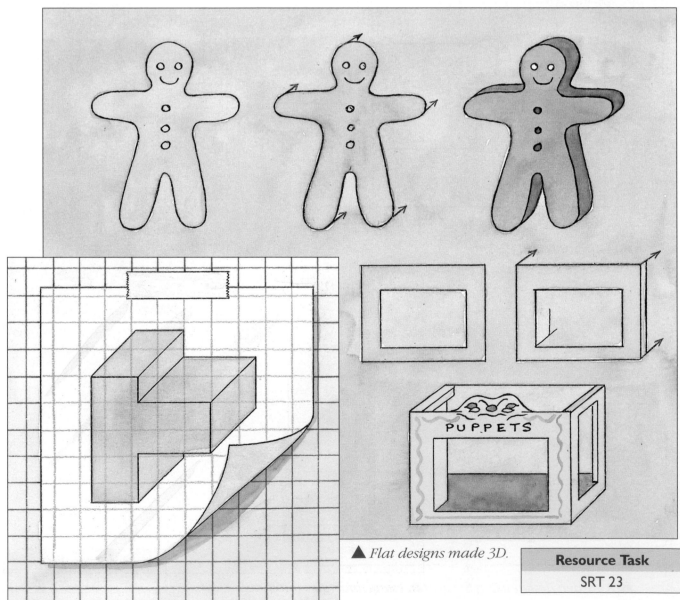

▲ *Flat designs made 3D.*

Resource Task

SRT 23

...Modelling product appearance on paper

Crating

This is useful for drawing more complicated objects. Imagine that the object is in a box or crate, and use that as a starting point for your sketch.

   Draw the box as a 3D view (see page 20), then draw your object by taking parts away from the box.

   You may need to break the object down into several boxes to create the shape you want.

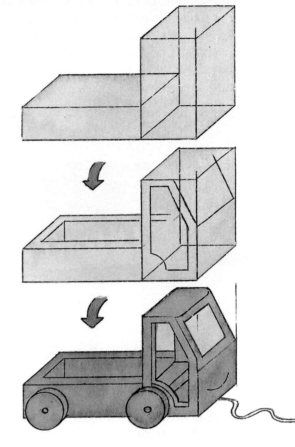

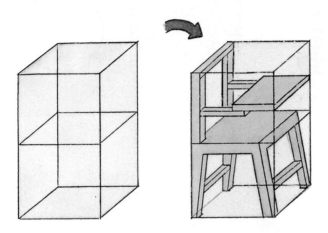

▲ *Using crating for 3D sketches.*

Thick and thin lines

When you are using guidelines and crating, it is important to make your final outlines stand out from other lines on the paper. A darker outline distinguishes the shape from the construction lines.

   Vary line thickness to help make the object you have drawn look more solid and three-dimensional. But do not overdo this. Use the simple rules in the picture as a guide.

Resource Task
SRT 24

1 Add a thick line to an edge where only one surface is visible.

2 Leave a thin line where two visible surfaces meet.

3 For extra impact, draw in the thickest line around the outline of the object.

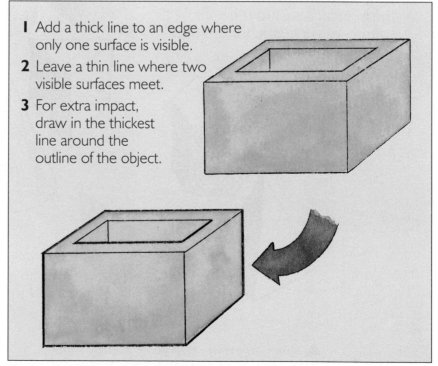

▲ *Using thick and thin lines.*

Making things look solid

Line drawings can describe flat shapes and 3D forms, but lines only show a framework. In reality, we cannot see these lines on objects.

Instead, we notice that one surface is darker than another because of the effects of light and shade.

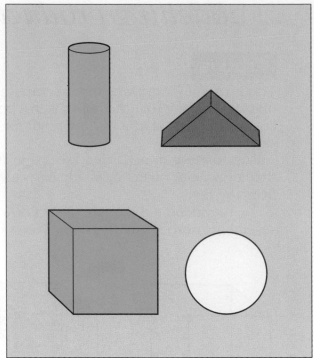

Shading makes the object you have drawn look more solid. It shows the effect of light falling on its surface.

The variations of light and dark are called **tone**.

The simplest way to show difference in tone is to use pencil or pencil-crayon shading. This will go from very light, for the side of the object closest to the light source, to very dark, for the part that is in shade.

▼ *Shading can make objects look solid.*

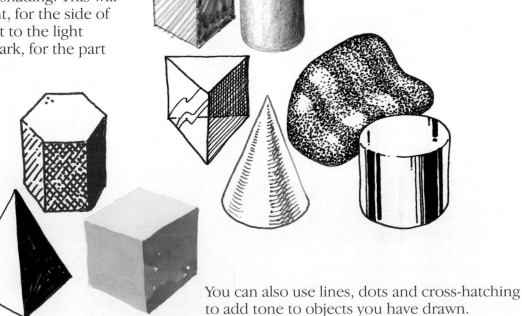

You can also use lines, dots and cross-hatching to add tone to objects you have drawn.

▲ *Some different methods of adding tone to your drawings.*

Resource Task

SRT 25

Modelling product appearance in 3D

Rapid model making

Making a 3D model, using quick techniques and easy-to-work materials, is a useful way of finding out whether your ideas look right. It may also help you see whether the proportions and scale of your design are right.

Seeing your idea in 3D at an early stage may help to avoid expensive mistakes later on.

These kinds of models are often called **sketch models** because you can make them quickly.

Trying out ideas for a piece of jewellery using paper taped on to wire. ▶

Key points:

- Decide on the level of detail you need. (Remember, these are only intended to give quick impressions.)
- Use the most appropriate materials for the model. (For example, you would not use Plasticine to see what a pop-up card would look like!)
- Choose a suitable scale for the model.
- Choose materials that are easy to work or assemble.

Using foam models to help make a decision about scale. ▶

Materials for rapid model making

Plastic foams

Foam is light but rigid and good for making block models. It is easy to cut with any blade and can be shaped with a file or rasp.

SAFETY

Beware of dust particles – use a mask.

A hot-wire cutter is effective for shaping foam blocks, but can result in dangerous fumes, so, again, great care is needed. **The heating wire should never become red-hot. Keep a window or door open to prevent fumes building up.**

To join pieces together, use a special adhesive – the wrong sort will attack the plastic foam. Temporary joints can be made with cocktail sticks.

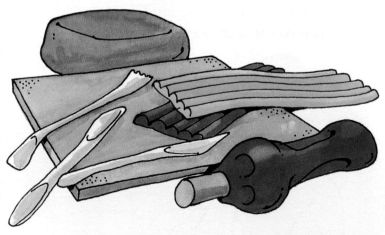

Found materials: packaging, fabrics

Cans, bottles, polystyrene foam, card and cardboard tubes are useful sources of shapes and forms for experimenting.

Reclaimed fabrics or remnants can be used for ideas for textiles or to make sketch models of fashion items.

Paper, newsprint, wrapping paper, wallpaper

These are suitable for rapid modelling of ideas involving textiles or where patterns and templates might be used. They are also good for quick packaging models.

Work quickly: cut, tear and fold. Fix using a glue stick, stapler or tape. Double-sided tape is particularly useful.

Plasticine and clay

These are easy to mould into shape, and so are good materials for modelling a small, irregular object. Details and texture can be added by pressing onto the surface with cocktail sticks, pencils or textured boards.

Plasticine can be reused. Clay is easy to mould, but can be messy and will set hard.

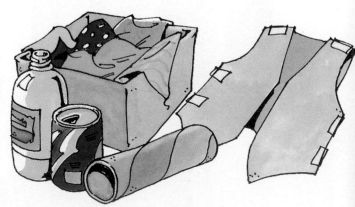

Modelling product performance on paper

Sketches and diagrams can help you to see how your design might work, as well as look.

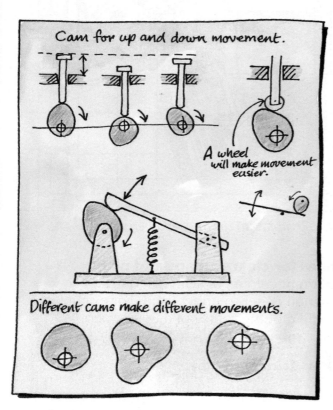

▲ *Thumbnail sketches of how a design might work.* ▼

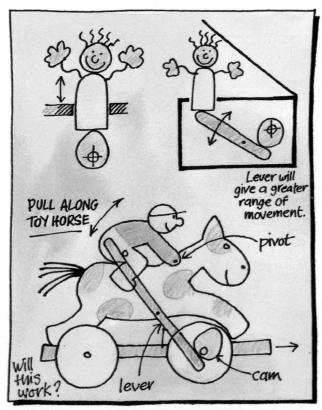

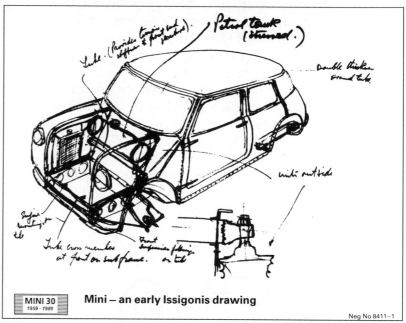

MINI 30
1959–1989

Mini – an early Issigonis drawing

Neg No 8411–1

▲ *A thumbnail sketch by Issigonis, the designer of the Mini.*

Thumbnail sketches

As you begin planning your design, it is enough to sketch the main parts.

These rapid sketches are called **thumbnails**. They should show very little detail and help you sort out your thinking on paper. Because thumbnails allow you to put ideas down quickly, they do not slow down the flow of your design thinking.

Remember to:

- keep the drawings or diagrams quick and simple;
- use a pencil, fine line marker or biro – whatever you find easiest;
- draw flat, 2D outlines without taking time to shade and colour;
- use only stick figures for people;
- use a word or notes to make things clearer;
- use symbols such as arrows to show movement or direction.

Try out any 'shorthand' techniques that you can think of to help you put down *only* the essential information.

As you become more practised at quick sketching, you will find that the drawings can actually suggest new ideas (see page 15).

Maps and plans

As your design idea becomes clearer, you may need to make more accurate 2D drawings that show greater detail.

Maps and plans can show the location of objects or components. A plan is a view of an object or area seen from above. It is sometimes called a bird's-eye view. It may be used to show the position of objects in a room, or the layout of smaller details, such as the buttons on a remote control unit or components on a circuit board (see page 19).

A map can be useful for plotting the movement of people or traffic, or for locating places at a distance.

▲ *Using a plan to arrange kitchen units.*

Guidelines for clearer maps and plans

- Use different colours or symbols to make information easier to understand. For example, you could plot the routes of different people around a room using different colours to avoid confusion.
- Use symbols to indicate objects.
- Use dotted lines or arrows to show movement.
- Always include a key to explain your symbols.
- If possible, include an indication of scale or size.

50 mm

▲ *The layout of an easy-to-use remote control unit.*

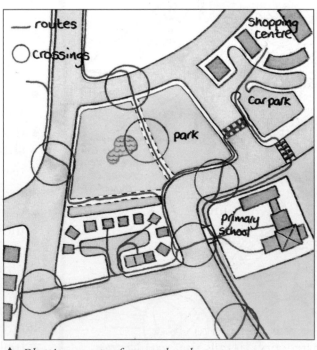

▲ *Plotting routes from school.*

...Modelling product performance on paper

Sometimes you will need to draw a 3D view of your design to see how it might fit together and work. These two pages describe some techniques that you could use.

Hidden details

Often the working details of an object are hidden inside. You can show these hidden details on a drawing in several ways:

- Draw dotted lines to show the outline of the shapes hidden inside the object.
- Make a **see-through drawing** of your design.
- Draw what you would see if you cut through the object – a **section drawing** of your design. This can show the thickness of the construction material.

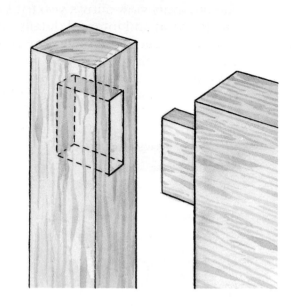

▲ *normal view*

▲ *'see through' view*

▲ *sectional view*

Magnified details

The smaller details on a drawing may be difficult to see or understand. You can overcome this problem by imagining that you are holding a magnifying glass over the detailed part and draw an enlarged view of it.

Drawing a frame around the magnified detail helps to focus attention on it.

Use this method to show construction details that would not normally be seen.

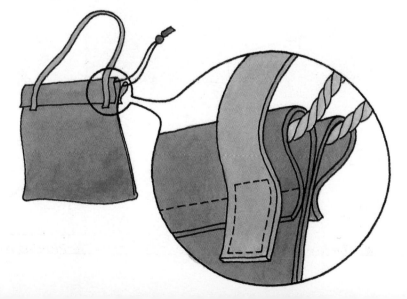

Cut-away views

The cut-away view allows you to show the construction and internal details of your design. Layers or parts of the object are removed or **cut away** to enable these details to be seen.

A cut-away view should only be a sketch. There is no point in producing a highly finished illustration.

Exploded views

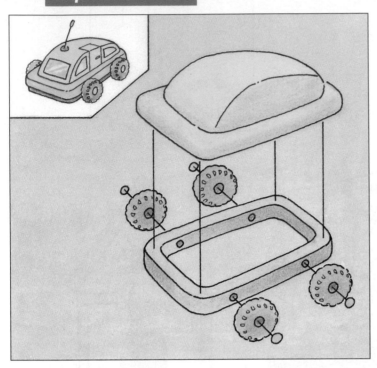

An **exploded view** is a useful way of showing how all the parts of a design idea fit together.

The title suggests an explosion, but the drawing really shows the object as if it had been pulled apart.

The pieces should be organized to show how they fit together. Arrange the parts along straight lines and put faint lines in to show the connections, if necessary.

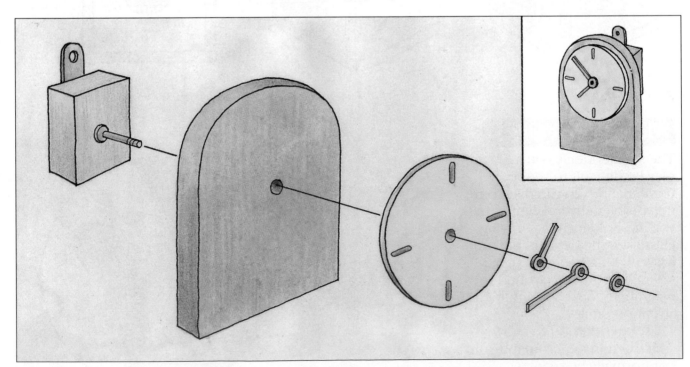

Modelling product performance in 3D

Three-dimensional models are a good way of exploring how a design idea will work as well as how it will look (see page 23). Sometimes these will be quick **sketch models** made with inexpensive materials. Sometimes they will be more complicated models made with construction kits.

Ergonomic modelling

In designing things for people to use we need to take the human form into account. The study of how easy it is for people to use objects and environments is called **ergonomics**. The ergonomics of your design proposal will show how safe, comfortable and easy to use it will be.

People come in different shapes and sizes and they move in different ways. If your model is life-size you can ask people to test it and record their responses.

Using easily worked materials like Plasticine or foam, you can adapt your model and find the design that suits most people.

Anthropometric data

Charts and tables can show average measurements for people in different age-groups for things like height, reach, grip and sight lines.

▲ *Card models used to test designs for handles.*

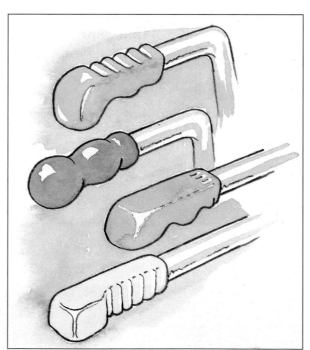

▲ *Plasticine models used to find the best grip.*

Such information is called **anthropometric data**. You can use it when you are making models to work out the details of, for instance, handles, or how your design might be held.

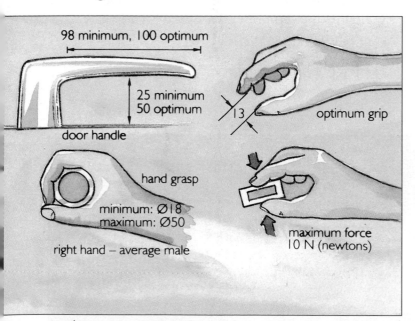

98 minimum, 100 optimum

25 minimum
50 optimum

door handle

13

optimum grip

hand grasp

minimum: Ø18
maximum: Ø50

right hand – average male

maximum force
10 N (newtons)

▲ *Making handles fit hands.*

Resource Task

RMRT 17

Modelling movement

Some designs involve moving parts and mechanical components like **cams**. Drawing these design ideas may not be enough. A working model can show actual movement and help you to see if your idea will work.

Remember:

- Keep your working model simple. Do not add unnecessary detail. Concentrate on the parts that move.

- Work on a scale that will let you model quickly. Tiny details of complicated parts are time-consuming to assemble. It may be easier to work on a much larger scale.

- The model should work in the same way as the final product. Choose materials and fixing techniques that behave like those you plan to use for the final design.

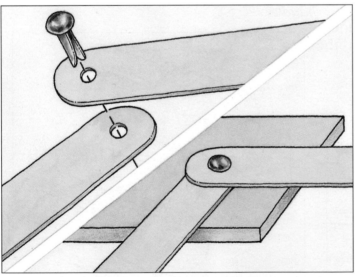

▲ *Making links between card components.*

Materials

Card, paper and thin plastics are the most common materials used for this type of working model. They can behave like rigid materials, but are easy to cut and modify.

Pins, paper fasteners, and eyelet-type fastenings can be used as pivots. They allow movement and are easy to adjust.

You can also explore moving parts using easy-to-assemble construction kits (see page 34).

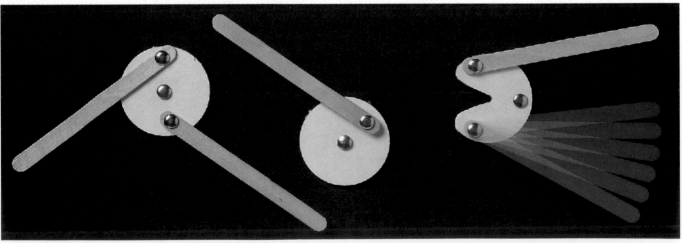

▲ *Models of different types of mechanisms.*

...Modelling product performance in 3D

Modelling structure

Many of the objects that you design will involve a structure. They may be based on a framework (like a pylon), a solid structure (a dam), or a shell structure (a domed roof). For all of these, **strength**, **stiffness** and **stability** are important.

A 3D model will show you very quickly whether your design is sound. By adding loads to your model, you can see how it resists stress, how stable it is, and you can discover the points of weakness.

It is also easier to identify the parts that are not functional, so they can be removed.

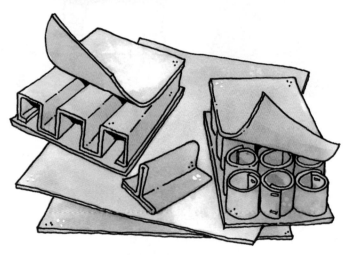

▲ *Two ways of making strong beams from card.*

Choosing the best materials

Structural models are usually small in scale, so it is important to use modelling materials that behave in a realistic way and show up problems in your design. Use a material that will show up lack of stiffness or weaknesses when tested. Materials that bend and snap easily will tell you about a structure under test situations.

- Suitable materials are paper, card, art straws, pipe-cleaners, spaghetti, cotton, wood, paperclips and thin wire.

- For rapid joining use a hot-melt glue gun; PVA glue is stronger but takes longer to set.

SAFETY ⚠
Care is required when using a glue gun.

- Only use adhesive tape in small quantities. If you use too much you may not be able to tell whether it is the structure or the tape that is strong!

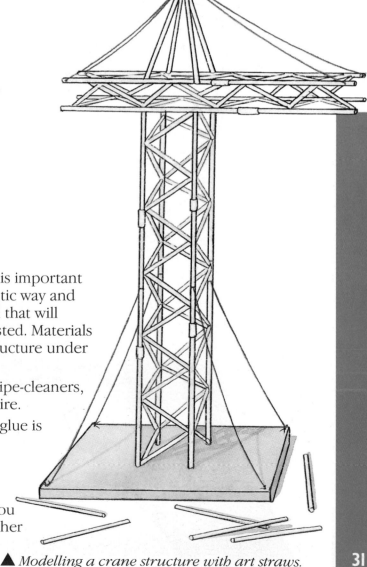

▲ *Modelling a crane structure with art straws.*

Resource Task
RMRT 16

Modelling for fit

Sometimes you will need to find out how your design idea will fit *onto, into* or *around* something. For example, if you are designing something to be worn, a simple paper pattern is a good way of testing for size and shape.

Paper is easy to cut, fold and join, and can be modified time after time until the fit is correct.

A paper pattern is usually drawn to actual size so that tracings can be taken from it at a later stage in the design process.

Developments

Most packages or boxes are made up from flat sheets of card that have been folded up to make a 3D form. This is known as a **development** or **net**.

Open out a cardboard package to see how it has been folded. Notice the flaps that allow the box to be neatly joined together.

You can use developments for designing objects to be made from sheet materials. Paper or card developments allow you to see whether you have the correct size, shape and fit.

Simple forms can be fitted together to make more complicated ones.

If you are working on a scaled-down version of your idea, you can transfer the development to grid paper and enlarge the shapes to give you a pattern or template to draw around.

| **Resource Tasks** |
| SRT 26, TRT 11 |

...Modelling product performance in 3D

Environmental modelling

When designing for an **environment** such as a bedroom, you will need to consider how objects are positioned within the space. It can be difficult to work out the impact of 3D objects on a space if you use only a 2D plan.

It is better to make simple, scaled, **block models** of the objects, and move them around on a plan to explore different layouts.

▲ *A set model used to plot movement.*

Block models can be quickly made from foam or card. You can use junk or found materials to give quick impressions.

Modelling like this will help you to imagine how people might use the space and move around within it.

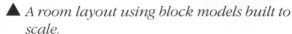

▲ *A room layout using block models built to scale.*

Full-scale models

With small-scale models, it is difficult to get a true picture of how the layout will affect people. You can get a better impression with a full-scale model, using lightweight materials such as large empty cardboard boxes and fabric draped over poles.

You can test whether the layout works by getting people to move around in it and to pretend to perform tasks. Is there enough space for the doors to open properly? Can you walk comfortably between the units?

▲ *Full-scale modelling of an environment.*

Modelling with kits you can buy

Construction kits are designed to enable parts to be quickly assembled, taken apart and used again.

You can model structures, mechanisms, electronic circuits and pneumatic and hydraulic systems without having to spend time producing the individual parts.

As with any modelling, it is important to understand exactly what you are trying to work out before you start using kits like these.

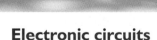

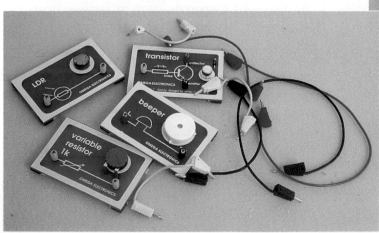

Mechanisms

Models using **gears**, **pulleys** and **axles** can be put together very quickly using a kit, so that you can experiment with different combinations of gear wheels or pulleys to achieve the results you want.

Electronic circuits

It is much easier to assemble circuits from ready-prepared 'systems boards' than with individual parts. The boards connect together simply and you can try out many different ideas quickly.

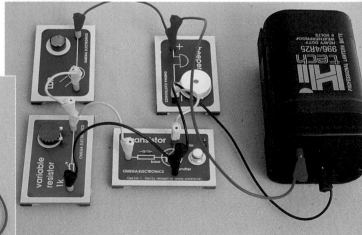

Resource Tasks

MCRT 9, ECRT 10–12

Modelling with computers

Modelling product appearance

Modelling on computers is sometimes called **computer assisted design (CAD)**. There are two main advantages to computer modelling:

- You can produce some sorts of drawings more quickly than with pencil and paper.
- You can make changes without doing the drawing again.

Thus you can build up a series of design drawings quite quickly and compare alternative designs more easily.

Most school software is *not* suitable for doing rough sketches and notes; it is much better to use pencil and paper for these.

However, it takes time to learn computer modelling and you will need to find time to practise.

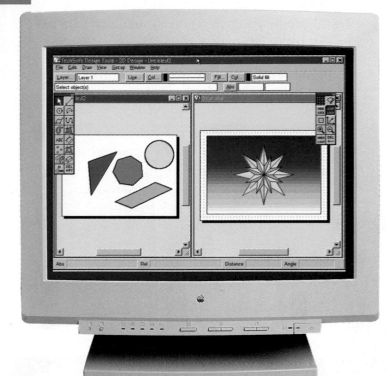

▲ *You can draw many shapes on a computer.*

Modelling shapes

You can use draw-and-paint programs to produce geometric shapes, curves or freehand lines.

Some software enables any part of the design to be enlarged or reduced in size, rotated, copied, or turned into a mirror image of itself.

Modelling surface decoration

You can easily use draw-and-paint programs to produce patterns.

You can select from a 'tool box' of pens, brushes or airbrush which can all be adjusted for thickness, spread and shape. Colour can be mixed on a 'palette' to fill in shapes or add shading or spray effects.

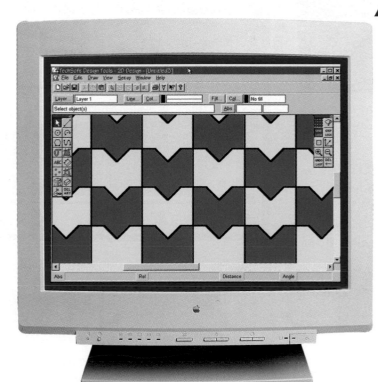

▲ *You can easily produce decorative patterns on-screen.*

Resource Tasks
SRT 9 and 10

Modelling form

You can use solid-modeller programs to produce 3D forms. These can appear on the screen as simple wire frames or solid objects.

Usually you can rotate these images to see them from all angles.

You can also colour the surfaces to show light and shaded areas to reflect the position of the light source.

▲ *You can experiment with different forms on-screen.*

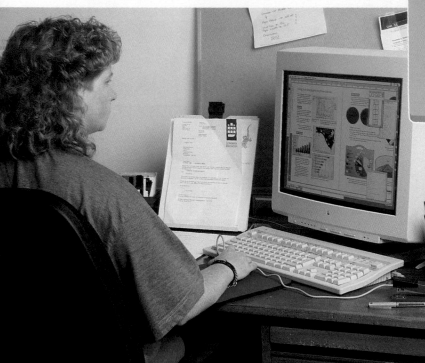

▲ *Use a computer to get your work to look good.*

Modelling page layouts

You can use **desk-top publishing (DTP)** software to produce different layouts for a given text and illustrations. You can vary the number of columns of text, the size and shape of the illustrations, and the style and size of the lettering.

You can use a layout that you like as a template for every page in a document, making your work look professional.

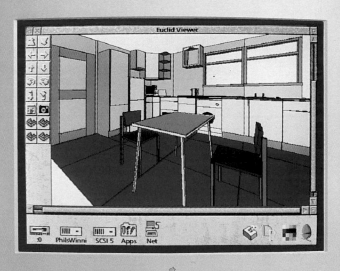

▲ *You can explore different interior designs with a computer.*

Modelling built environments

You can use architectural modelling software to produce on-screen the image of an interior design. You can experiment with this design until you find the most suitable model. You can alter the proportions of a room, making it taller or wider. You can alter the colour scheme. You can experiment with different furniture layouts.

...Modelling with computers

Modelling product performance

Modelling how your design will work using computers (CAD) will save time.

Modelling mechanical action

You can design mechanisms on-screen and see whether they work as they need to for your design.

You could do this modelling using a construction kit, but it would probably take longer and you would be limited to the parts in the kit. On-screen a wider range of parts is available and you can even design your own.

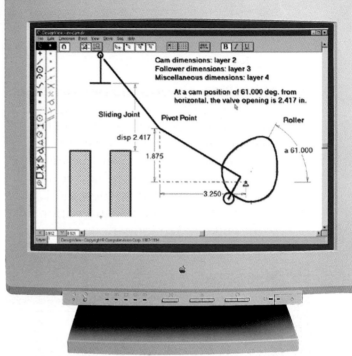

▲ *Modelling the action of a cam.*

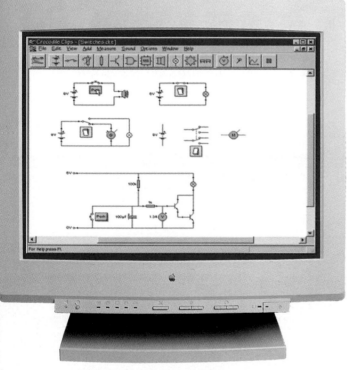

▲ *Testing circuits on-screen.*

Modelling the behaviour of electronic circuits

You can design **circuits** on-screen and see whether they do what you want. Once you have designed a circuit that works on-screen you can build it knowing that it will do the job. Using an electronics kit would probably take longer and you would be limited to the parts in the kit.

Modelling energy transfers

The need to save energy is particularly important in the design of buildings, where heating uses a lot of energy.

It is quite easy to find out just how much energy would be saved by using double-glazing, draught-proofing, roof insulation, different construction materials and even changing the shape of a house by using a computer.

Resource Tasks

SRT 28, 29

Testing energy efficiency on-screen. ▶

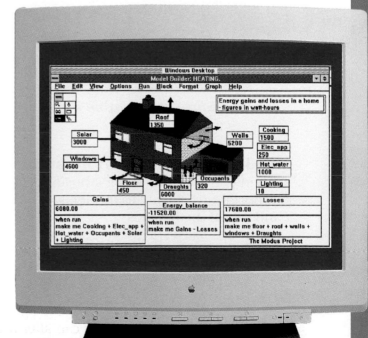

Modelling nutrition

You can use a nutrition database to identify and calculate the food values of ingredients for meals. You can compare these values with the dietary requirements of people eating the meals.

Modelling ergonomic performance

It is easy to show different workspace layouts on-screen and to draw in the movements needed to carry out particular jobs. In this way, the most efficient layout, the one that requires least movement, can be identified.

To do this with pencil and paper would take much longer.

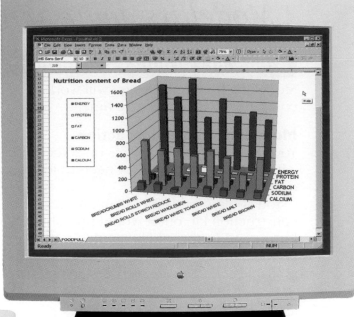

▲ *Exploring the nutrition of different breads.*

▲ *Finding the best layout using a computer.*

Modelling business performance

When you are developing a business plan, it is important to be able to model how money moves in and out of the business.

You can use a spreadsheet to help you do this. Put in figures for all your costs and expected sales, and in just a few seconds the spreadsheet will be able to calculate whether you make a profit or loss. Doing all the necessary calculations by hand would take a very long time.

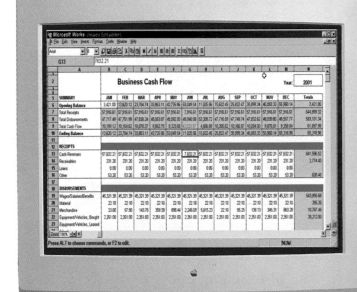

▲ *Using a computer to check on money movement.*

Resource Task

FRT 9

Using a systems approach

A way of thinking

You can think about anything that is made up of a collection of parts that work together to do a job as a **system**. The parts of the system might be objects, people or both.

Systems thinking helps you think about what something has to do, rather than how it is done. So you might think of a torch as a (very simple) system:

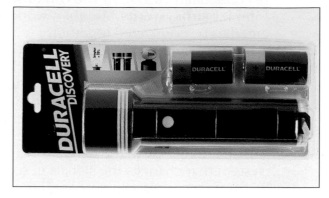

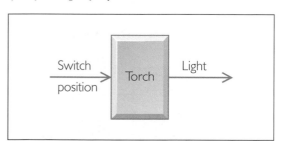

▲ *A system diagram.*

This system diagram tells you that a switch will control the light output from the torch. But it does not tell you how this will happen. However, because a torch is a fairly simple device, the number of (sensible) ways to make the circuit is limited.

Systems thinking will help you understand complicated situations and design complex products.

The system boundary

The **system boundary** is like the borders of a country. Everything inside the boundary belongs to the system. Anything outside does not. The signals into and out of the system pass across the system boundary. However, unlike the borders of a country, with a system boundary you can choose to put the boundary where it helps your understanding or design thinking.

If you were designing just the internal workings of a radio your system boundary would not include the case, battery-changing arrangements, tuning dial or switches. If you were designing the case as well you would draw the boundary to include all of these. So whenever you are designing a system the first thing you need to do is decide on its boundary.

Some unusual system boundaries

Gas fire and boiler manufacturers must include the house as part of their system.

▲ *Cinema owners include nearby houses in their system boundary.*

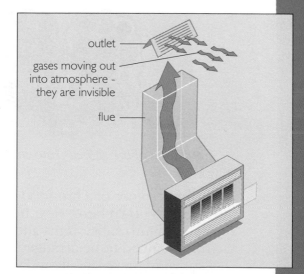

outlet

gases moving out into atmosphere - they are invisible

flue

▲ *Waste and poisonous gases must be removed from the house.*

Systems and subsystems

To understand a system you can divide it up into simpler **subsystems**. You then work out how these need to be connected together.

A music centre can be divided into several subsystems – such as the record deck and the tuner.

A **system diagram** shows how the subsystems are connected together to make the complete system. The **arrows** show where information, or a **signal**, leaves or enters a subsystem. Each subsystem **block** in the diagram is a part of the system that changes the signals in some way. Each subsystem can also be described by dividing it into further subsystems.

Subsystem blocks which bring signals into the system are called **input** blocks; for example the tuner block in the 'music centre' system diagram responds to radio signals.

Subsystems whose signals leave the system are **output** blocks; for example the speakers produce sound and the mini disc player can produce magnetic recordings on a mini disc.

Other subsystems, like the amplifier, are called **process** blocks because they process (change) signals. This system diagram is not meant to look like a music centre only to help you to understand how a music centre works.

Signals

A designer beginning to design a complex product using systems thinking only needs to consider what signals go into the system and what signals come out. She does not need to worry about what happens inside the system just yet.

▲ *Some of the signals into and out of a fast-food service.*

The designer of a fast-food service might identify the signals shown here. Next he will break down the system into subsystems and see how the signals and blocks need to be arranged. A system diagram showing these signals and some of the subsystems is shown on the right.

You should be able to see that the signals from one subsystem often pass into another.

▲ *A music centre and its system diagram.* ▼

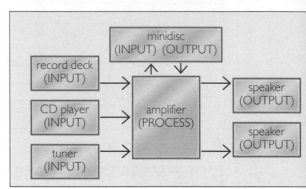

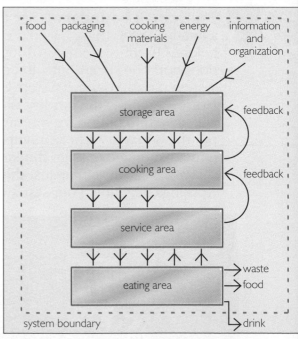

▲ *A fast-food service as a system diagram. Can you work out what is moving along each of the arrows?*

Resource Task

SRT 33

...Using a systems approach

Connecting systems to the outside world

The user

Many systems need to be used by people who have had no special training. For example, shoppers need to be able to tell the system what they want, collect their orders and pay. Or someone using a bank needs to be able to ask for and get money and information. Users do not need to know how a system works, just how to use it.

The parts of the system that they see, touch, talk to or handle are called the **user interface**. Sometimes this is another person, like a shop assistant or bank clerk. The advantage is that it is friendly. Users can easily ask questions if they are not sure what to do.

◀ Machine and human ▶ interfaces.

However, human interfaces need special training to enable them to deal with user enquiries and they are not available 24 hours a day. Often the user interface is a machine as in a soft drinks machine, or shopping across the Internet. There are written instructions to read and buttons to press or click instead of someone to talk to. The advantage is that it is always available. The disadvantages are that it can appear unfriendly and difficult to use. The user interfaces for such machines must be designed so that they are self-explanatory and easy to use.

The operator

Some systems need to be controlled by a trained operator. The operator needs information about the system and a way of controlling it. For example, a car is controlled by its driver. The car driver needs to know how fast the car is going, how much petrol it has, and other detailed information. She needs to be able to increase the car speed, slow down and turn left and right.

The parts of the system that the operator looks at, touches, talks to or handles are called the **operator interface**.

An operator interface is usually more complicated than a user interface. An operator needs more information than a user and has to be able to do more things.

The operator must be able to put information into the system through easy-to-use controls. The operator interface should be as easy to use as possible.

Resource Task

SRT 34

The operator interface of a modern car. ▶

Feedback

Most systems need to respond to changes. A central heating system needs to be able to turn itself off if a room becomes too hot and on again when it becomes too cold.

To do this the system needs to know the room temperature. Of course this temperature is affected by the heating system. So the temperature controls the heating system and the heating system controls the temperature. This is called a **closed-loop system** because the signals travel in a loop round the system. The best way to see how this works is to look at the system diagram below. When signals travel in a loop like this it is called **feedback**.

A system without feedback is called an **open-loop system**. A room heated by an electric fire is an open-loop system. If the fire is left on it will carry on heating the room even if it is a hot day. There is no feedback signal telling the fire that the room is too hot and to turn itself off.

System diagrams for both of these systems are shown below.

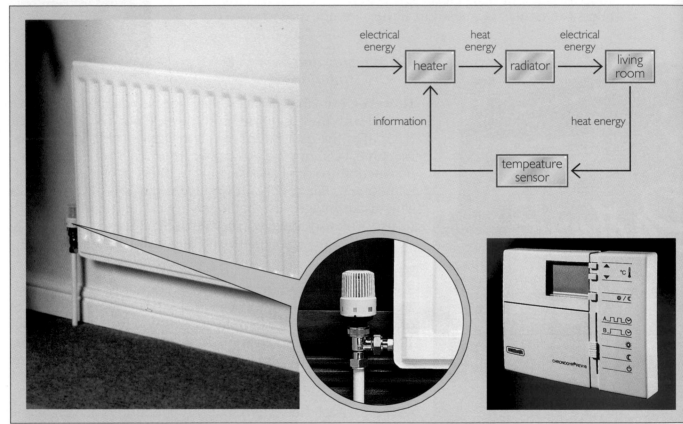

▲ *Closed-loop and open-loop systems.*

▲ *Can you draw a systems diagram for this electronic controller for a whole central heating system?*

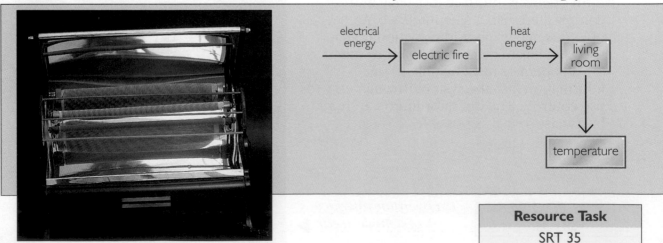

Resource Task

SRT 35

Digging deeper

System diagrams can be used to:

- help you design your own systems;
- help you describe existing systems.

Whether you are designing or describing a system, the following questions about signals will help you.

Signals going into the system

What signal(s) does the system need?
Are there any unwanted signals going into the system which will affect its performance?
Can you do anything to minimise the effect of unwanted signals? If not, is the system still useful?

Signals leaving the system

What signal(s) is the system designed to produce?
Are there any unwanted signals leaving the system which will affect its performance?
Can you do anything to minimise the effect of unwanted signals? If not, does the benefit of the system still justify its use despite these unwanted signals?

Signals inside the system

What types of signal are used inside the system?
Possibilities include: electronic, force (in mechanical systems), pressure (in pneumatic and hydraulic systems), a range of objects (e.g. in libraries or shops).

SIGNALS

Physical signals
can be provided by:

Light
Sound
Heat
Force
Magnetism
Electric current

Information
can provide signals.

The information is usually in the form of digital data.

The number or amount of
Physical objects
moving through a system can be signals. For example:

Books
Cars
Chemicals
Food
Paper
People

After you have decided the answers to these questions you are ready to think about the subsystem blocks.

Input subsystems

What input blocks can be used to accept the incoming signals?

Output subsystems

What output blocks can be used to produce the outgoing signals?

Process subsystems

What process blocks are needed to produce the desired signal changes within the system?

Using mobile phones can be treated as ▶ a system.

These system diagrams show how a systems analysis of a mobile phone might develop. The first diagram shows the desired inputs and outputs; the microwaves that carry the conversations to the phone and the sounds that the humans need to communicate.

microwave → mobile 'phone → microwave

sound → → sound

A general system diagram for a mobile phone. ▶

The second diagram shows the two main subsystems: one that allows the user to 'be heard' and one that allows them to 'hear'.

sound → be heard → microwave

microwave → hear → sound

Identifying the main subsystems. ▶

The third diagram shows the subsystems in the 'be heard' subsystem.

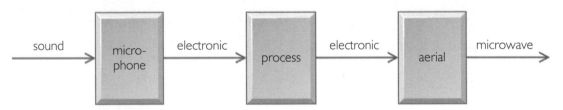

sound → micro-phone → electronic → process → electronic → aerial → microwave

▲ *The speaking subsystem.*

Finally, the fourth diagram identifies two of the outputs of a mobile phone that were, perhaps, not expected by their first developers.

mobile 'phone → cancer?

→ noise

Unwanted outputs. ▶

- Noise from users speaking into mobile phones is an irritant to some people. Are these irritated people simply behind the times, or are mobile phones being used thoughtlessly?
- **There** is now real concern that microwave radiation from the aerials of mobile phones could cause brain cancer in users. Should these phones be banned? Should the manufacturers make them safer? Should people use remote headphones so that the aerial is not so close?

Planning techniques

Sequence diagrams

Sequence diagrams show the order in which events happen.

Flow charts

Flow charts can look similar to system diagrams. But they show something different: **actions** and the **sequence** in which they should be carried out.

In a flow diagram boxes represent the actions.

Arrows indicate the order, or sequence, in which the actions should be taken. Decision boxes are used where there is a choice about the sequence of actions.

In contrast, system diagrams are about information or signals (arrows) and the changes (boxes) that happen to these signals. The panel below shows the differences between flow charts and system diagrams.

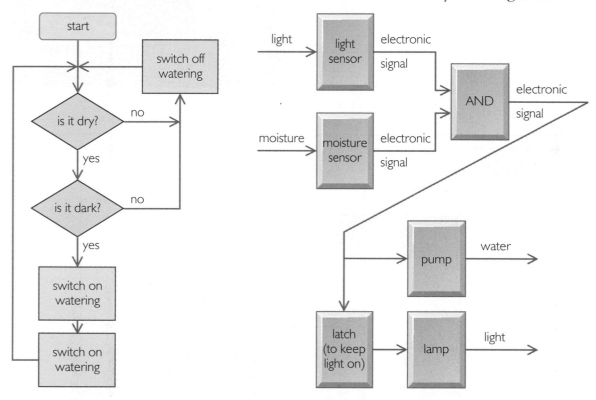

▲ *A flow diagram and a systems diagram both describing a watering device.*

	Flow charts	**System diagrams**
Boxes	represent actions to do or questions to ask	represent changes to signals (e.g. type of signal, size of signal, signals combining)
Arrows	show next action to carry out	show signals carrying information
Arrows joining	arrows can join when more than one action leads to another action	signals can only be combined by a box with a rule saying how they join
Arrows splitting	a split can only happen through a decision box which decides which action to do next	arrows can split if a signal is going to more than one box

Resource Task

SRT 36, ECRT 9

Gantt charts

Gantt charts are the most useful way of planning when several different things are going on at once.

The Gantt chart below shows the planning for a puppet play performance. Several pupils are involved. They know that they have to write the script, design and make the puppets, the theatre and scenery, develop any special effects, and rehearse the play for a performance in six weeks' time. Have they allowed enough time for all they have to do?

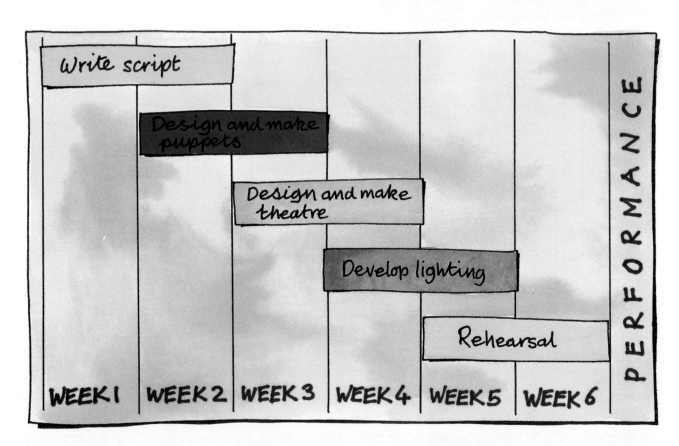

Storyboards

You can make a sequence diagram using pictures and notes. It is called a storyboard. It will help you work out the sequence of events and it is not intended to be an illustrated guide for a wider audience (see User Support, page 72).

Evaluating outcomes

The user trip

▲ *Whatever the product you can take a user trip to evaluate it.*

Four different outcomes of design and technology are shown on this page. The supermarket is a complex system. The telephone box is a complicated communications device. The tin opener is a simple tool, and the chicken tikka masala is a convenience food.

When you try to evaluate an outcome you are trying to find out its good and bad points. A simple way of doing this is to take a **user trip**. This just means using the product in an ordinary way and asking yourself the following questions:

- Is it easy or convenient to use?
- What is its job and does it do it?
- Do I like it?
- Would I want to own it or use it?

You would evaluate the four outcomes like this:

- the supermarket by going shopping there;
- the phone box by making a telephone call;
- the chicken tikka masala by heating and eating it;
- the tin opener by using it to open a tin.

While on the user trip you note down the answers to the questions. You can use them to make a list of 'improvement suggestions'.

Sometimes it helps to get other people to take user trips and for you to observe them and then ask questions. In this way you can collect views from users with different viewpoints. For example, a tin opener that works well for most of us may be quite difficult for someone with arthritis to use.

Resource Task
SRT 37, TRT 2

47

Performance testing

To evaluate an outcome you need to find out whether the product does what it is supposed to do. The specification will tell you what it has to do. So you need to compare what it does – its performance – with the specification. Here are two examples.

A child's hat

Look at the specification for a hat for children 3–5 years old. The designer tried to meet these requirements by providing an adjustable head strap plus a chin strap with a Velcro fastening. He used PVC for the outer covering.

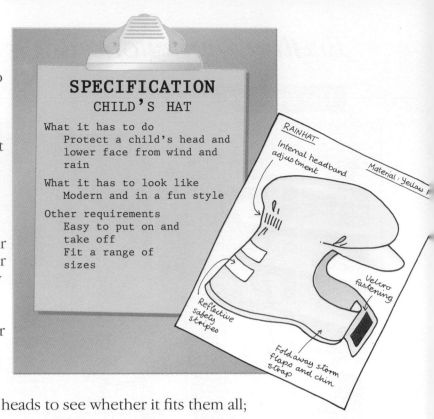

SPECIFICATION
CHILD'S HAT

What it has to do
    Protect a child's head and lower face from wind and rain

What it has to look like
    Modern and in a fun style

Other requirements
    Easy to put on and take off
    Fit a range of sizes

RAINHAT
Internal headband adjustment
Material: Yellow
Velcro fastening
Reflective safety stripes
Foldaway storm flaps and chin strap

To test the hat's performance you need to:

- try it on a range of different-sized heads to see whether it fits them all;
- observe children wearing it on a windy day to see whether it comes off;
- spray water on it to see whether it comes through to the lining;
- watch children trying on the hat to see if they can manage.

A toy car

Look at the specification for a toy car for children 5–8 years old.

The designer tried to meet all these requirements by designing a hand-held control unit which is attached to the toy by a ribbon cable. The control panel has an on/off switch to control the lights and switches to control the motor. The large tyres have a deep tread to provide the grip for climbing. The battery is housed in the control unit so that the motor only has to move the toy and not the battery as well.

A performance test will need to answer these questions:

- Can the car go forwards and backwards?
- Will it climb over obstacles?
- Will the headlights turn on and off?
- Can children use the hand-held unit to control the car?

SPECIFICATION
TOY CAR

What it has to do
    Travel forwards and backwards
    Climb over small obstacles

What it has to look like
    Resembles a real vehicle of some sort

Other requirements
    Operated by a battery powered electric motor
    Headlights that turn on and off
    Be suitable for children aged 5–8 years old

Thumb and finger controls
Control lead in roll bar to keep it clear of wheels
Battery Pack
Survival pack under spare wheel
Pop-up headlights
All-terrain tyres

... *Evaluating outcomes*

Winners and losers

Any technological change will affect lots of people, some directly, others indirectly. Some will gain from the change and others will lose. As part of your design and technology work you will need to evaluate your ideas and products. Identifying winners and losers will help you decide how good the designs are.

A pupil evaluated his design for a disposable waterproof hat for hikers, using a **target chart**.

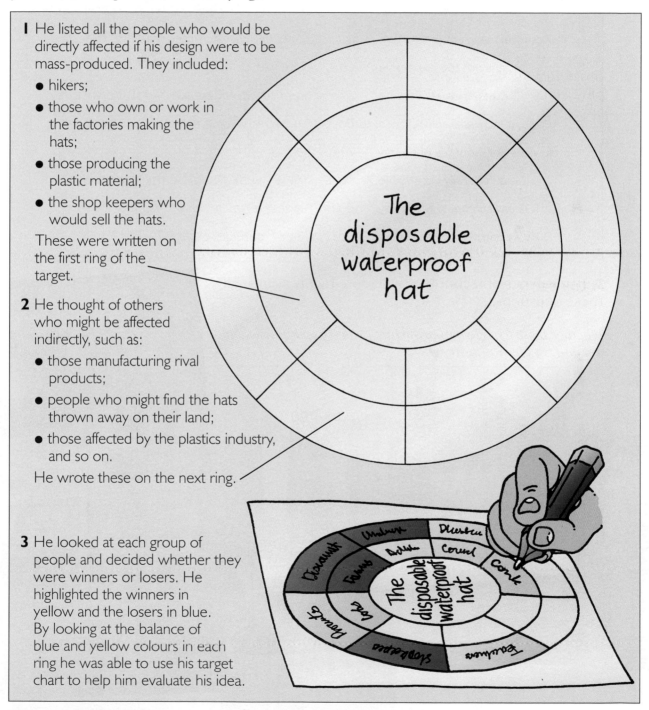

1 He listed all the people who would be directly affected if his design were to be mass-produced. They included:

- hikers;
- those who own or work in the factories making the hats;
- those producing the plastic material;
- the shop keepers who would sell the hats.

These were written on the first ring of the target.

2 He thought of others who might be affected indirectly, such as:

- those manufacturing rival products;
- people who might find the hats thrown away on their land;
- those affected by the plastics industry, and so on.

He wrote these on the next ring.

3 He looked at each group of people and decided whether they were winners or losers. He highlighted the winners in yellow and the losers in blue. By looking at the balance of blue and yellow colours in each ring he was able to use his target chart to help him evaluate his idea.

Resource Task

SRT 38

Is it appropriate?

Appropriate means 'suitable', so appropriate technology is suitable technology.

Is it appropriate?

Technology is appropriate if ...	You can check whether appropriate technology is being used by asking these questions:
... it suits the needs of the people.	Is it what the people need and want?
... it uses local materials.	Does raw material need to be transported?
... it uses local means of production.	Do local people make it near where they live?
... it is not too expensive.	Can the people afford to buy, run and maintain it?
... it generates income.	Are jobs created or people made redundant?
... it increases self-reliance.	Does it improve people's lives?
... it uses renewable sources of energy.	What fuels does it use?
... it is culturally acceptable.	Does it fit in with the way the people live?
... it is environmentally friendly.	Does it damage or improve the environment?
... it is controlled by the users.	Does it need outside experts?

Very few types of technology will score highly against all these questions.

Whether these tools are appropriate forms of technology will depend on the situation. ▼

Resource Task

SRT 39

Which strategy?

This Chooser Chart gives you information about strategies:

- when to use a strategy in a Capability Task;
- how long the strategy will take;
- how complex it is;
- whether it involves other people.

Use the chart to help you decide which strategy to use.

Strategy	Comments			
Identifying needs and likes				
Observing people	B	◔	☆	
Interviewing	B	◔	☆	大
Looking in books and magazines	B	◔	☆	
PIES	B	◔	☆	
Looking at aesthetics: style, colour, feel, space and harmony	B	◔	☆	
Image boards	B	◑	☆	
Using briefs and specifications				
Writing design briefs	B	◔	☆	
Writing specifications	B	◔	☆	
Generating design ideas				
Brainstorming	B or M	◑	☆	大大
Observational drawing	B or M	◑	☆	
Making connections	B or M	◑	☆	
Attribute analysis	B or M	◔	☆	
Modelling				
Modelling appearance	M	◑	☆	
Modelling performance	M	◑	☆☆	
Modelling with computers	M	◕	☆	
Using a systems approach	M	◑	☆	
Planning tools	B or M	◔	☆	
Evaluating by user trip	E or B	◔	☆	大
Evaluating by winners and losers	E or B	◔	☆	大
Evaluating by performance specification	E or B	◔	☆	大
Evaluating by appropriateness	E or B	◔	☆	大

Key

B = beginning

M = middle

E = end

◔ ◑ ◕ = short to long (for time)

☆ ☆ ☆ = simple to complex

大 大大 大大大 = one other to many (people)

2 Communicating design ideas

Why and how?

This chapter looks at ways of communicating your design ideas to different audiences.

Before starting any drawing or model during a design and make task you need to be clear about:

- the purpose of the drawing or model – what it has to communicate;
- the audience – who you are trying to communicate with.

Visualizing and developing ideas

In the earliest stages of designing, **thumbnail sketches** help you to visualize and record ideas for yourself.

Later, you will need to communicate your ideas to others. For this, the drawings are likely to be **rough sketches** that you need to explain for your ideas to make sense. In a design team, this may be an important stage in the development of your design.

unstable shape but good lift

← weak here!

easy shape to cut out

expensive to make but very strong

▲ *Thumbnail sketches help you to visualize your design.*

52

'Selling' your idea

When you are happy with your design idea you need to 'sell' it to persuade the client (or teacher) that it is worth producing. For this you make **presentation drawings** or **models**. These should show how your idea will look and explain how it will work.

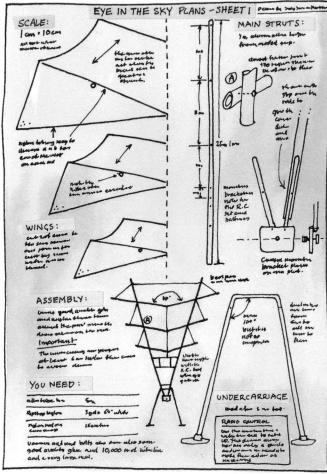

▲ *Working drawings.*

Informing the user

Often, you will need to give information to the user of your design. You might need to make a model showing how the design works, to produce instructions explaining how to use it or a guide to repair and maintain it.

You may be involved in marketing, producing materials to persuade people to buy your product.

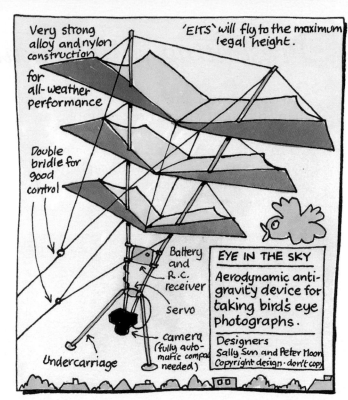

▲ *A presentation drawing.*

Drawings for making

Before a design can be made, a 'drawing for making', a **working drawing**, is needed. It must communicate the exact details of the design.

It specifies the materials needed, the shapes and sizes of all the parts to be made and how these fit together. Someone should be able to make the design from your working drawing without having to ask you any questions.

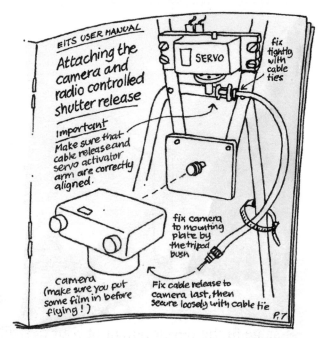

▲ *Diagrams can help others to use your design.*

Presenting your product idea

You can produce presentation drawings in many different ways. Three examples are shown here.

It may take several drawings to present your idea well. Just one of these bicycle alarm drawings would not be as effective a presentation as all three.

BICYCLE ALARM

BICYCLE ALARM
FRONT VIEW

BICYCLE ALARM
SEE THROUGH VIEW

OOEEOOEBOOE

Using isometric views

An **isometric view** is a way of showing three dimensions on a drawing. You can use special grid paper.

- Draw the object at an angle, with one corner as the closest point to you.
- Draw all vertical (upright) lines on the object as vertical lines on the drawing.
- Draw all lines which are horizontal on the object at 30° to the horizontal on the paper.

These step-by-step drawings show how the isometric view of the camera is constructed. You can use the crating method (page 48) to add details. Practise drawing isometric views on grid paper before you try to draw them freehand.

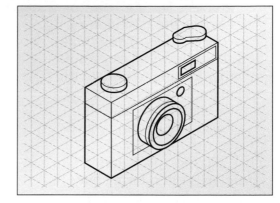

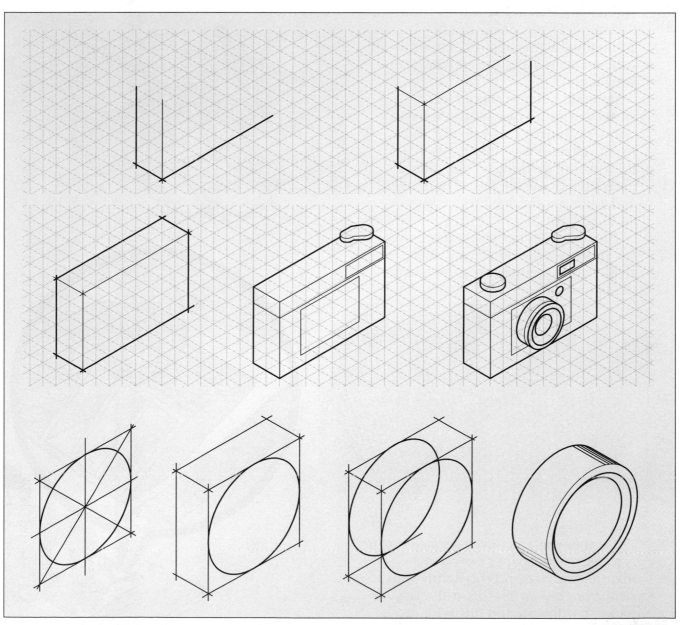

...Presenting your product idea

Giving surfaces texture

Choose the best view of your product. Then think about how you can colour the drawing to imitate the material the product will be made from, and the finish you intend to give it.

Plastics, glass and metals often have shiny surfaces. We see these surface finishes in the way they reflect light. Show this by adding highlights and reflections to your drawing using the techniques shown here.

Materials such as rubber, card, wood and some plastics often have only a dull surface and do not show harsh reflections or highlights. Show this on your drawing by applying an even tone of pencil, pastel or marker, and adding soft-edged reflections and highlights.

The texture is not applied evenly, but more heavily on areas that are in shade, and sparingly on areas facing the light source.

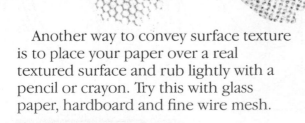

Another way to convey surface texture is to place your paper over a real textured surface and rub lightly with a pencil or crayon. Try this with glass paper, hardboard and fine wire mesh.

Resource Task
CRT 2

Giving surfaces depth

Step 1

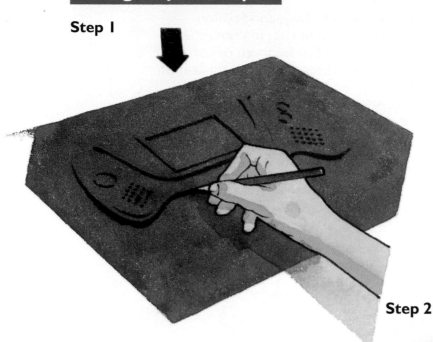

You can convey depth and 3D on a flat view of an object by adding highlights and shadows. You need to understand how light falls onto an object and creates areas of light and shade.

This flat view of a games console has added highlights and shadows to give depth.

This technique works best on coloured paper, as you do not have to colour in the whole surface, just the shadows and highlights. If you use white paper you will need to colour the body of the object with markers or water colour.

Step 2

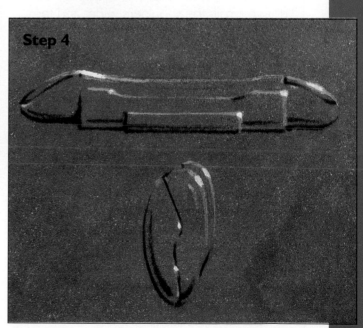

Follow these steps:

1 Decide where the light is coming from. Darken all the edges facing away from the light.

2 Use a white pencil-crayon to lighten the edges facing the light source.

3 Add sharper highlights using the crayon or a fine paint brush and white poster paint or gouache.

Step 3

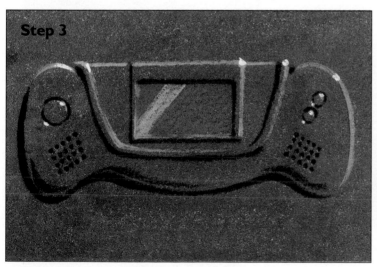

Step 4

4 You may need to include more views to show the shape of the product.

Resource Task
CRT 3

Presentation drawings for textile designs

Your design work with textiles will often involve clothing and fashion accessories. These are nearly always presented as if in use, to convey size and proportion, and show how the design is meant to be worn or carried. It can also suggest the image and effect that the design creates as a fashion item.

Drawing people can be difficult. There should be spaces between the clothing and the body – unless you are designing a skin-tight item like a swim suit! Here are some hints.

Trace over a photograph of a model in a magazine. Draw your design over it.

Simplify heads, hands, feet and the body, if you are designing items for them.

Fashion drawings sometimes show models with false proportions. The head may be drawn small, the shoulders wide, and the arms and legs extra long. This gives an elegant, stylish effect.

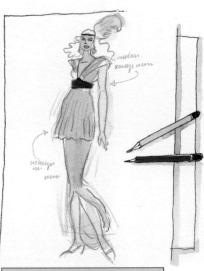

An outline of a figure will be enough if you only want to present an idea for an item like a rucksack.

Resource Task
CRT 8

Using different media

Your presentation drawing should show the most important features of your design. If you have given special attention to details, include a magnified close-up (see page 27).

Attach samples of materials, called **swatches**, buttons and small samples of decoration to the drawing to give a more detailed picture of the final design.

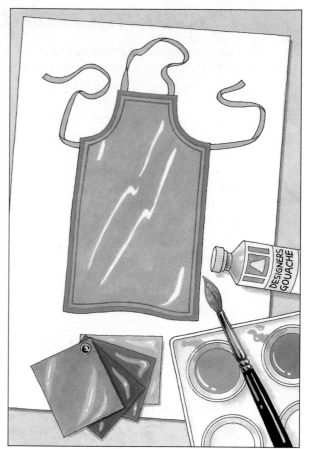

Your presentation also needs to suggest the 'feel' of the material used in your design. Mix different media to obtain the effect you want. Try these:

- **water-colour paints** – use water-resistant wax crayon before using the paints to make a pattern;
- **gouache** – good for strong, flat colours;
- **pencil-crayons** – good for hinting at detail and texture on top of colour washes;
- **pastels** – give a soft, matt effect, especially if rubbed on with a tissue or cotton wool;
- **brush pens** – give strong, flowing outlines to clothes;
- **felt-tip pens** – for fabric designs and decoration if you can get a good range of colours.

Resource Tasks

CRT 9, 10

Presenting food product ideas

The best way of presenting a food product idea is to prepare the real thing. Drawings and models lack taste and smell, which are so important.

In industry, home economists usually present a number of variations on a product for tests involving taste, appearance and texture. The test results could form the basis of a presentation along with photographs of the product and descriptions of the content.

A video record of taste tests or a survey could also be used.

Taste testing 3 varieties of icecream:-
Vanilla icecream
Cornish vanilla icecream
Vanilla water ice

Criteria for taste testing:-
soft – hard
smooth – gritty
creamy – watery

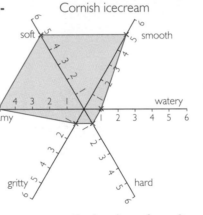

Cornish icecream

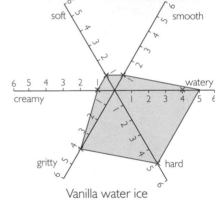

Vanilla water ice

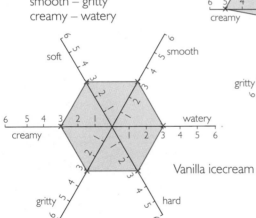

Vanilla icecream

Evaluation of results

The three icecreams involved very different characteristics and properties. The Vanilla icecream scored an average star profile. The Cornish vanilla icecream scored high on soft/creamy/smooth, with the Vanilla water ice high on hard/watery/gritty criteria. You now have to look at recipes for the three icecreams to try to work out what causes these differences.

Packaging and advertising are important, as are data connected with nutrition and user preferences (see page 159).

Photographs on the packet, and in cookery books and advertisements, present food in the most attractive way possible.

You may need to use photographs or a videotape recording to keep a record of the appearance of the food products that you design.

Resource Tasks
CRT 11

Presenting your idea in a context

Backgrounds

Your presentation drawing may have much more impact if the product is shown against a background, rather than 'floating' on a sheet of white paper. Even a simple frame attracts the eye. Here are some ideas.

Draw a frame around or under the image.

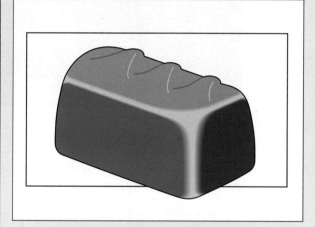

Add a shadow under the object. Use pencil or a grey marker.

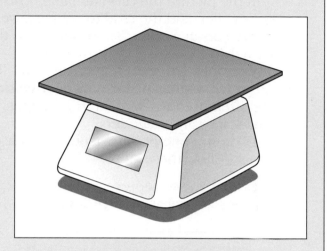

Draw a rectangle behind the image. This may suggest a horizon line or a landscape.

Cut out the shape you want from coloured paper or use pastels with masking tape for a clean outline.

Paste a cut-out of your design drawing over the top.

Place it into a 'real' environment. You could use a ready-made magazine picture or one of your own photographs.

Paste a cut-out of your drawing on the picture, or on a tracing paper overlay if the drawing is 'lost' against the background.

Fruit and nut snack

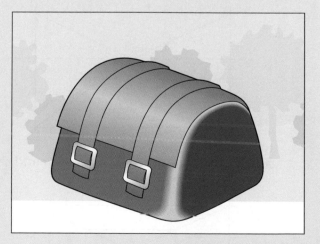

Resource Task

SRT 29

...*Presenting your idea in a context*

Putting it in a picture

For your presentation, you may want to show your design in a drawing of the place where it will actually be used. A technique often used to do this is **perspective drawing**. It gives an impression of depth as well as height and length, as we see them in real life.

In the picture the cars and lamp posts seem to get smaller, and the road to get narrower until it disappears at a point. This is known as the **vanishing point**.

A perspective drawing recreates this illusion on paper. **Single-point perspective drawings** are often used to show interior designs, landscapes and stage sets.

To draw a one-point perspective view of a room, follow these steps:

1 Draw a line to represent the horizon. This line is known as the **eye level**.

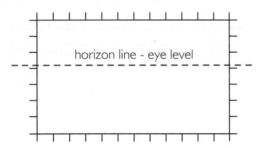

horizon line - eye level

2 Mark a vanishing point on the horizon and draw in lines to it from the corners.

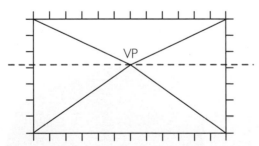

VP

3 Estimate the depth of the room and draw in the back wall.

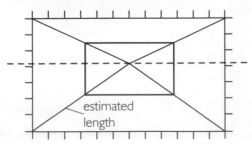

estimated length

4 Draw in guidelines using a scale taken from the front of the frame.

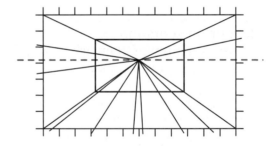

5 Add details and rub out the guidelines.

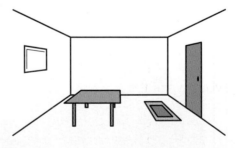

▲ *A finished single-point perspective view.*

ResourceTask
CRT 4

Displays and exhibitions

An important part of your presentation may be a display.

Whatever the product, the most important question you can ask yourself is, *'How can I get my ideas across?'*

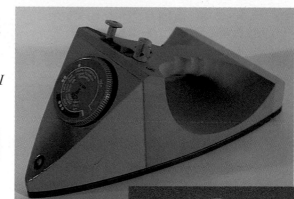

◄ *This 'block model' of an iron is made of polystyrene foam but gives a good idea of how the finished product would look.*

Presentation models

A good way to put over your idea may be to build a presentation model or **prototype**. These are accurate, detailed models that show exactly what the final design will look like, and sometimes how it will work.

They can be made of any material that is easy to work with and will give a realistic finish. A few coats of spray paint and the addition of details like switches and lettering can help.

▲ *A prototype working model of a toy car.*

Mounting a display

If your presentation consists mainly of 2D work, consider mounting it for display.

An easy way is to **surface mount** the work, fixing it on to sheets of mounting paper or card.

Or you can **window mount** the work behind a mounting sheet with a hole or 'window' cut in it.

Choose the colour of the mounting material to show your work to the best effect.

Add headings, labels or captions to help explain the display. Lettering should be neat and easily understood (see page 64).

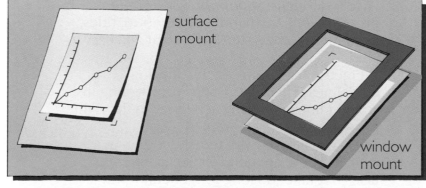

surface mount

window mount

When you mount sheets together, keep the layout simple. One technique is to line up one or two edges of a sheet with others on the display. ▶

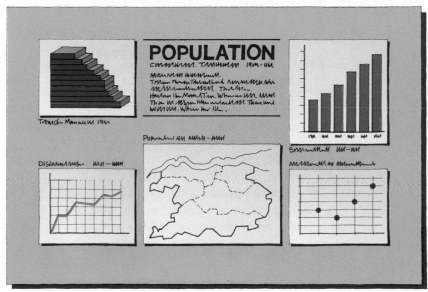

Presentation reports and documents

If written material forms an important part of your presentation, it should be laid out clearly and attractively to help others understand your proposals.

Lettering

Using computers

Choose lettering styles that are easy to read. These can often communicate as much as the words themselves. One style may suggest seriousness while another may give a more light-hearted impression.

There are many different designs of lettering – called **fonts** or **typefaces**. If you use more than two or three on one document it can look messy.

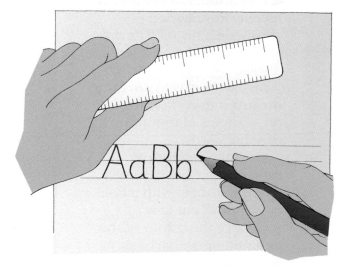

Hand lettering

Poor lettering can spoil your design presentation. Any hand-written notes, titles, headings or labels should be clear and easy to read.

Practise hand lettering by drawing guidelines. These help keep your writing in a straight line and form each letter to the right proportions.

You can also use dry transfer letters or a stencil. These are good for small lettering tasks but take too long for general work.

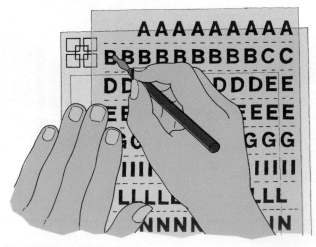

Photographs

Photographs can record the progress of a design task. They may help to explain how you arrived at your proposal.

With an overlay of tracing paper or clear film, a photograph can be used to show proposed changes. ▶

▲ *Photographs can be pasted together to show a panoramic or composite view.*

Layout

Layout is the arrangement of words and pictures on a page.

Designers may use a **grid**, which lets them place words and pictures together in different ways, but still keep the same basic 'look' for each page.

If you are using a DTP or word-processing system, investigate the use of grids to present your work. Some examples are shown here.

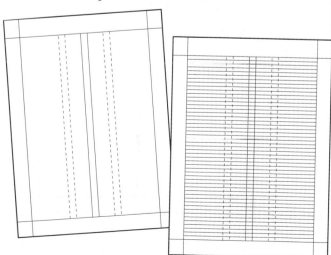

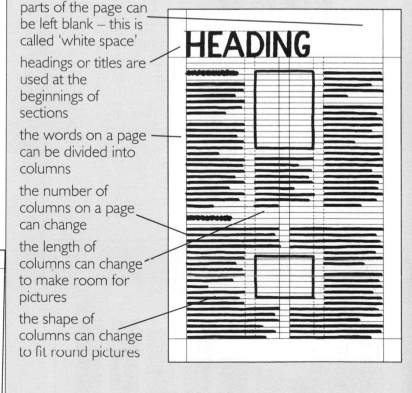

parts of the page can be left blank – this is called 'white space'

headings or titles are used at the beginnings of sections

the words on a page can be divided into columns

the number of columns on a page can change

the length of columns can change to make room for pictures

the shape of columns can change to fit round pictures

HEADING

Using facts and figures in presentations

Facts and figures collected during your design research should be presented accurately but in an attractive and clear way.

You can do this by presenting them as pictures or **graphics**. Here are some ideas.

Graphs

A graph can show how something changes over a period of time. For example, you could use one to show temperature changes during a day.

If you have more than one line to plot, code each in a way that clearly identifies them.

This gives the same information as the other graph but in a more interesting and attractive form. ▶

Bar charts

A bar chart is a way of comparing different amounts. The simplest bar chart is a single column divided up to show each item as a proportion of the whole.

Different amounts can also be shown as vertical or horizontal blocks drawn to scale along an axis.

Whichever method you use, choose a scale that makes it easy to 'read off' the amount accurately.

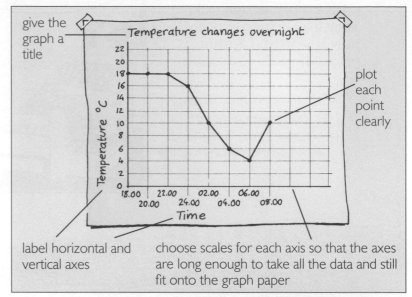

give the graph a title

plot each point clearly

label horizontal and vertical axes

choose scales for each axis so that the axes are long enough to take all the data and still fit onto the graph paper

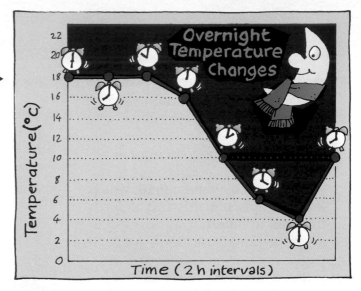

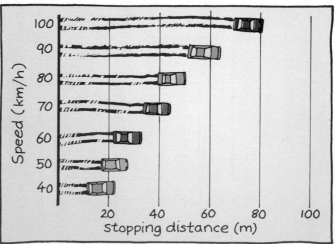

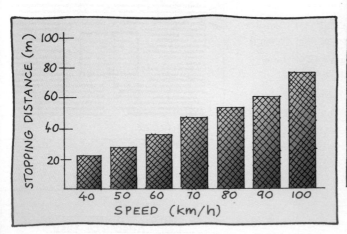

▲ *This bar chart has more visual impact than the one on the left.*

Pie charts

A **pie chart** is a good way to present data graphically, when you want to show the proportions of the parts making up a whole.

It is usually a circle divided into portions like the slices in a pie. The circle represents 100% – the whole. The size of each portion shows its percentage of the whole.

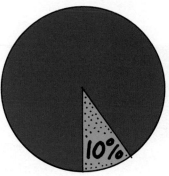
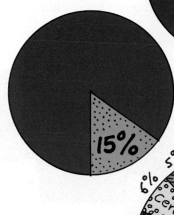

To draw a pie chart:

- work out the percentage size of each quantity;
- turn this percentage into an angle: 100% is 360°, so 10% would need a 36° slice, 15% a 54° slice, 25% a 90° slice and so on;
- label each slice and add the percentages or values so that it is clear what each represents.

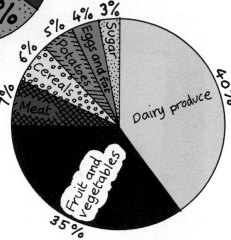

▲ *A pie chart comparing food purchases.*

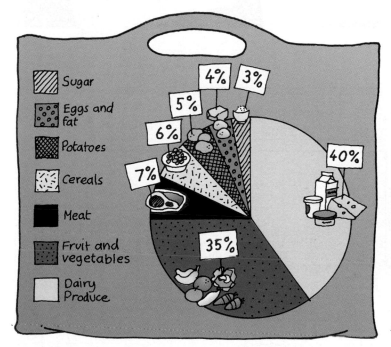

▲ *A pie chart must present information accurately and clearly, but it will have more impact if it is drawn in an interesting way.*

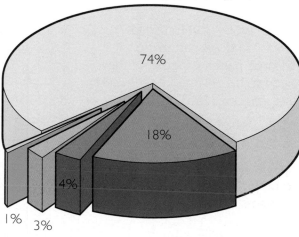

▲ *You can use computer programs to do the calculations and draw pie charts for you. Some programs will draw the pie chart in 3D.*

Resource Tasks
SRT 31, RMRT 4

Information for making

When your design proposal is ready to be made, you need to put together the 'information for making'. This includes all the working drawings and instructions that you, or someone else, need to make the design.

Putting this information down on paper is also a useful check on how well you have thought through your idea.

Recipes

You will need planning tools when you are working with food (see page 45), but also you will probably want to record your design idea as a detailed recipe.

The recipe lists the ingredients, and gives step-by-step instructions on how to make the product.

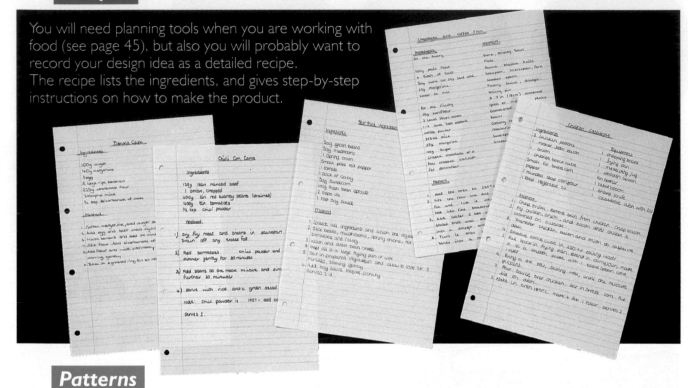

Patterns

When working with textiles, it is helpful to draw patterns on squared paper, especially if they need to be enlarged or reduced (see pages 132–3).

Mark allowances for joining materials on your patterns.

Special fixings or fastenings need to be highlighted, using sequence diagrams if necessary.

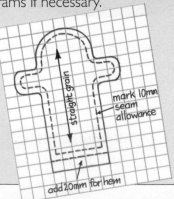

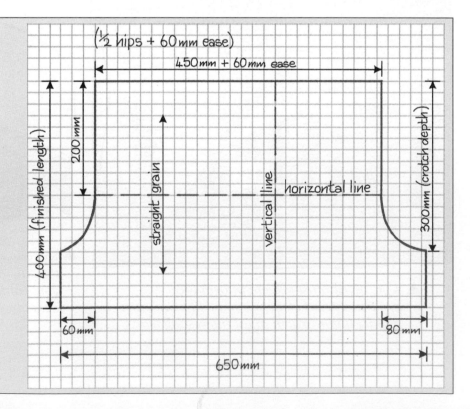

Orthographic views

Working drawings usually show some square-on views (or elevations) of the product that is to be made. These views, drawn as a related group, are known as an **orthographic projection**.

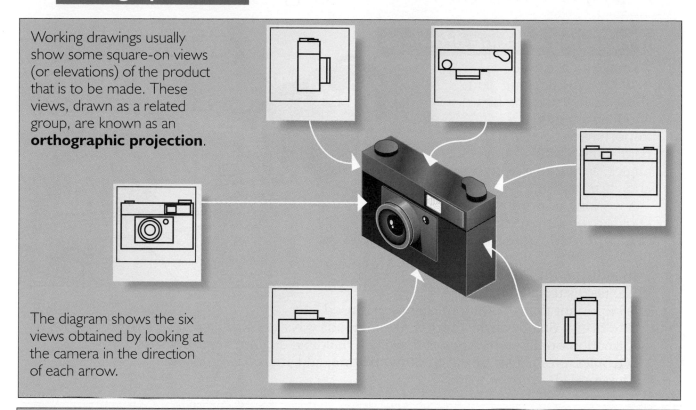

The diagram shows the six views obtained by looking at the camera in the direction of each arrow.

You need only draw three views to give enough detail about your design. The names given to each are:

- **the plan** – the view looking down;
- **the front elevation** – the main view giving the most information;
- **the end elevation** – the remaining side view(s).

Each view must be drawn so that its relation to the others is clear. Using grid or graph paper makes it easier to line the views up with each other.

It can also help to imagine that the product is suspended inside a transparent box. Draw the views as if traced on the sides and top of the box, which is then opened out flat.

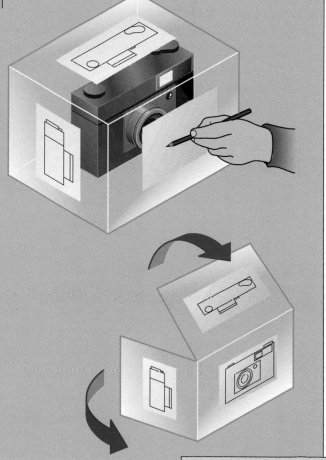

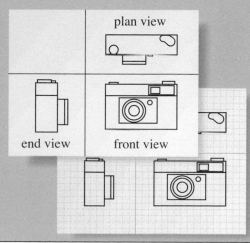

▲ *This arrangement of views is called third angle projection.*

Resource Task

CRT 5

... *Information for making*

Producing working drawings

To make an accurate orthographic drawing, you should use a drawing board and instruments. It is important to be able to draw parallel lines and accurate angles, as part of a neat, clean and clear drawing.

A working drawing must show all the dimensions and details needed for a product to be made.

In industry the design and make task is usually shared, so it is important that a common 'language' is used.

The British Standards Institution recommends ways of showing information on different types of drawing – building, engineering, electronics, etc. These are called **conventions**, and are recognized and understood all over the world.

A complete working drawing includes:
- exact sizes with measurements, usually in millimetres, for each part;
- the materials to be used for each part;
- detailed construction and assembly instructions;

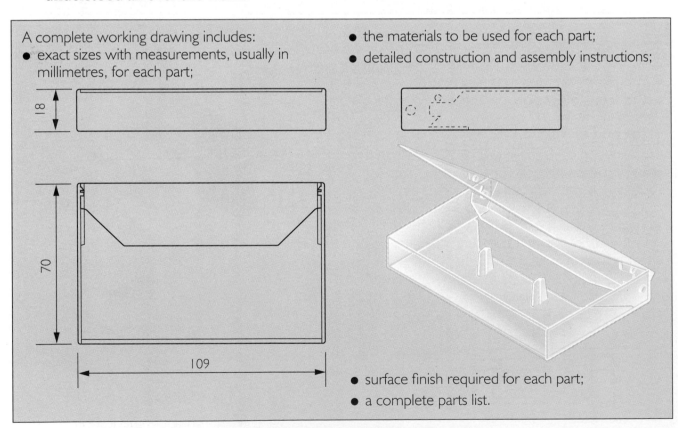

- surface finish required for each part;
- a complete parts list.

It may not always be possible to make a full-size drawing of your design. It may be too large to fit on the paper, or so small that you would not be able to see the detail.

Choose a suitable scale and write it on the drawing. A full size drawing is 1:1, an object drawn at half size is 1:2, and one shown at twice the size is 2:1.

Resource Tasks
CRT 5, 6

Assembly details

Most products you design are made up of several **components** (parts). On a working drawing each must be identified and shown in its correct position for **assembly**.

A good way of doing this is by drawing an accurate 'exploded' view of the product (see page 28). These views may be 2D or 3D. Label or number each component to help with identification.

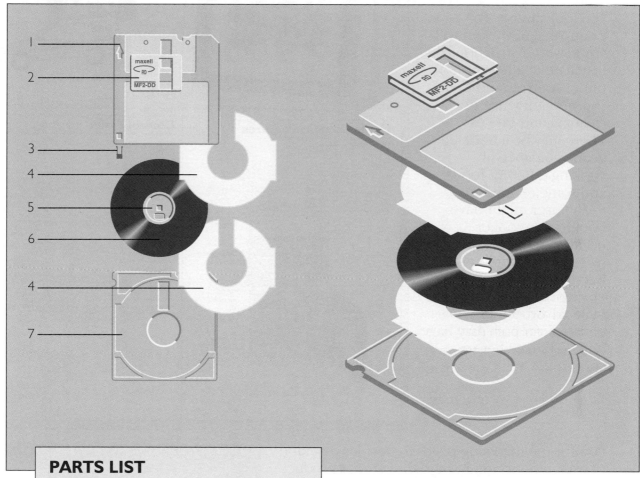

PARTS LIST
  1 Shell top × 1
  2 Auto-shutter × 1
  3 Write protect slider × 1
  4 Liner × 2
  5 Metal hub × 1
  6 Disc × 1
  7 Shell bottom × 1

Parts list

A parts list is a table of information. For each component it gives:

- part number;
- description;
- quantity needed.

If it is on a working drawing it will also list:

- size;
- material it is made from;
- surface finish.

Resource Task

CRT 7

User support

Now you have designed and made your product you need to persuade someone to buy it.

You will need to make sure that the person using it understands how to use and look after it. For example, a new oven will come with instructions on installation, a description of the controls and their use, and guidance on cleaning and safe use. There may be a booklet giving guidance on cooking different foods and some recipes.

The user might have bought this cooker because a model showed how new technology had been used to improve its efficiency. Or information in an advertisement or consumer report may have helped him or her to choose it.

Different sorts of user support. ▶

Look at the following pages to decide what kind of user support might be right for your product.

Demonstration models

Demonstration models are used to show exactly how a final design will work. They can help to explain an idea, a process or a system, often using a simplified version of the actual design.

Sometimes it is helpful to scale-up the model (for instance, a small mechanism). At other times the model can be scaled-down (for instance, a hydro-electric plant).

The model may be a graphic representation of a system or process, and may take the form of a diagram, such as a flow chart (see page 45).

Small-scale model of a wind turbine on a farm. ▶

Guides and instructions

Many products are supplied with a **user guide**, a set of instructions to ensure that the product is used effectively and safely. This information must be clear and easy to understand, so care needs to be taken in the production of the guide.

Communicating information graphically – using pictures or diagrams – can be very effective.

Step-by-step instructions for some self-assembly furniture. Note the use of 'exploded' views and no words. ▶

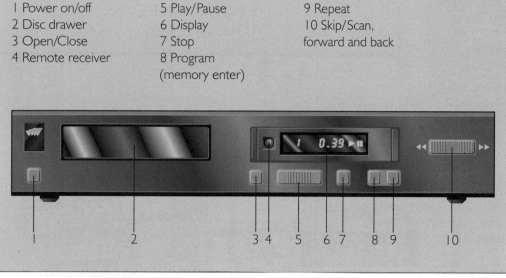

1 Power on/off
2 Disc drawer
3 Open/Close
4 Remote receiver

5 Play/Pause
6 Display
7 Stop
8 Program
(memory enter)

9 Repeat
10 Skip/Scan,
forward and back

▲ *The layout of controls on a compact disc player. Note the use of a front view and key.*

EL TORO RESTAURANT OPTIMAL KITCHEN MANAGEMENT SYSTEM . DRAFT WORKSHEET 3

Date: 25/8/95   Operative/s: PABLO   Unit: C3

Menu No: 64

Item: Spanish Rice

PROGRESS

INGREDIENTS

Item	Quantity
Long grain rice	150g
Onion	1
Green pepper	1
Margarine	25g
Tomatoes	395g tin
Salt	to taste
Sugar	1 t/spoon
Bayleaf	1
Cheddar cheese	50g
Water	500 ml

UTENSILS

Item	Size/Qty
Saucepan	6pt 1

A.M.

Time	PREP.UNIT	COOK UNIT
10.00	Gather all utensils and ingredients to hand	
10.05	Grate cheese	Put water in saucepan. Add salt to taste. Bring to boil
10.10		Add rice to water
10.15	Deseed pepper and slice. Peel and chop onion. Open can of tomatoes	
10.20	Melt margarine in	Turn on oven to heat up. check rice to see if cooked

▲ *Part of a sequence diagram showing stages in the preparation of some food.*

Resource Tasks
SRT 32, RMRT 4

...User support

Choosing the best buy

The results of product evaluations can be useful to people who are choosing which product to buy. Meeting a demanding specification can convince people that the product is a good buy.

You will often see specifications for a product used in advertising – especially for cars. It is more helpful for the user to find information about available products in a consumer report. *Which?* and other consumer magazines test and compare products and services, and publish the results with suggested best buys. The consumer knows their advice is independent and objective.

THE NEW 4 LITRE XJS.
SAME CLASSIC LINES BUT WITH 2 NEW CURVES.

The information in consumer reports needs to be accurate, but also clear and readily understandable to non-technical people.

Charts, diagrams and good graphics help the user to understand the results of any tests, and to decide on the best buy.

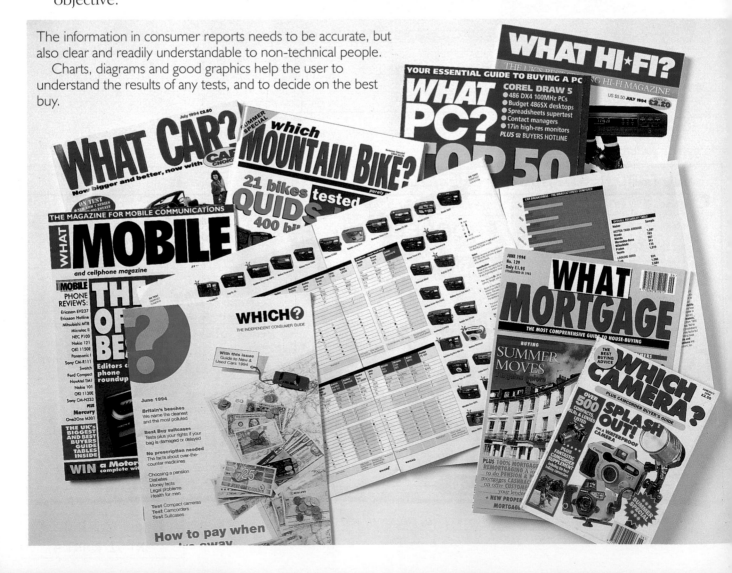

Communication Chooser Chart

Use the chart to decide which technique or drawing system to use.

What you want to communicate	Techniques or drawing systems to use
Realistic appearance of products	rendering on perspective or isometric views
Realistic appearance of clothing	fashion drawing
Realistic appearance of food	photography
Giving impact	put drawing opr photograph against a background
Putting the product in a picture	single point perspective
Plans for food products	recipes
Plans for textile products	patterns
Plans for other products	orthographic views (suitable for CAD)
Assembly details	exploded views
Using a product	simple annotated drawings

3 Designing and making with resistant materials

Choosing resistant materials

What are they like?

'Resistant material' is the term used for materials such as wood, plastic and metal. To describe a resistant material think about its physical properties, appearance and keeping qualities.

▲ *Can you describe and name the materials shown here?*

Physical properties
These govern what the material can do.

- **Strength** – a strong material will carry a heavy load without breaking.
- **Stiffness** – a stiff material will not bend or stretch easily.
- **Electrical conductivity** – an electrical **conductor** allows an electric current to flow through it.
- **Thermal conductivity** – a good **thermal** conductor allows heat to pass through it.
- **Heaviness** – a **dense** material will weigh a lot for its size.
- **Toughness** – a tough material withstands blows without breaking; a brittle material is easily broken.

▲ *The effect of surroundings on materials.* ▼

Appearance
You can describe the appearance of a material by asking questions:

- Does it look natural or manufactured?
- Is it rough or smooth?
- Is it shiny or dull?
- Is it **transparent** (see-through) or **opaque**?
- Is it coloured?
- Is it patterned?

Keeping qualities
Many materials are affected by their surroundings. Many metals are **corroded** by air and water. Wood is attacked by insects and fungus. Many plastics become discoloured and brittle with age. Some materials are meant not to keep, such as **biodegradable** materials.

Questions to ask yourself

When you are deciding which materials to use for your design you will need to consider all these questions. The information on pages 79–80 will help you. This example will help.

Tom chooses the materials for a steady-hand game

Tom had designed this game for his school fête. He had to choose the materials for each of the parts. He used the resistant materials information on pages 79–80. His choices and the reasons for them are shown below. Do you agree with him?

What does it need to do? What physical properties will be important?

What's available?

What materials have these properties?

How do I want it to look?

What keeping qualities will it need?

What's the best starting form?

How much can I afford?

What consequences will my choice have?

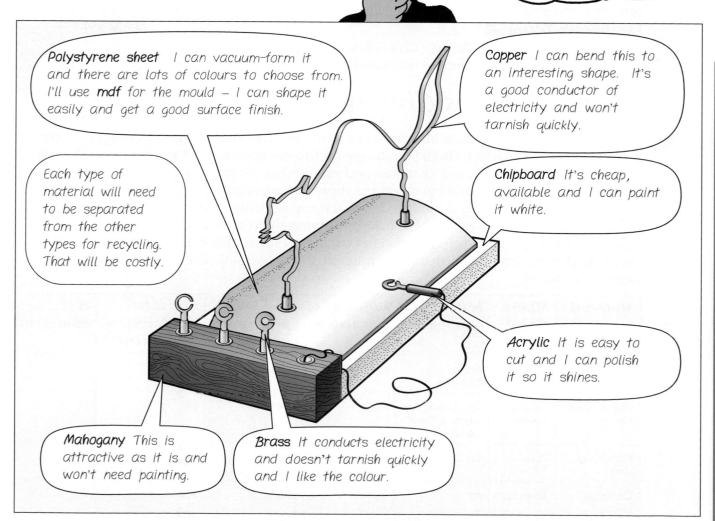

Polystyrene sheet I can vacuum-form it and there are lots of colours to choose from. I'll use **mdf** for the mould – I can shape it easily and get a good surface finish.

Copper I can bend this to an interesting shape. It's a good conductor of electricity and won't tarnish quickly.

Each type of material will need to be separated from the other types for recycling. That will be costly.

Chipboard It's cheap, available and I can paint it white.

Acrylic It is easy to cut and I can polish it so it shines.

Mahogany This is attractive as it is and won't need painting.

Brass It conducts electricity and doesn't tarnish quickly and I like the colour.

...Choosing resistant materials

Consequences

In choosing materials, consider these important questions:

● Where does the material come from?

Some materials are grown and are renewable. Others are found underground and are not. The way both sorts of materials are obtained can harm the **environment**.

● Where will it go when the useful life of the product is over?

The design of your products should encourage the non-renewable materials to be recycled and reused. You can find out more about this in *Meeting needs and wants*.

The harmful effects of material production. ▶

Resistant materials information

Choosing wood

The information in the Chooser Charts and the available forms panel will help you decide whether to use wood and if so what sort.

Consequences Chooser Chart

The chart below summarizes information about the environmental cost of using certain materials. You can use it to help you decide on the environmental impact of your designs. There is concern that the use of metals and plastics has a high environmental cost because it takes lots of energy to extract and process these materials into useful forms. There is also concern that because they are not renewable these valuable resources may become used up. So it is important that we use these materials sparingly, in ways that enable them to be reused or recycled efficiently. It is also important to ensure that the industries producing them do all they can to improve the extraction and processing so it has minimal impact on our environment.

Material	*Where from?*	*Is it renewable?*	*Difficulty of extraction*	*Amount of processing required*	*Can it be easily reused or recycled?*	*Is it biodegradable?*
Natural timber	forests	yes, if managed	low	low	yes	yes
Manufactured boards	natural timber	yes, if natural timber is from managed source	low	medium	yes	
Metals and alloys	ores	no	high	high	sometimes	no
Common plastics	fossil fuels	no	high	high	sometimes	no

Available forms
These forms of timber are readily available.

Manufactured Board and Wood Chooser Chart

Material	Important properties	Making tips	Cost	Typical uses
Plywood	tough doesn't warp exterior plywood is water-resistant	can split when cut	high	containers flat cut-out figures mechanical parts – links, cams, wheels
Hardboard	brittle goes soggy with water	tears easily difficult to finish edges	low	covering panels
Medium density fibreboard (mdf)	hard keeps edges well goes soggy with water	blunts tools shapes easily finishes well drills well	medium	block models vacuum forming moulds small bases
Chipboard	brittle edges easily damaged	difficult to shape blunts tools finishes poorly catches on drills	low	large bases
Red deal (often called pine)	softwood, cream and pale brown colour, often knotty, rots unless protected	moderately easy to cut, trim, shape and join	low	simple frameworks, block models
Jelutong	hardwood, light colour, no knots, more durable than red deal	easy to cut, trim, shape and join	medium	simple frameworks, block models, moulds for vacuum forming
Balsa	hardwood, whitish pink, very soft, very light, not durable	very easy to shape, cut and trim for joining use balsa cement	high	rapid model-making light-weight structures
Mahogany	hardwood, red-brown colour, durable	more difficult to work than red deal or jelutong	medium	containers, indoor furniture, items requiring decorative finish

Resource Task

RMRT 11

... *Resistant materials information*

Choosing metals

The information in the Metals Chooser Chart and the available forms panel will help you decide whether to use metal and if so what sort.

Metals Chooser Chart

Material	Important properties	Making tips	Cost	Typical uses
Mild steel	silver-grey colour stiff and strong rusts in moist air ferrous alloy of iron and carbon	easy to join using heat (brazing) difficult to deform or melt and cast quite hard to shape	low	mechanical parts such as axles and linkages frameworks from both strip or tube
Aluminium	silver-white colour low density non ferrous	difficult to join using heat easy to deform, shape and cast	medium	castings for jewellery, decorative items and fittings
Copper	pinkish-brown colour good conductor tarnishes slowly in moist air non ferrous	easy to join using heat (solder) very easy to deform and shape	high	decorative items electrical contacts
Brass	yellow colour hard tarnishes slowly in moist air alloy of copper and zinc non ferrous	easy to join using heat (solder) fairly easy to cast	high	mechanical parts such as couplings and bearings decorative items

Available forms

These forms of metal are readily available.

Choosing plastics

The information in the Plastics Chooser Chart and the available forms panel will help you decide whether to use plastics and if so what sort.

Plastics Chooser Chart

Material	Important properties	Making tips	Cost	Typical uses

Acrylic	stiff and strong but not tough
	scratches easily
	wide range of colours
	thermoplastic
		good for strip heating
		polishes well
		join using Tensol
		    cement
			medium	containers and storage
				    devices
				flat cut-out figures
				mechanical parts –
				    links, cams, wheels

PVC
(poly vinyl
chloride)
	stiff, strong and tough
	more scratch-resistant
	    than acrylic
	thermoplastic
		join using liquid solvent
		    cement (sold as
		    plumbers' material)
			medium	containers and storage
				    devices

Polystyrene
(high impact
polystyrene)
	not tough
	wide range of colours
	thermoplastic
		good for vacuum forming
		join using liquid
		    polystyrene cement
			low	shell forms for
				    containers, model
				    boats, model cars

ABS
(acrylonitrile
butadienestyrene)
	stiff, strong and tough
	scratches easily
	wide range of colours
	thermoplastic
		easy to cut and trim
		join using liquid solvent
		    cement
			medium	frameworks and
				    mechanical parts –
				    links, cams, wheels

Nylon	stiff, strong and tough
	self-lubricating
	thermoplastic
		machines well
		difficult to join with
		    adhesives
			high	good for bearings and
				    mechanical
				    components

Polyester resin	liquid, sets to a hard
	    solid
	Wide range of colours
	thermosetting plastic
		important to use
		    the correct
		    amount of catalyst
		    for hardening
			medium	solid, decorative
				    castings reinforced
				    with glass fibre to
				    give strong shell
				    structures

Available forms

These forms of plastics are readily available.

Resource Task
RMRT 11

Marking out and checking that it's right

You will need to transfer your designs to the materials carefully so that you can cut and shape accurately. Unless you mark out and check thoroughly you will not be able to make your design well.

Check for the straightest part first

Usually your material will have at least one surface or edge which is already accurate. Check for this with a steel rule. Mark out using this surface or edge as a starting point.

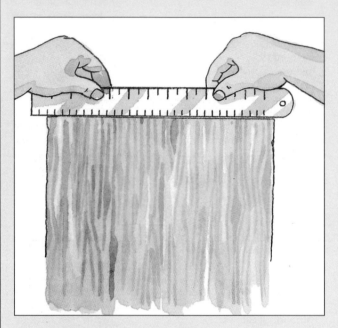

Marking and checking angles

Tools to help you mark out and check 90° angles:

- For wood use a try-square.
- For metal or plastics use an engineer's square.
- Draw or check angles other than 90° with an adjustable bevel.

Making marks

Use different markers for different materials.
Use a sharp pencil for wood or the paper protection on plastic sheet.
Use a scriber or spirit-based felt pen for metal or bare plastics.

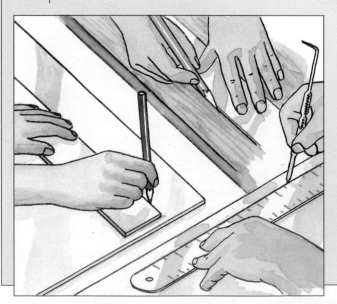

Marking out lines parallel to a straight edge

Use a marking gauge on wood.
Use odd leg callipers on metal or plastic sheet.

Marking out and checking circular parts

Mark circular curves with a pencil compass on wood or paper protection on plastic.
For metal use a pair of spring dividers and mark the centre with a centre punch.

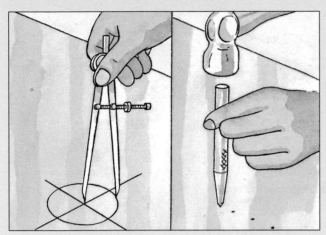

Check the inside and outside diameters of circular objects with inside or outside callipers which can then be measured against a rule.

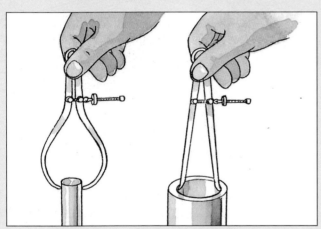

Use a centre square to draw in a diameter. To find the centre of an 'unknown' circle, draw two diameters and see where they cross.

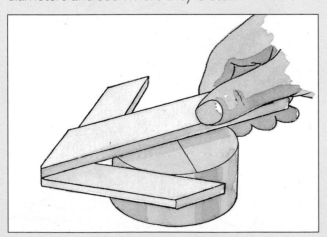

Marking out irregular shapes

To mark out irregular shapes use a card template. They are useful if you want to mark out more than one shape.

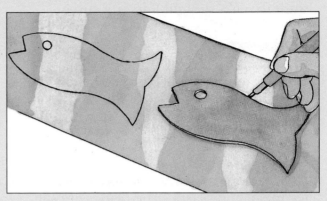

Marking out the position for drilling holes

To drill a hole you only need to mark out the centre. Use a small, accurate cross.
To stop the drill bit from wandering away from the centre of the cross, mark it with a centre punch on metal and a bradawl on wood.
For plastics mark the cross on a piece of masking tape.

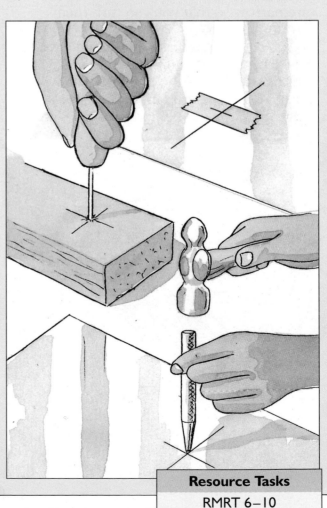

Resource Tasks
RMRT 6–10

Cutting the pieces and trimming them

The cutting tool you choose to use will depend on the material you are cutting – wood, metal or plastic – and whether you want to cut a straight line or a curve.

Sawing

Hard or thin materials have to be cut with a saw which has many small teeth. Thicker and softer materials can be cut with a saw with larger teeth.

Sawing straight

Use a tenon saw for wood and a hacksaw for metal and plastic. The blades are stiff and wide and cannot be twisted to follow curves.

Sawing curves

Use a coping saw to cut curves in wood and plastics. The blade is set so that it cuts when it is pulled.

Use an abra file for metal. The blades are narrow so that you can turn them around the curve.

You can also use a small machine fret saw. This will cut thin wood and metal. To cut plastics, cover the part to be cut with masking tape to stop the plastic's waste sticking in the cut behind the blade.

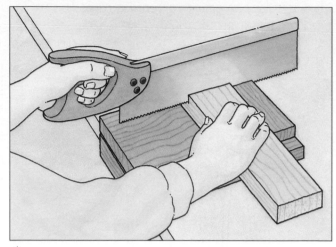

▲ *A tenon saw cuts a piece of wood held against a bench hook.*

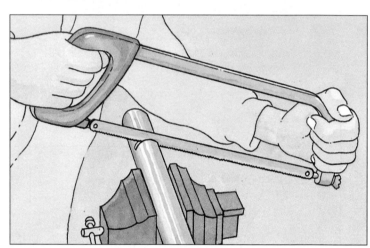

▲ *A hacksaw cuts a mild steel bar held in an engineer's bench vice.*

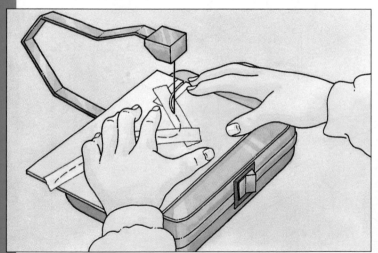

▲ *A small machine fret saw cuts a curve.*

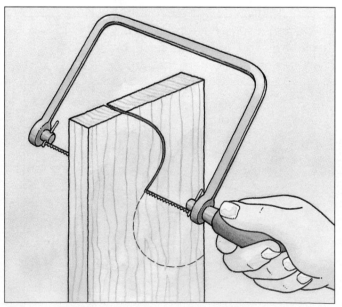

▲ *A coping saw cuts a curve.*

Shearing

Thin sheet metal can be difficult to cut with a saw. You can cut it more easily by using tin snips which **shear** through the metal.

Trimming

It is difficult to saw or shear materials accurately. To get the exact shape you want you will need to **trim** the material down to the line after it has been cut off or cut out.

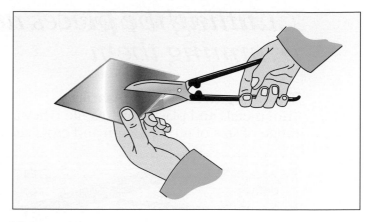

Using chisels

Use a chisel to clear away material neatly and make slots and grooves.

Remember the following safety points:

- Hold the work firmly in a cramp or vice, leaving both your hands free.
- Use a wooden mallet to tap the chisel, so that you don't make your hand sore.

- Keep both hands behind the cutting edge of the chisel. Then, if it slips, your fingers are safe.

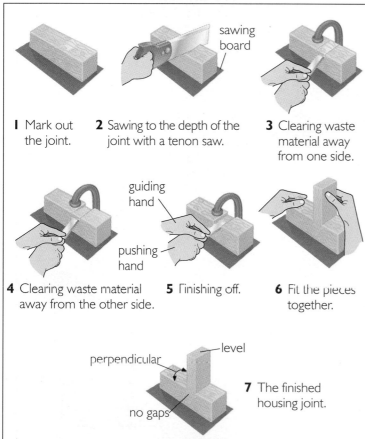

1 Mark out the joint.

2 Sawing to the depth of the joint with a tenon saw. — sawing board

3 Clearing waste material away from one side.

4 Clearing waste material away from the other side. — guiding hand, pushing hand

5 Finishing off.

6 Fit the pieces together.

7 The finished housing joint. — level, perpendicular, no gaps

▲ *Making a simple housing joint.*

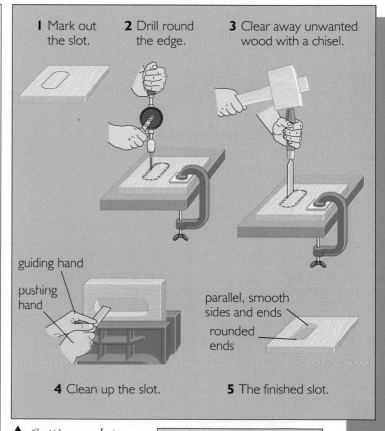

1 Mark out the slot.

2 Drill round the edge.

3 Clear away unwanted wood with a chisel.

guiding hand, pushing hand

4 Clean up the slot.

parallel, smooth sides and ends, rounded ends

5 The finished slot.

▲ *Cutting a slot.*

Resource Tasks

RMRT 6, 7

...Cutting the pieces and trimming them

Trimming metals and plastics

Trim metals and plastics with a file. They are available in a range of size of teeth, length and cross-sectional shapes.

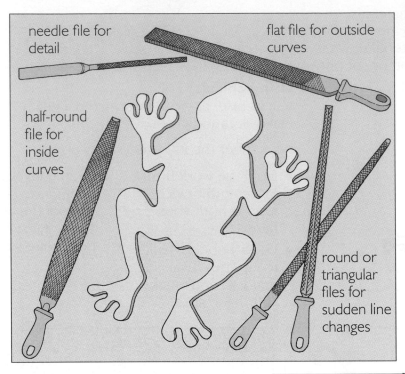

needle file for detail

flat file for outside curves

half-round file for inside curves

round or triangular files for sudden line changes

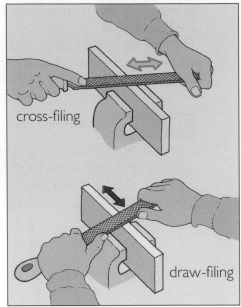

cross-filing

draw-filing

Which file you use will depend on the shape you are making. Most trimming is done by cross-filing, followed by draw-filing to a good finish.

Sawing and shearing materials is an approximate process. For an accurate shape, trim the material down to the line after it has been cut off or cut out.

Trim the straight edges on a piece of wood or manufactured board ▶ with a plane.

Trimming wood

To plane the end grain of solid wood you must plane in half-way from each end to prevent the corners from breaking.

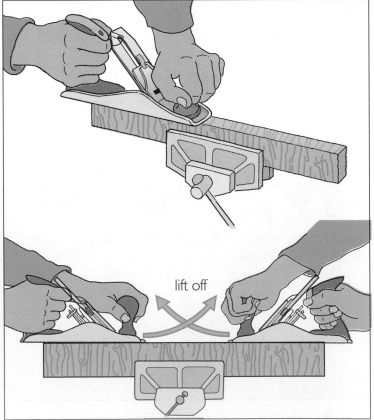

lift off

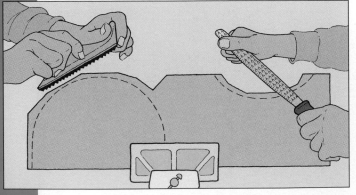

▲ *For inside and outside curves use a surform or wood rasp.*

Using a sanding machine

Small pieces of wood and plastics can be trimmed on a sanding machine. You can make a simple **jig** to trim circular pieces of material. Remember to mark out a line to which you can work.

A belt sander. ▶

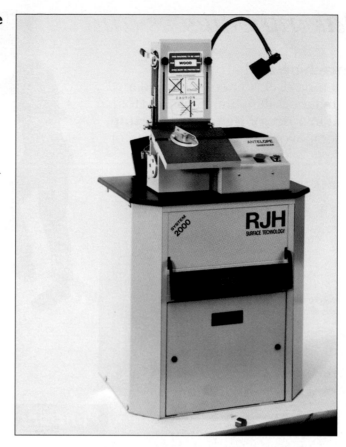

Making holes

Drilling holes

Using hand drills

You can drill small diameter holes (1–6 mm) by hand with a wheel brace (hand drill) and twist drill. This method is suitable for small holes in wood, plastics and softer metals.

Hold the work firmly so it does not move or bend.

Put scrap wood under your workpiece to prevent the material splitting or tearing.

Larger holes in wood can be made with a brace and twist bit. In this case bore until the point just breaks through.

Turn the work over and, using the small hole made by the point as a guide, bore through from the other side.

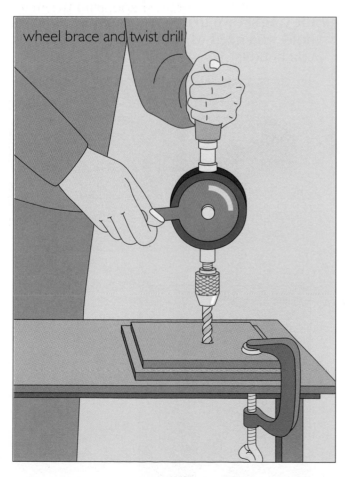

wheel brace and twist drill

Resource Tasks
RMRT 6, 7, 8

87

... *Making holes*

Using a machine drill

Using a machine drill, sometimes called a pillar drill, makes drilling much easier. Hold the material in a vice or **jig** or with a **cramp**. Rest it on scrap wood to prevent splitting or tearing.

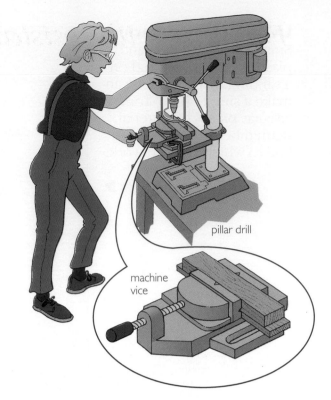

pillar drill

machine vice

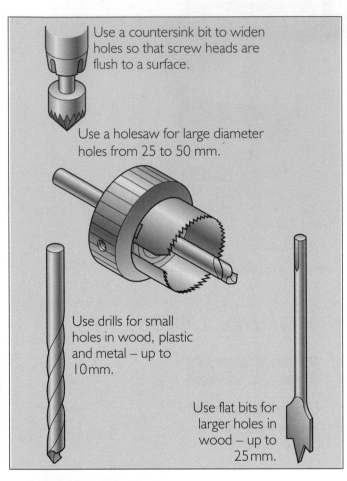

Use a countersink bit to widen holes so that screw heads are flush to a surface.

Use a holesaw for large diameter holes from 25 to 50 mm.

Use drills for small holes in wood, plastic and metal – up to 10mm.

Use flat bits for larger holes in wood – up to 25mm.

Punching holes

It is often easier to punch a hole in thin material. You can use a simple punch tool like the one shown to do this. You must punch any holes you need while the material is flat; before you bend it.

Sawing holes

You can use a coping saw or abra file. These can be taken apart and reassembled with the blade through a hole so that a shape can be cut from the centre of the material.

Mark out the shape, drill a 3mm hole, fit the blade through the hole and secure in a vice.

Reassemble the saw and cut out the shape. Remove the saw.

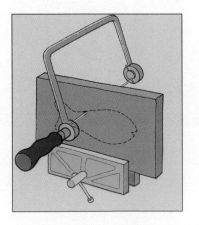

Resource Tasks
RMRT 6–8

Forming with resistant materials

Folding and bending

You can use simple folds or bends in some materials to make interesting forms.

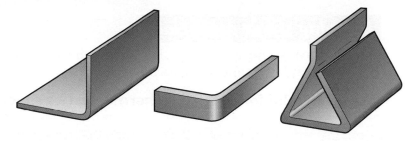

Bending thermoplastics with a strip heater

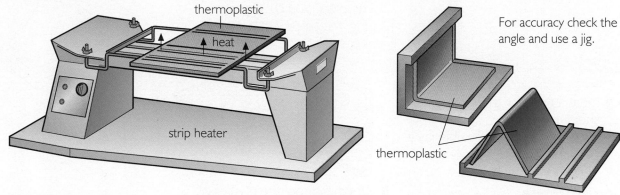

thermoplastic

heat

strip heater

For accuracy check the angle and use a jig.

thermoplastic

Mark the position of the fold onto the outside of the plastic with a marker or chinagraph pencil.

Heat both sides of the material where it is marked, using a strip heater.

When it feels soft enough, fold it to the required angle. If it is hot, use protective leather gloves.

When cool the plastic will retain its new shape and the marking out can be cleaned off.

Using a folding machine

The best way to fold or bend sheet metal is to use a folding machine like the one shown. This gives a clean fold along a straight line. It is much easier to do it this way than by using a vice or folding bars.

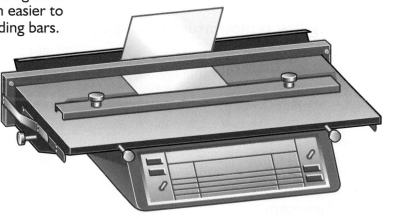

Resource Task

RMRT 6

...Forming with resistant materials

Forming sheet materials

You can form some sheet materials into shell forms by vacuum forming, hollowing and plug-and-yoke forming.

Plug-and-yoke forming thin thermoplastics sheet

1 Mark out the required piece of mdf or plywood.

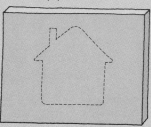

2 Cut around the shape with a coping saw starting in from the outside. Make sure that the edges are made smooth. The piece you cut out is the plug, the piece you leave becomes the yoke.

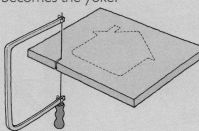

3 Glue another piece of plywood or **mdf** underneath the yoke.

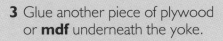

4 Heat a piece of thermoplastics sheet in an oven.
When it is soft and flexible lay it over the yoke and press the plug into the yoke.

SAFETY △
Wear protective leather gloves.

5 When it is cool the plastic will retain its new shape. Cut away the excess material, and trim the edges. Then smooth them using a sheet of glasspaper on a flat work-top.

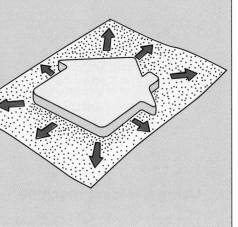

Using low temperature moulding material

You can use this material to produce small solid 3D shapes easily and quickly. The material comes as granules. Place these in a bowl and pour on hot water. After a few moments the granules will coalesce in a blob which you can take out and shape by squeezing it between your fingers. As it cools it becomes stiffer and eventually sets hard. If you haven't got the shape you want by then just put it back in the hot water until it softens and try again.

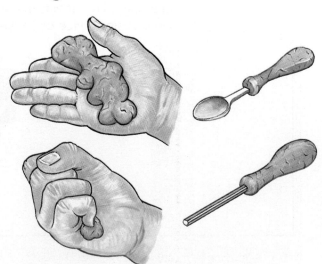

Vacuum forming thermoplastics sheet

1 Prepare a mould of the form you want to make. Use plywood, solid wood or mdf.

The sides of the mould must slope slightly to help remove the form from the mould after completion. The mould should be smooth and polished.

Moulds can also be made from dried and hardened clay.

2 Place the mould on the bed of the vacuum-forming machine.

3 Clamp the sheet of thermoplastics into place. Heat it until it is soft and flexible.

4 The machine will bring the mould and the thermoplastics sheet together. With the vacuum pump withdraw the air from between the mould and thermoplastics sheet. Air pressure on the outside will press the sheet against the mould.

5 When it cools, the thermoplastics sheet will keep its new shape. Tap out the mould, cut away the excess material and trim and smooth the edges.

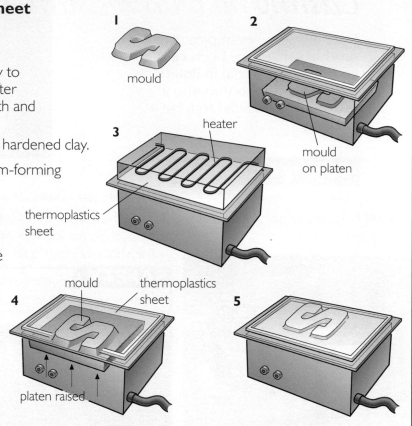

Forming sheet aluminium alloy or copper by hollowing

1 Mark out and cut the required outline shape from the flat sheet with tin snips.

2 **Anneal** the metal by heating it. This makes it easy to work. Copper will glow cherry red when it is hot enough. Aluminium alloy needs less heat but gives no tell-tale glow. Smear some soap onto the cold metal and heat it until the soap goes black.

3 Cool the metal in cold water. Form a dish by hammering the metal into a sandbag with a bossing mallet. Start from the outside and work into the middle.

4 This will give a rough shape which can be made true by using a blocking hammer to hammer the form into a hollow carved into the surface of a heavy piece of wood. Or hammer the shape from the outside with a flat-faced mallet over a domed metal stake.

5 Clean up the metal and polish it.

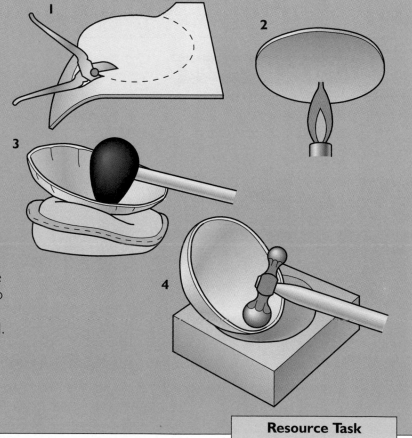

Resource Task

RMRT 9

Casting

Here are some examples of products that have been **cast**. In each case a material in liquid form has been poured into a **mould** and set solid to form a **casting**.

▲ *All these objects have been produced by casting.*

Casting with metal

1 Melt the metal by heating it in a ladle.

2 Pour the molten metal into the heatproof mould. It takes up the shape of the mould.

SAFETY △ Care is required when pouring molten metal

3 The metal cools in the mould and freezes solid.

4 Split open the mould to get the casting out.

5 Trim the spare metal off the casting.

6 You can paint the finished casting.

Casting with resin

1 Mix the liquid resin with the correct amount of catalyst and any colouring.

2 Pour the mixture into the mould.

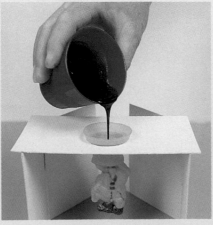

3 The liquid resin sets solid to form a thermosetting plastic.

4 Strip the mould off the casting.

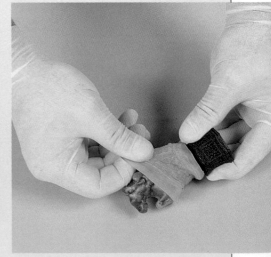

Using machine tools

You can use lathes and milling machines to make components with complex shapes.

The lathe

Using computer-controlled tools

You may be able to use a machine tool that is controlled by micro-computer. You can produce the design on-screen using a computer. This is CAD – computer assisted design.

The computer uses this information to control the cutting machine that makes the design. This is CAM – computer aided manufacture.

The mill

The vinyl cutter

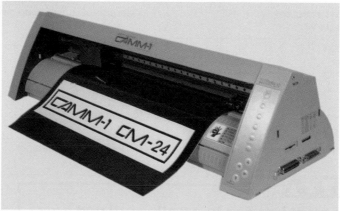

Resource Task
RMRT 10

Joining

Describing joining

Four important terms you will need to use when describing how two pieces of material are joined together are:

- **temporary**;
- **permanent**;
- **rigid**;
- **flexible**.

These examples will help you understand what they mean.

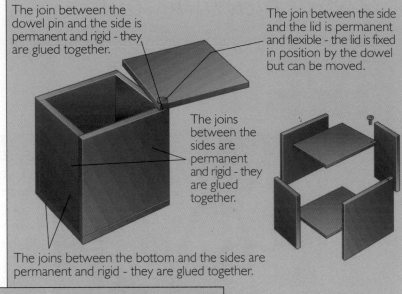

The join between the dowel pin and the side is permanent and rigid - they are glued together.

The join between the side and the lid is permanent and flexible - the lid is fixed in position by the dowel but can be moved.

The joins between the sides are permanent and rigid - they are glued together.

The joins between the bottom and the sides are permanent and rigid - they are glued together.

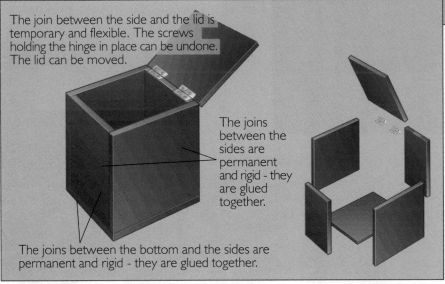

The join between the side and the lid is temporary and flexible. The screws holding the hinge in place can be undone. The lid can be moved.

The joins between the sides are permanent and rigid - they are glued together.

The joins between the bottom and the sides are permanent and rigid - they are glued together.

Adhesives

You will often need to join materials together using **adhesives**.
The Adhesives Chooser Chart will help you make the right choice.

Adhesives Chooser Chart

Adhesive	Uses
PVA (polyvinyl acetate) e.g. Evostik Resin W	a general-purpose wood glue; not water-resistant
Synthetic resin e.g. Cascamite	for joining wood; waterproof and stronger than PVA; must be made up immediately before use
Epoxy resin e.g. Araldite	for joining metals and acrylic plastics; waterproof; must be made up immediately before use
Contact adhesive e.g. Dunlop Thixafix	for joining polystyrene, fabrics and leather
Acrylic cement e.g. Tensol	for joining acrylic plastics

SAFETY

Adhesives must be used in a well-ventilated area.

Resource Task

RMRT 8

Fittings

You will often need to fix materials together using **fittings** such as nails, screws or nuts and bolts. The Fittings Chooser Chart will help you make the right choice.

Fittings Chooser Chart

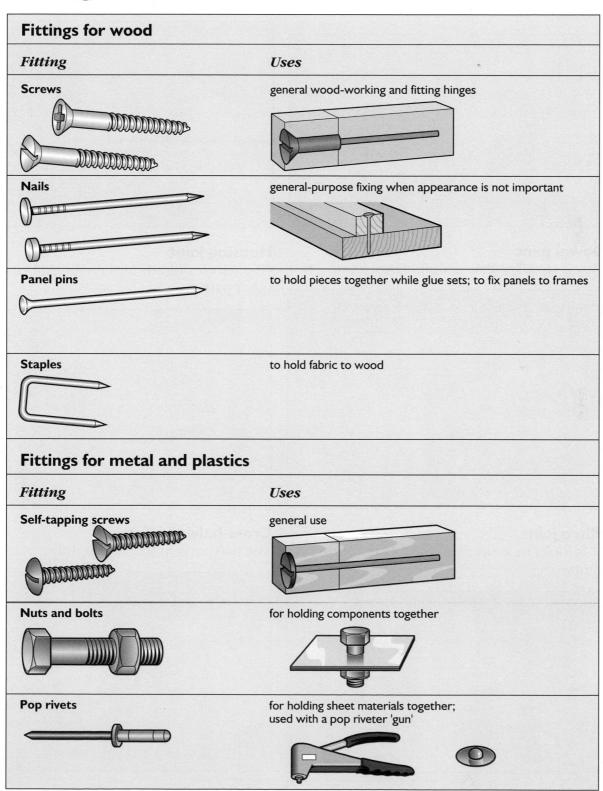

Fittings for wood	
Fitting	*Uses*
Screws	general wood-working and fitting hinges
Nails	general-purpose fixing when appearance is not important
Panel pins	to hold pieces together while glue sets; to fix panels to frames
Staples	to hold fabric to wood

Fittings for metal and plastics	
Fitting	*Uses*
Self-tapping screws	general use
Nuts and bolts	for holding components together
Pop rivets	for holding sheet materials together; used with a pop riveter 'gun'

... *Joining*

Ways of joining wood

Here are some different ways of joining pieces of timber or manufactured board.

Simple butt joint
The two pieces have been pinned and glued together.

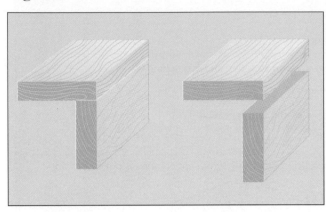

Lapped joint
This is stronger than a simple butt joint.

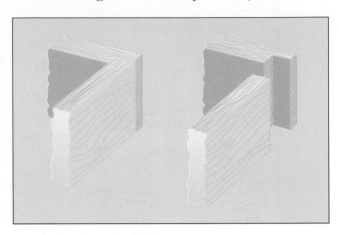

Dowel joint
This is stronger than a simple butt joint.

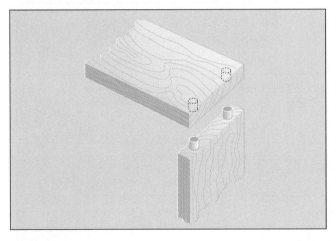

Housing joint
One part fits tightly into the housing in the other part.

Mitre joint
This looks more attractive than butt or dowel joints.

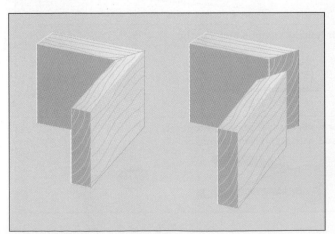

Cross-halving joint
The two parts fit together tightly.

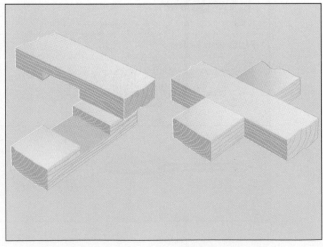

Brazing and soldering

You can join two metals by using a different metal with a lower melting point as the 'adhesive'. When you heat the joint, the low melting point metal melts and flows into the gap. As the joint cools this metal turns solid, joining the other two pieces of metal together in a permanent, rigid joint.

It is important to clean the pieces of metal to be joined. Use a **flux** to keep them clean when heating the joint. If they are dirty, the liquid metal will not stick to them properly so the joint will be weak or will not form at all.

The table shows the different solders you can use.

Materials to be joined	Solder	Strength of joint
Copper, brass or tin-plate	soft solder m.p. 185 – 230 °C	weak
Copper or steel	silver solder m.p. 720 – 800 °C	strong
Copper or steel	brazing spelter m.p. 900 °C	very strong

▲ *Soft-soldering tin-plate.*

▲ *Silver-soldering a copper ring.*

▲ *Brazing a steel cross-piece.*

Assembling different parts

You can often make a product by assembling parts.
You might use wood screws or nuts and bolts, so that it can be taken apart again. Here are three other methods of assembly.

Producing a carcass with knock-down fittings

1 Mark out, cut and trim the panels needed for the **carcass.**

2 Hold the carcass together using cramps.

3 Place the knock-down joints in position and mark out.

4 Take the carcass to pieces and attach the fittings.

5 Reassemble using the fittings.

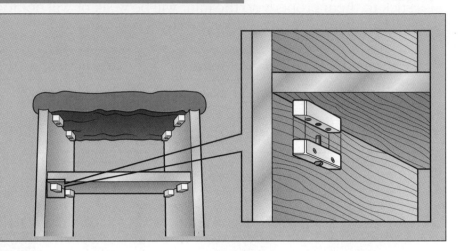

Producing frameworks

A framework from wood strip

1 Mark out, cut and trim the lengths of wooden strip needed for the frame.

2 Mark out and cut joining corners from stiff card or thin plywood.

3 Hold the framework together using cramps.

4 Apply glue to the joining corners and place in position on the framework. Leave to dry. When dry, turn it over and repeat the process.

You may have to work in stages if the framework is complicated.

A framework from PVC tubing

1 Mark out, cut and trim the lengths of tubing needed. Use a file to remove the sharp edges at the ends.

2 Assemble the framework with the corner and T fittings, without adhesive first to check that everything is correct.

3 Take it to pieces and reassemble using a plastic adhesive.

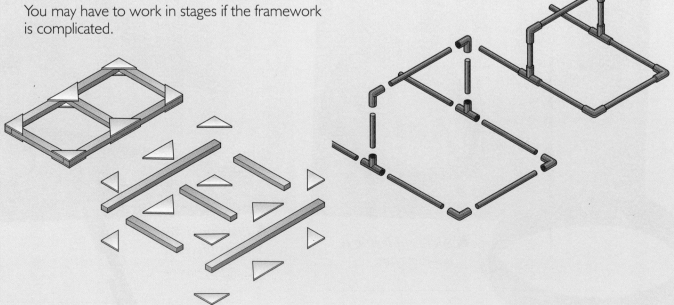

Making resistant materials look good and stay good

Heat treatment

Hardening and tempering

You can **harden** tool steel by heating it to red and then **quenching** (cooling) it in water or oil. This also makes the steel brittle. If parts of the steel need to be tough as well as hard then you need to re-heat it carefully in a process called **tempering**.

To temper a piece of steel heat it very gently so that the surface gets hot enough to combine with the oxygen in the air and form a layer of coloured oxide. Different colours of oxide are formed at different temperatures. The colour of the oxide formed tells you the temperature. The steel gains different properties at different temperatures.

Tempering is used to give steel tools the properties they need as shown in the panel.

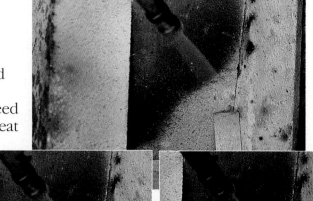

▲ *Careful heating tempers steel.*

Tempering colour chart

Oxide colour	Temperature reached
Yellow	230 °C
Dark yellow	245 °C
Brown	260 °C
Purple	270 °C
Blue	295 °C

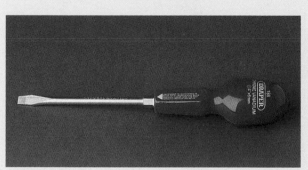

▲ *The screwdriver blade needs to be hard – it is tempered to 270 °C. The shaft needs to be tough – it is tempered to 230 °C.*

▲ *This steel tape needs to be springy – it is tempered to 295 °C.*

...Making resistant materials look good and stay good

Cleaning up

You apply a finish to a resistant material to protect it from the environment and to make it look good.

The first step in applying a finish, called cleaning up, is getting the surface of the material as smooth as possible.

Any surface or edge on which you have used tools will be marked. You should remove these marks.

You can use **abrasives** to wear down the material. Start with coarse abrasive to remove the deepest marks and work down to a fine abrasive, which should leave the material smooth and free of marks.

To clean wood

Use glass paper wrapped around a cork block. The finest grades of paper are called flour paper. Work with the direction of the grain. If you cut across the grain it will leave scratches that are difficult to remove.

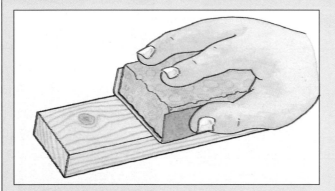

To clean metal

Use emery cloth, working down through the grades. It is often wrapped around a file to keep it flat. A drop of oil will help to remove the waste metal produced.

Final polishing of copper and aluminium alloy can be done with a buffing machine or by hand with metal polish.

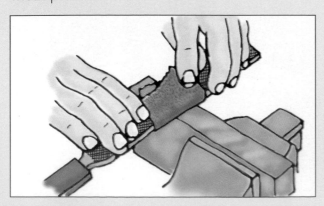

To clean plastics

Use 'wet and dry' (silicon carbide) paper, with water. The water helps remove the waste plastic and stops it clogging up the paper. It also prevents friction heating and spoiling the surface.

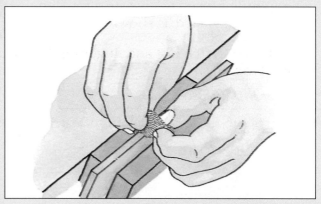

A tightly rolled ball of 0000 grade steel wool can be used as an alternative.

Final polishing can be done with a buffing machine or by hand with metal or plastics polish on a cloth or leather pad.

SAFETY
Care is required when buffing.

Applying a finish

Most woods and some metals will need to have a finish applied. There are two basic types:

- a substance that coats the surface forming a protective skin;
- one that is applied to the surface and soaks into the material.

Plastics do not require a finish other than polishing.

PROTECTIVE LAYER

PENETRATIVE

Protective skin finishes

Paints, varnishes and lacquers

These form protective skins on wood and metal. Paints usually hide the material and provide the surface decoration as well as protection. Some paints require an undercoat.

Varnish and lacquer are usually transparent so the material they are applied to can show through. You can apply them with a brush or a spray.

Leave them to dry somewhere undisturbed and dust-free so that dirt and finger marks do not spoil the finish.

Enamelling

Use enamelling for a highly coloured, tough and attractive finish on copper.

To enamel onto copper:

1 Mark out, cut and trim the required shape of copper blank.
2 Slightly dome the blank with a bossing mallet.
3 Clean the copper blank thoroughly with emery cloth.
4 Place the blank on paper. Mix the enamel powder to a paste with water. Paint the paste onto the blank.
5 Heat the blank in a kiln or on a mesh over a flame until the enamel powder fuses.
6 Set the piece aside to cool down slowly.

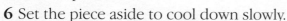

...Making resistant materials look good and stay good

Dip-coating

Use dip-coating for a coloured finish that protects metals from air and moisture.

To dip-coat a piece of mild steel with plastic:

1 Ensure that there is a means of attaching a wire hanger to the object.

2 Clean the object with emery cloth.

3 Hang the object in an oven set at 180° Celsius.

4 Carefully dip the object into a fluidizing tank containing polythene or nylon powder.

SAFETY ⚠
A face mask is essential.

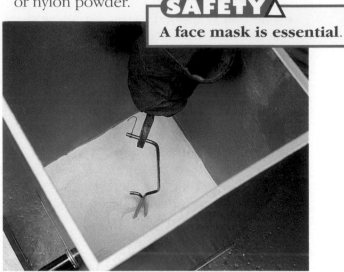

5 Put the object back in the oven until the grains of plastic fuse together.

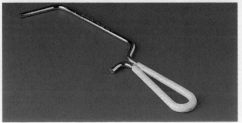

Finishes that soak in

Each of these products uses a finish that soaks in.

▲ *The oil used here makes the wood darker and protects it from water.*

▲ *This stain decorates but does not protect the wood.*

▲ *The finish used here protects but does not alter the appearance.*

This chart will help you choose the finish needed for your product.

Finishes Chooser Chart

Finish	Does it alter appearance?	Does it protect the material?	Can I use it on wood?	Can I use it on metal?
Paint	Yes	Yes	Yes	Yes
Varnish	No	Yes	Yes	No
Lacquer	No	Yes	Yes	Yes
Enamelling	Yes	Yes	No	Yes
Dip-coating	Yes	Yes	No	Yes
Coloured stain	Yes	No	Yes	No
Linseed oil	No	Yes	Yes	No
Sanding sealer	No	Yes	Yes	No
Oil quenching	Yes	Yes	No	Yes

Choosing tools

The information in the Tools Chooser Chart will help you choose the right tools for the job.

Tools Chooser Chart

Process	Wood	Metal	Plastics
For marking out	pencil	scriber	felt-tip pen or scriber
• at right angles	try-square	engineer's square	engineer's square
• parallel to an edge	marking gauge	odd-leg callipers	odd-leg callipers
• an irregular shape	card template	card template	card template
For holding	woodwork vice	metalwork vice	metalwork vice
	G-cramp	G-cramp	G-cramp
	machine vice	machine vice	machine vice
For cutting			
• straight lines	tenon saw	hacksaw	hacksaw
• curves	coping saw	tin snips	abrafile
	fret saw	abrafile	coping saw
For trimming			
• to a straight line	plane	flat file	flat file
	sanding machine		sanding machine
• to a curve	rasp	flat file	flat file
	surform	round file	round file

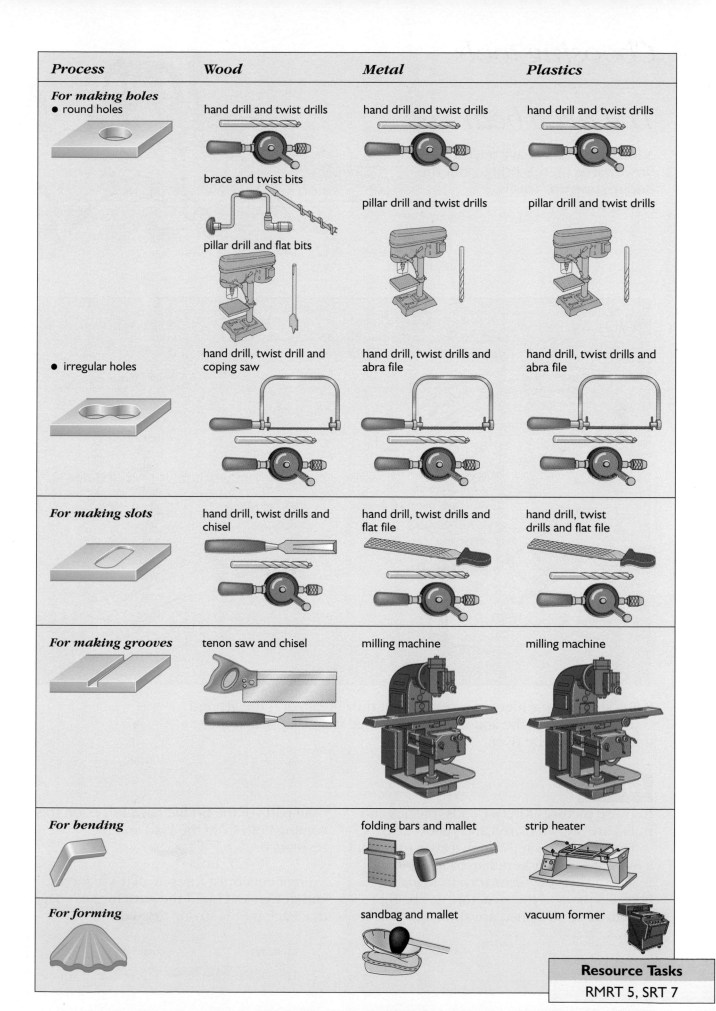

Process	Wood	Metal	Plastics
For making holes ● round holes	hand drill and twist drills brace and twist bits pillar drill and flat bits	hand drill and twist drills pillar drill and twist drills	hand drill and twist drills pillar drill and twist drills
● irregular holes	hand drill, twist drill and coping saw	hand drill, twist drills and abra file	hand drill, twist drills and abra file
For making slots	hand drill, twist drills and chisel	hand drill, twist drills and flat file	hand drill, twist drills and flat file
For making grooves	tenon saw and chisel	milling machine	milling machine
For bending		folding bars and mallet	strip heater
For forming		sandbag and mallet	vacuum former

Resource Tasks
RMRT 5, SRT 7

The arch bears up

A load such as a heavy tractor pushes downwards on this bridge, but the bridge stays up. This is how it works.

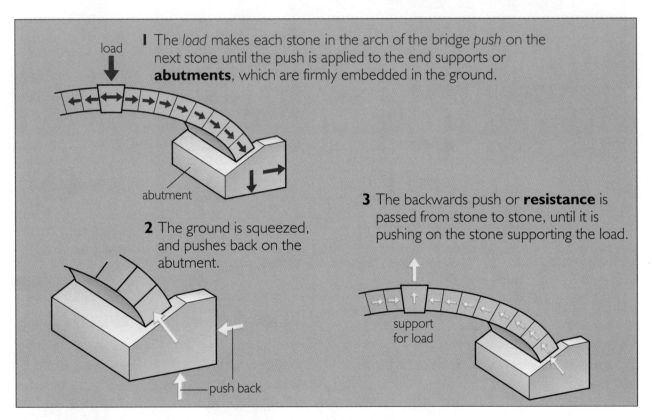

I The *load* makes each stone in the arch of the bridge *push* on the next stone until the push is applied to the end supports or **abutments**, which are firmly embedded in the ground.

load

abutment

2 The ground is squeezed, and pushes back on the abutment.

push back

3 The backwards push or **resistance** is passed from stone to stone, until it is pushing on the stone supporting the load.

support for load

If any stones are squeezed so much that they break, or if the ground is pushed away by the abutments, the bridge will collapse and the tractor fall into the river.

Forces

In these pictures forces (loads, pushes and pulls) are shown by red and yellow arrows.

Those passed on through a structure from a *load* are shown as red arrows. ◀

Those showing *resistance* to loads because parts of the structure are being squeezed or stretched are shown as yellow arrows. ⇨

All parts of the bridge have forces on them coming both from the load and the resistance. ⇨ ◀

Engineers must foresee all these forces, and design and build the structure to ensure that each part is strong enough.

Aloft on the aerial ropeway

The gang's hideaway is in the branches of an old beech tree. Now they are building a rope-and-pulley system for exciting rides. William has offered to test the rope.

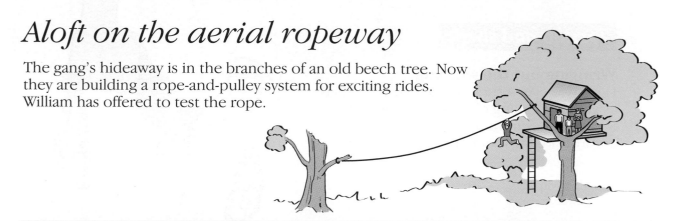

1 As soon as William hangs his full weight from the rope, it stretches. He drops a few feet and the rope becomes tighter.

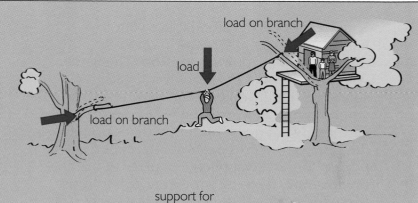

load on branch

load

load on branch

2 The increase in tightness is passed on to the tree branches, making them bend. The bent branches pull backwards on the ends of the rope.

support for William

pull back on rope

pull back on rope

3 These pulling forces are passed back along the rope, right back to where William is hanging.

Ropes in tension

In a tug-of-war, the rope between the teams is stretched by a pulling force from each team.

Stretched, the rope tries to pull its ends inwards.

What happens if team A pulls harder than team B?

What happens if the rope is not strong enough?

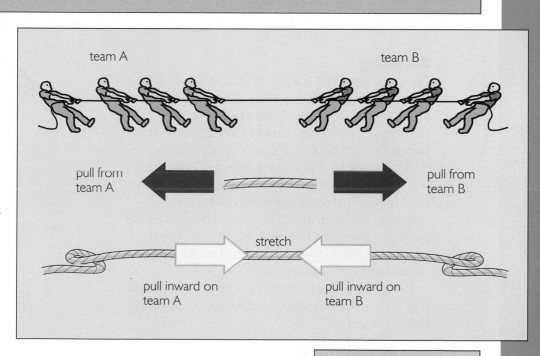

team A

team B

pull from team A

pull from team B

stretch

pull inward on team A

pull inward on team B

Torsion and shear

Wringing out the washing

Have you ever wrung out wet clothes, such as your swimming costume perhaps, or some clothes from the washing machine before hanging them out to dry?

You may not have realised it but your two hands gripping and twisting in opposite directions were applying **torsion**. The harder you grip and twist the more water gets squeezed out. If you grip and twist really hard you can force almost all the water out of a wet garment. What does this tell us that's useful for designing structures. It shows that when torsion forces are applied to a piece of material the material has to be strong enough to resist these forces. If not the material will break. This can sometimes happen when you turn a key in a lock that has become very stiff. The torsion you apply in your efforts to turn the lock are so great that the thin part of the key is not strong enough to resist and it breaks. In very large structures such as pylons which have to withstand strong winds and the pull of cables it is important that the designer plans for the structure to withstand torsion forces.

Unable to resist the torsion forces, the thin part of the key breaks. ▲

Shearing

Has anyone ever told you that scissors don't cut? Strictly speaking, they are right. Knives cut by digging a sharp edge into the surface of a material. The knife can do this because it is harder than the surface it is cutting into. Scissors cut by a shearing action. That is why they are sometimes called shears. It involves two blades moving towards each other in opposite directions as shown. The top blade pushes down on the material as the bottom blade pushes up – as a result, the material is separated into two pieces.

Being strong enough to resist these **shear** forces is important for the fixings that hold things together.

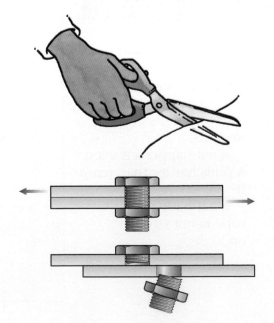

Resource Tasks
RMRT 12

Unable to resist the shear forces, the bolt breaks. ▲

Walking the plank

The cabin boy had been sentenced to 'walk the plank'. As he steps onto it, the plank begins to bend. The further he walks the more it bends, until ...?

The *load* of the cabin boy makes the plank bend.

The top of the plank is stretched and resists by pulling itself inwards. The bottom is squeezed and resists by pushing itself outwards.

The *pulling* effect along the top of the plank may be so strong that the fibres of the wood are torn apart. The plank snaps in two and the cabin boy is tipped into the sea.

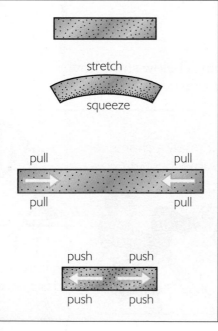

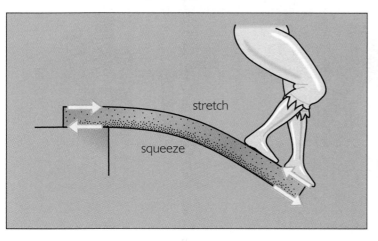

When a plank bends, one side stretches while the other side gets shorter.

stretch

squeeze

When anything is stretched, it becomes tight (like the aerial ropeway), and pulls back on its ends.

pull · · · · · pull

pull · · · · · pull

When something is squeezed, it pushes outwards on its ends (like the stones in the arch bridge).

push · · · push

push · · · push

What happens to planks that bend?

The plank resists bending by pulling in on the ends along its top and pushing out along its bottom.

This happens whenever something bends. It may be a beam simply supported at each end or a cantilever (like the gang-plank). It may be horizontal, vertical or at an angle. Whatever the form, the designer has to foresee the effect of different load sizes and make sure the beam is strong enough to provide the pulling and pushing forces along its length without breaking.

Resource Tasks

RMRT 13, 16

Upsetting the apple-cart

A market trader stacked his cart with apples. The apples sold fast and soon the barrow was nearly half empty.

Suddenly, the barrow tipped up and the apples poured onto the ground. Why?

Structures suddenly overbalance when the distribution of a load changes little by little.

The combined load of the weight of the apples and the cart causes upward resisting forces on the wheels and legs, from the ground.

As the apples are sold from the leg end of the cart, the combined load on the barrow moves away from that end until the upward resisting force is only on the wheels (and no longer on the legs). The cart is now exactly balanced.

combined load

Stable or unstable?

Structures usually need to be stable. The drawings below show how pairs of forces may cause things to topple over or to stay balanced.

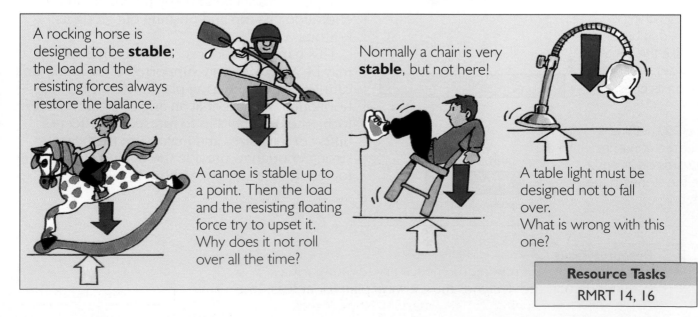

A rocking horse is designed to be **stable**; the load and the resisting forces always restore the balance.

A canoe is stable up to a point. Then the load and the resisting floating force try to upset it. Why does it not roll over all the time?

Normally a chair is very **stable**, but not here!

A table light must be designed not to fall over.
What is wrong with this one?

Resource Tasks

RMRT 14, 16

Step-ladders that won't stay up

This painter tried to use an old step-ladder to reach the top of the wall. But whenever he tried to climb up, it slipped on the floor and went flat.

What was going wrong? As he climbed onto the steps, his weight provided a load, which was passed down, through the pieces of wood and their joints, to the floor. The floor, squeezed like the abutments of the arch bridge on page 106, responded with a resisting force upwards on the feet of the ladder, but....

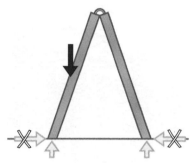

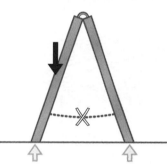

- there was no resisting force to stop the feet of the ladder from slipping out sideways;

- there was no connection between the parts of the ladder to stop it splitting apart;

- there was no stop on the hinge at the top to prevent its opening wide.

On a slippery floor any one of these would have been able to stop the step-ladder falling flat.

Then the painter tried to use the ladder for outdoor work. At first he succeeded. He set up the steps on the grass.

The feet of the ladder stuck into the soil, squeezed it and obtained a resisting force which stopped it moving any further.

Then he set it up half on grass and half on a path. This time there was resistance for one part of the ladder but not for the other... so, whoops!

Strengthening frameworks

Any framework, like this step-ladder, must have some way to keep its shape under a load. Almost always, there will be many possible ways of creating the necessary resisting forces.

Remember, the designer must always plan for at least one method of producing the necessary resisting forces.

Resource Tasks
RMRT 15, 16

Strength in hollow boxes

A well-made box has great strength. Box construction is often used in the design of heavily loaded structures such as ships, motor-car bodies and bridges. But it sometimes goes wrong, as these stories show.

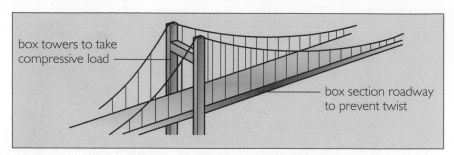

box towers to take compressive load

box section roadway to prevent twist

The bus shelter that blew down
The wind blew off the back of the shelter. Then the walls and roof could no longer support each other and the shelter collapsed.

The car that crumpled
This box was designed to crumple. The energy used in crumpling the car during the crash is not available to injure the travellers.

The soap box that collapsed
Because one side of the box was missing the other sides began to sag. They could no longer support the load of the speaker.

The tower that toppled
The walls and floors of this tower block supported each other. When one wall was blown out, the rest collapsed.

What happens to loaded boxes?

The sides of boxes are very thin compared with their length and breadth. So why is a well-designed box so strong?

The sides are strong in tension. It is difficult to break a side by pulling along it. But it is easy to cause buckling by pushing on it.

Good design takes advantage of the strength in tension and ensures that the walls are supported to prevent buckling.

load

The pieces joining opposite walls prevent buckling.

If two sides come apart at a join the box becomes very weak because it cannot provide a force to resist the load.

resist

If you try to twist a box the walls go into tension and resist.

load

Resource Task

RMRT 16

Lara Sparey – designer/maker of architectural metalwork

Lara was educated at the East Barnet Secondary Comprehensive School in North London, and studied design and technology to A level. Her enthusiasm for the subject was rewarded when her final A level design project, a fabric arm support for stroke victims, won the national Young Designer of the Year Award in 1986.

Lara went on to study the foundation course in art and design at Middlesex Polytechnic, before moving to the West Surrey College of Art and Design to take a degree course in 3D design, specializing in metals. This course provided her with the rich experience of working in a wide range of metals, processes and different scales, from jewellery to architectural metalwork. Her final degree show consisted of a collection of exquisite vessels made from sheet metal, each exploiting the natural properties of the materials to create interesting connections and forms.

Lara Sparey. ▲

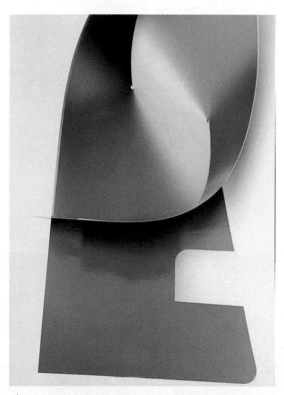

▲ *Lara experimented with sheet metal.*

After leaving college, Lara set up a workshop at Spitalfields in London, working in collaboration with a fine art metal sculptor. One of their first joint commissions was to produce the Spitalfields gates, a large pair of decorative gates marking the entrance to the regenerated old fruit and vegetable market. For Lara, this proved to be the first of a number of large-scale projects, and she went on to further commissions and to design and manufacture other sets of market entrance gates within Spitalfields.

Running alongside these large architectural commissions, Lara undertakes a variety of smaller works, such as small residential gates, furniture and prototyping products for other designers and architects. These smaller projects are important for Lara as they enable her to keep afloat financially on a day to day basis and to develop the skills required to run her own business. In recent years, she has become increasingly involved in undertaking community-led art projects, working within the area of architectural metalwork on commissions which encourage local people, such as residents, retailers, schools and youth groups, to become actively involved in the designing process.

The Cathall Road Archway, Leytonstone, East London

An advertisement in the *Artists' Newsletter*, a monthly publication for artists and designers, invited submissions and suggestions for a project to enhance a covered brick entrance to a housing development in Leytonstone, as part of an urban regeneration scheme. Following interviews by a residents' committee, Lara was pleased to be awarded the commission.

Lara soon set about researching and investigating the site. She built up her knowledge of the local environment through conversations and discussions with local residents and visits to the local museum. She sketched and modelled many alternative designs. Her research revealed the presence of a natural water source on the site, and it was this feature that eventually provided the inspiration for the abstract use of fish, leaves and water lily shapes, and the rippling effect of the waves, to create the overall image for the archway.

The final design. ▲

In order to share her ideas with local residents, Lara prepared an exhibition of her proposals on site and was able to seek their views first-hand. Eventually, a meeting of the residents' steering group approved the final design and gave Lara the go ahead to manufacture the archway. She decided to construct it as a series of panels, to make both fabrication and final installation easier. The curved components, representing waves, were rolled into a number of identical circles and then cut to the required lengths. The motifs were cut from steel sheet using CADCAM, to ensure that they were of a consistent shape and size. Prior to assembly, the frames were hot-dip galvanized to prevent corrosion, and the motifs colour powder coated in enamel before being riveted to the 'waves'.

Installing the arch. ▲

The erection of the completed archway involved a team of steel erectors to ensure that the heavy panels were safely bolted into position. The Mayor of Leytonstone duly opened the archway at a gathering of residents, marking the culmination of four months, hard work from commission to completion and the successful creation of a public work of art to be enjoyed by the local community.

▲ *The completed arch.*

Research

Locate a piece of contemporary 'public art' in your area (for example a piece of sculpture, a mural or a gateway) and try to find out the name of the designer.

Try to find out about other designs he/she has produced.

Write a few sentences to describe your feelings about this piece of work.

Stonebridge Park, North West London

Lara's most recent community project has involved a commission for the Stonebridge Housing Action Trust who are responsible for the development of the Stonebridge Park Estate. The brief was to create an entrance feature for the recreation ground that would provide a focal point for the local community and focus public attention on the recreation ground and its various activities.

▲ *The original railings.*

The project provided an ideal opportunity to involve local people in the design and selection of a piece of artwork for their area. After contacting a number of local community groups, Lara set up a series of workshops to begin the design process and to provide a platform for generating ideas and collating people's concerns and demands for the site. Many workshops were held, involving local children of all ages, from the Gujarati Association, the Adventure Centre and the Youth Club. Lara encouraged them to develop their own ideas and to draw images to express their views, and a wide range of ideas were put forward, from totem poles, seating, lighting and climbing frames. By the time the workshops were completed, Lara had collected a large selection of drawings and designs for the entrance. The next stage was to collate these proposals and evaluate those which could be adapted to the site.

Using children's drawings as railings. ▲

The creation of a piece of 'public art' can often become a target for criticism and it was felt that the involvement of local residents was essential to create a feeling of ownership and to reduce the threat of vandalism and negative criticism. At all stages of the project the local people were involved and kept informed of progress. Exhibitions were mounted at tenants' meetings and comments and suggestions recorded. The most popular solution was to replace the proposed railings at the entrance to the recreation ground with forged metal panels inspired by the drawings of the children from Stonebridge. The workshops had produced endless images, and the naïve childrens' drawings provided the perfect inspiration for the entrance. By the careful juxtaposition of their images, Lara was able to create a lively and humorous entrance to be enjoyed from both inside and outside the park, the fabrication in forged steel providing a marked contrast to the row of plain railings originally planned.

▲ *Lara's work – the idea is successful.*

Pause for thought

Why do you think people might criticize a piece of 'public art'?
What might be the benefits of having a piece of 'public art' in your area?

Lara continues to work on community-led art projects. She has been working with the Crafts Council to share her ideas and enthusiasm for designing and making in this way, and also with students in schools and teachers on training courses.

Research

Within your own area, consider a site that would benefit from the addition of a piece of 'public art'. Describe your reasons for choosing this site and why it would benefit from such a scheme.

4 Designing and making with textiles

Where do textiles come from?

All textiles are made from fibres. The fibres may be natural and come from animals or plants. Or they may be synthetic and come from minerals such as coal or oil.

▲ *Fibres from these three sources are twisted to make yarns.*

▲ *The yarns are made into fabrics in different ways.*

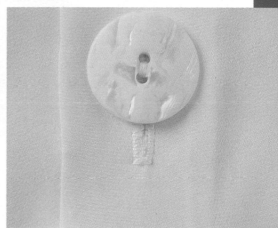

Most fabrics are made by weaving or knitting. **Yarn** for weaving is twisted tightly to make it strong. Yarn for knitting is twisted more loosely to make it stretchy.

A few fabrics are non-woven, made from fibres that are meshed together in no particular order. Felt is a non-woven fabric; so is Vilene which is used for stiffening other fabrics.

What are textiles like?

Words to describe fabrics

To describe a fabric you should be able to say something about its performance, feel and appearance.

Performance		Feel	Appearance
Physical properties	**Aftercare**		
strong	hard-wearing	warm to touch	plain
flexible	easily cleaned	soft	patterned
stretchy	washable	hard	bright
non-slip	non-iron	smooth	dark
absorbent	quick to dry	rough	shiny
insulating	crease-resistant	cool to touch	dull
flameproof	easy to iron	stiff	coloured
waterproof	stain-resistant	crunchy	neutral
windproof	disposable	scratchy	pastel
lets light or heat or	biodegradable	fluffy	stripy
moisture through	easily dyed	floaty	checked
		furry	flecked
		hairy	see-through

Fabrics Chooser Chart

This chart describes the important properties of different fabrics. Use it to help you choose the fabric that is right for your design.

Fabric	Performance	Feel	Appearance	Cost
Medium calico (undyed cotton)	strong dyes easily	crunchy	neutral/plain	low
Cotton drill	strong hard-wearing	quite stiff	plain/coloured	medium
Cotton poplin	absorbent biodegradable	cool	coloured/patterned	medium
Polyester cotton	crease-resistant lets moisture through	smooth	coloured/patterned	medium
Cotton T-shirt jersey	absorbent stretchy	soft	coloured/plain	high
Cotton corduroy	absorbent hard-wearing	soft ribbed	coloured/plain	very high
Wool light-weight tweed	insulator	warm quite hairy	coloured/patterned	high
Wool crepe	insulator stretchy	soft	coloured/patterned	high
Ripstop nylon	waterproof strong, does not tear	smooth	highly coloured	high
Acetate lining	dries easily frays easily	silky	coloured/plain	medium
Net	stretchy non-absorbent	scratchy	coloured/plain see-through	low
Polyester satin	crease-resistant frays easily	very silky	coloured/plain	high

Resource Tasks
TRT 1, 14

Testing fabrics

You can check whether a fabric has the properties you need for your design by testing it. Here are some examples.

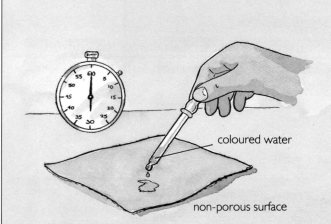

coloured water

non-porous surface

Absorbency

To stay cool, you might need an absorbent fabric that will soak up sweat. Absorbent fabric cleans up liquids as well.

2 drops of strong tea

non-porous surface

B3

B4

2 drops of orange fruit juice

washing bowl

Stain resistance and washability

You might need a stain-resistant fabric. For easy care, a washable fabric will clean and dry better.

Wear resistance

For durability, you might need a wear-resistant fabric that will not go fluffy or bobbly too quickly.

thermometer

test tube wrapped in fabric held in place with 2 elastic bands

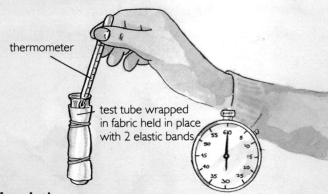

Insulation

To keep warm, you will need a good insulator that will keep warm air in and prevent too rapid cooling.

Windproofing

To keep cold air out, you will need a windproof fabric.

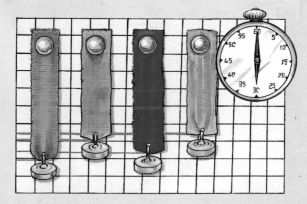

Strength and stretch

For supporting loads or taking strain, you will need a strong fabric. To allow movement, you might choose a fabric that will stretch and then return to its original shape.

Resource Tasks

TRT 17–20

Explaining choices

When you design a textile item you should choose a fabric that will perform well, feel good and look right.

The exact properties of a fabric depend on:

- the fibre it is made from;
- the way the yarn has been spun;
- the way the fabric has been constructed – whether it is woven, non-woven or knitted.

Clothes are made from many different fabrics with different properties. You can see some of the reasons for particular choices below.

Woven fabrics

Woven fabrics do not stretch along the length or width.

The **shirt** is made from mixed polyester and cotton. It is comfortable because the cotton feels cool and absorbs moisture.

This **tie** is made from smooth, shiny and luxurious silk. Silk is expensive but only a small amount of fabric is used.

Mixing cotton with polyester makes the fabric easier to wash and iron. The **soft touch shirt** is woven from 70% Tencel® and 30% polyester. Tencel® is an advanced, new fibre manufactured from cellulose. The addition of Tencel® to mthe mixture improves the feel and drape of the fabric.

The **parka** is closely woven from a mixture of 60% cotton and 40% polyester. The polyester makes it showerproof. The main lining is woven from 100% polyester which is lighter than cotton. In between the lining and the outer there is wadding composed of 50% feathers and 50% down.

The **cargo pants** are closely woven from cotton and heavily washed for softness. This fabric, called twill, is hard wearing and easy to care for. The way the fabric is woven gives the trousers a characteristic appearance.

Knitted fabrics

Knitted fabrics are stretchy.

The **top** is made from knitted fleecy fabric which acts as a good insulator.

The **T shirt** is made from cotton jersey, the most common knitted fabric. It stretches more sideways than downwards. It is comfortable because cotton absorbs moisture.

Note that the girl is carrying an envelope. It is made from polythene fibres bonded together by heat and pressure. The resulting material is called Tyvek. It is waterproof, provides a good printing surface and is very difficult to tear.

Aran knitwear has a stitch pattern that gives a raised effect. The yarn is wool and some of the natural oils are retained. This makes the pullover warmer and shower-proof.

The fabric for the **leggings** is knitted from a mixture of cotton for comfort and Lycra to prevent bagginess and give stretchiness.

Resource Task

TRT 16

Preparing and caring for fabrics

Before you cut out

Pressing the fabric before you pin it to the pattern or mark it out will make it easier to handle. Iron your fabric using a little steam. Make sure that you have the correct temperature for the type of fabric.

All pattern pieces should have a large arrow showing the way the pattern has to be laid on the fabric. With woven fabric, this arrow must be lined up with the lengthwise threads of the fabric – the **warp** or **straight grain**. Look for the neat edges of the fabric, where the cloth does not fray, which are called the **selvedge.** They run parallel to the warp.

woven fabric   knitted fabric

selvedge

straight grain

warp

On woven fabric the warp is parallel to the selvedge. This is the neat edge that will not fray.

On knitted fabric each line of stitches is called a row. To unravel knitting - by pulling a loose end - you will unpick a row.

The thread at right angles to the selvedge is called the **weft.** Knitted fabric stretches most along the row. For clothes, jersey fabric is usually cut with the stretch round the body for comfort.

During making

Take care of your fabric while you are making something and your product will look more professional. Press carefully at each stage and fold neatly at the end of work time. Press each seam open after you have sewn it. Hems and edges will be easier to sew if they are pressed before stitching and neater if they are pressed after they are sewn too.

These are some of the common standard fabric care symbols and their meanings.

You will find them on washing machines and garment labels. Those on older machines and clothes may differ slightly.

Washing
The numbers in the tubs give the maximum water temperature that can be used. The bars under the tubs indicate the strength of the wash.

 95 / 60 / 40   maximum strength wash for cottons

 50 / 40   maximum strength wash for synthetics, easy-care cotton and blends

 40   a gentle wash for wool and wool mixtures

 hand wash only

 chlorine bleach may be used

Drying and ironing

 may be tumble dried

 cool iron

 warm iron

 hot iron

Dry cleaning

 may be dry cleaned

 A cross through any symbol means 'DO NOT'

Look out for 'wash separately' on labels too - it means what it says!

Caring for finished garments

Bought garments always contain labels explaining what fibres they are made from and give instructions for cleaning.

Construction techniques

Most textile products are made from separate pieces of fabric which have to be joined together. This section of the book describes how to do this.

Facings

to neaten raw edges at necklines, armholes and fronts

Edging

binding to prevent fraying

attached ribbing

Seams

curved joined to straight edge

curved seam

straight seam

Fastenings

hooks and press studs   toggles and buttons   cords   zips   elastic   Velcro

Construction techniques – seams

A seam is a line of stitching that joins pieces of fabric together. Seams can be sewn with a sewing machine or by hand. Machines are quicker.

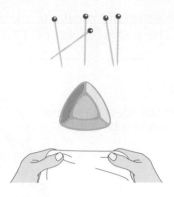

Tips to help you sew successfully

- Mark out the line where you want to sew with tailor's chalk or tacking stitches.
- Use pins or tacking (large running stitches) to hold the pieces of fabric together.

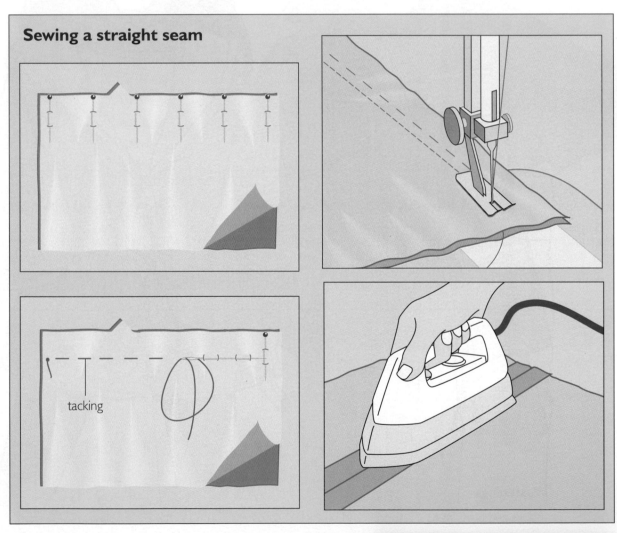

Sewing a straight seam

tacking

Does your fabric fray easily?

If it frays easily you will have to decide how best to stop this happening. See page 126 for ways of finishing edges.

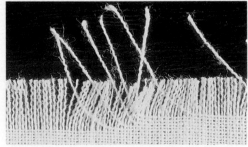

Seam allowance

When patterns are cut they allow extra fabric for joining pieces together. This is the seam allowance. Usually it is 15 mm.

If you cut your own patterns you should include seam allowances, and note on the pattern how much you have allowed. If you forget, your design will end up too small.

When you sew the seams, remember to leave the correct seam allowance. Otherwise, your finished product will be too big or too small.

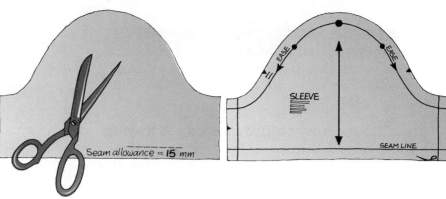

Seam allowance = 15 mm

Sewing thread and stitch size

Choose the right sewing thread

To get the best results choose a thread to suit the kind of fabric you are using. Threads come in different thicknesses and fibres. Common ones are polyester and cotton.

Match like with like:

- fine fabric to fine thread;
- thicker fabric to thicker thread;
- synthetic fabric to synthetic thread;
- natural fabric to natural thread.

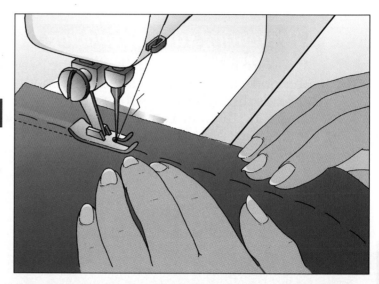

Choose the right stitch size

Most modern sewing machines have a dial to adjust stitch length. Some show a recommended length. It is best to check your stitch length on a spare piece of fabric. Measure the stitches.

As a rough guide, you should use:

- for very fine fabric like acetate lining – 2 mm stitches;
- for medium fabric like poplin or light woollen crepe – 3 mm stitches;
- for thick fabric like cotton duck or corduroy – 4 mm stitches.

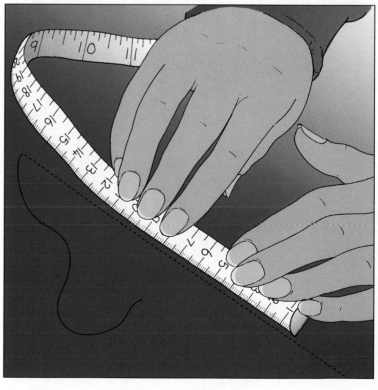

Resource Tasks
TRT 7–13

Construction techniques – edges and edging

Preventing edges from fraying

Many fabrics will fray along the cut edges. If you leave the seam edges to fray the item may fall apart.

Choose how to prevent edges fraying

An overlocker is your best way to stop fraying. When you have cut out your pattern, you overlock each piece before joining the parts together.

Preventing stitches undoing

If you are not stitching right up to the edge of the cloth, use a pin and carefully pull both threads through to the wrong side of the fabric. Tie them in a strong knot and snip the ends short.

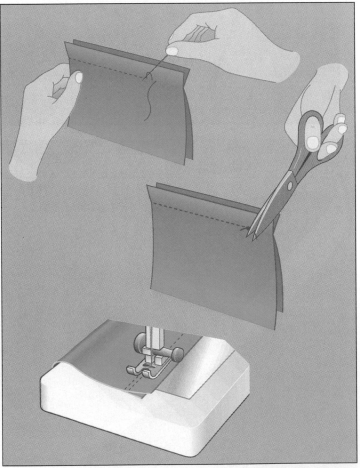

At the beginning of a seam, start 5 mm from the edge, sew a few stitches backwards, then sew the seam. At the end of a seam sew backwards for a few stitches. Cut the ends of thread off.

Most bought garments have the inside edge neatened with stitching called **overlocking**.

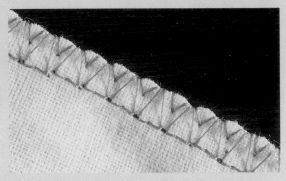

Garments made from knitted jersey fabric, like T-shirts, often have their seams stitched and edged in one operation. This is called **interlocking**.

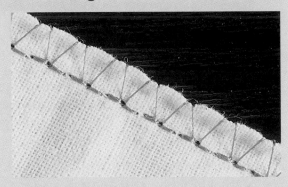

Zig-zag stitching

If you don't have an overlocker, use the zig-zag stitch on the sewing machine. Stitch near the raw edges of each piece.

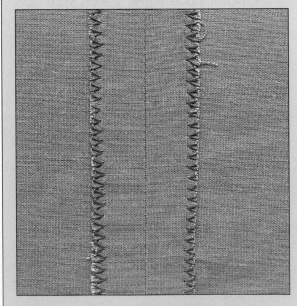

Edging techniques

Some edges need to be treated to stop them fraying and make them look neat.

Hemming

One way of neatening an edge is to turn it under and stitch it firmly on the wrong side. This is a hem. You can make hems wide or narrow and sew them by hand or by machine.

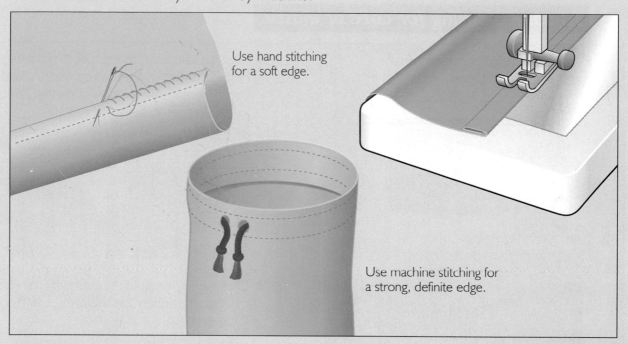

Use hand stitching for a soft edge.

Use machine stitching for a strong, definite edge.

Adding trimmings

You can hide raw edges by adding bindings. These can make the edge more attractive as well as preventing fraying.

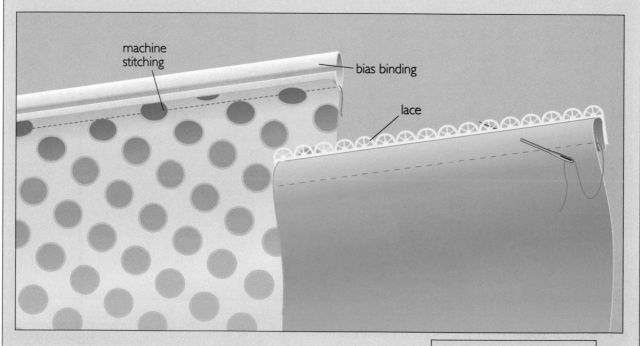

machine stitching

bias binding

lace

Resource Tasks
TRT 7–13

Construction techniques – cords and elastic

You can use cords or elastic:
- to make garments fit round the waist or cuffs;
- to stop garments falling down;
- to keep a bag closed.

You thread the cord or elastic through a channel called a **casing**.

Making a casing for cord or elastic

1 Turn the top edge of the material under 5 mm and press.

2 Then turn the material under 15 mm and pin in place.

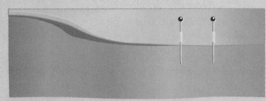

3 Tack the lower edge of the casing in place then machine stitch. Leave a small opening for threading the elastic. Remove the tacks. Machine stitch close to the top fold.

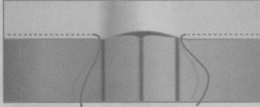

4 Press.

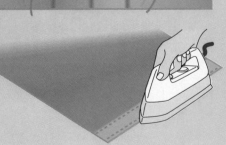

5 Attach a safety pin to each end of the elastic. Pin one to the material as shown. Push the other pin and the elastic trough the casing. Take care not to twist the elastic.

6 Overlap the ends of the elastic by 10 mm and pin. Stitch a square on this area. Stitch across it for strength.

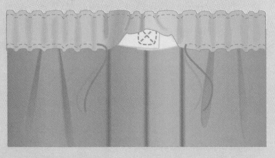

7 Stitch the opening shut. Keep the area flat by stretching the elastic as you sew.

 1 How would you change this method if you wanted to use cord rather than elastic?

Resource Tasks
TRT 7–9

Construction techniques – fastenings

Types of fastenings

Fastenings are used to make temporary joins. For example, on a cardigan, buttons allow you to open or close the front; on a rucksack, clips allow you to fasten pockets and straps.

Choosing fastenings
Your choice of fastenings will depend on many factors:

- they look interesting or attractive;
- they are invisible;
- they are wind- or waterproof;
- they can be opened and closed easily or quickly;
- they hold something up;
- they are strong;
- they are long-lasting;
- they are washable or dry-cleanable.

Fastenings Chooser Chart

	Ease of use	Ease of fitting	Variety of types	Strength	Ease of care	Cost
Buttons	●●	●●●● holes ●	●●●●	●●	●●	▲▲
Toggles	●●●	●●●	●	●●	●●	▲▲
Zips	●●●	●	●●	●●●●	●●	▲▲▲
Velcro	●●●●	●●●●	●	●●●●	●●●	▲▲
Hooks/eyes	●	●●	●●	●	●●●	▲
Eylets and laces	●●	●●●	●●	●●●●	●●	▲▲
Press studs	●●●	●●●	●●	●	●●●	▲
Clips/buckles	●●	●●●	●●	●●●	●●●	▲▲▲

● = few blobs for worse, ●●●● = more blobs for better

▲ = cheap, ▲▲▲ = most expensive

Resource Task

TRT 15

Ways to decorate fabrics

Tie dyeing

Tie small beads or stones into the cloth before it is dyed. The dye cannot go where fabric is tightly tied.

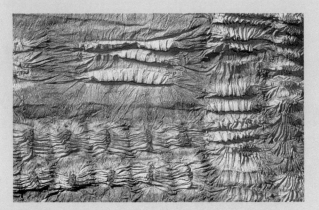

Batik

Trickle or paint wax onto the fabric before dyeing it. The dye cannot go where the wax is. You can make more complex patterns with layers of wax and different dyes.

Transfer painting and direct painting

Brush fabric paints directly onto the fabric. Transfer paints must be painted onto paper. Then place the painted paper over the cloth and iron it. This transfers the pattern onto the cloth, but back to front.

Block printing

Cut or carve a pattern into a block made from lino, potato or wood. Roll ink onto the block and press the block onto the fabric. This transfers the pattern onto the cloth, but back to front.

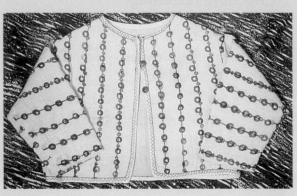

Appliqué

Cut pattern shapes out of different coloured fabrics. Arrange them on the main fabric and sew them down using a close zig-zag stitch and coloured threads.

Embroidery and quilting

In embroidery, you stitch a pattern onto the fabric with coloured silky threads. In quilting, you sandwich a layer of spongy wadding between two layers of fabric. Sew on patterns by hand or with a machine.

Choosing the best form of decoration

In deciding which technique to use to decorate your fabric, you should consider all these factors.

Use this Chooser Chart to help you decide on the right technique for your design.

Fabric Decoration Chooser Chart

Technique	One-off or repetitive	Time needed	Simple or complex	When to do it
Tie dyeing	one-off	quick (check time for dyeing and drying)	very simple	before cutting, when in parts, or the finished item
Batik	one-off	varies depending on the detail of motif and number of colours to be dyed	varies, needs practice	before cutting or onto cut parts
Fabric marker pen	one-off	quick for simple motifs, slower for more fiddly ones	simple	onto cut parts or finished item
Transfer painting	one-off	quick for simple motifs	simple, lettering must be reversed	onto cut parts or finished item
Block printing	repetitive	slow – block must be prepared first, but printing is quick	simple	before cutting
Appliqué	one-off	slow – for careful cutting, positioning and stitching	complex, needs practice	onto cut parts
Embroidery	one-off	varies depending on the detail	simple with practice	the finished item
CAM Embroidery	one-off and repetitive	varies depending on the detail	simple with practice	the finished item
Screen printing	repetitive	slow – screen must be prepared first but printing is quick	varies – depends on complexity of screen	before cutting when in parts or on the finished item

Introducing patterns

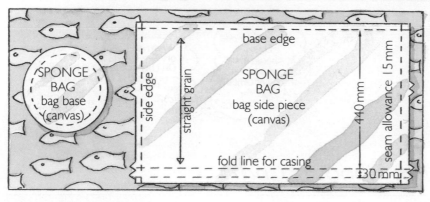

SPONGE
BAG
bag base
(canvas)

base edge

side edge

straight grain

SPONGE
BAG
bag side piece
(canvas)

440 mm

seam allowance 15 mm

fold line for casing

130 mm

Once you have made notes on the sketch of your design you will need to prepare a paper or card pattern. This is used to mark onto the fabric the exact shape and size of all the pieces you need to make up the design.

Preparing a pattern is called **drafting**. So as not to make mistakes, write all the important information on the pattern.

Use this checklist to make sure that you include all the necessary instructions on your own patterns.

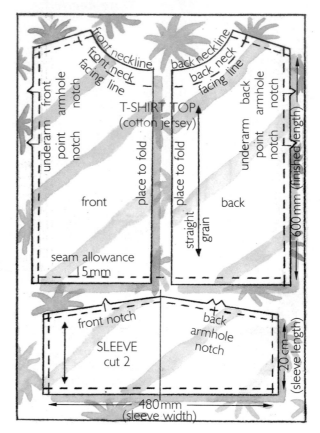

front neckline

front neck
facing line

back neckline

back neck
facing line

front
armhole
notch

underarm
point
notch

T-SHIRT TOP
(cotton jersey)

back
armhole
notch

underarm
point
notch

place to fold

place to fold

front

back

600 mm (finished length)

straight grain

seam allowance
15 mm

front notch

back
armhole
notch

SLEEVE
cut 2

20 cm (sleeve length)

480 mm
(sleeve width)

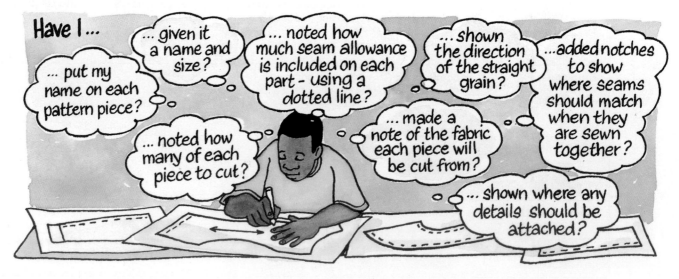

Have I...

...put my name on each pattern piece?

...given it a name and size?

...noted how much seam allowance is included on each part - using a dotted line?

...shown the direction of the straight grain?

...added notches to show where seams should match when they are sewn together?

...noted how many of each piece to cut?

...made a note of the fabric each piece will be cut from?

...shown where any details should be attached?

How to draft a pattern

1 Checking the design

Your design shows you its shape, its fit, the different parts it should have and where they will be joined together.

Check these details by drawing an exploded view and discuss it with others.

2 Measuring

Now work out the size of each part. Use scrap paper to model your design and estimate sizes. If you are making a garment to fit someone, measure them carefully.

3 Rough draft

Draw each part onto paper as accurately as you can. Add an extra 15mm all round for seam allowance. Cut the parts out and pin or tape them together with masking tape to make a model. If you are using one of the Resource Task basic patterns, draw them out life size and alter them to fit.

4 Checking the draft

Make any changes needed on the rough paper model. Plan where notches could be used to help with sewing. Work out whether extra fabric will be needed to neaten edges and hems. Note where any extra parts will be attached.

Ask yourself these questions:

Is it the right size?

Is it the right shape?

Do all the pieces fit together well?

Does it fit the wearer?

5 Final draft

Undo your paper model and lay it flat on pattern paper. Use it to draw a neat final draft. Then cut out the pattern pieces.

6 Pattern information

Use the checklist to make sure you have included all the important details.

grain of fabric

7 Planning the layout

Fabric comes in standard widths (900 mm or 1150 mm). Join some sheets of newspaper together to these sizes so that you can plan how to lay out the pieces without wasting fabric. Measure how much fabric you will need.

Designing bags

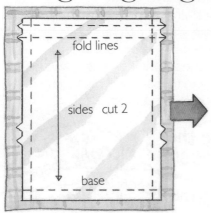
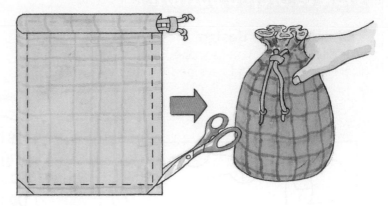

Bags are for carrying things. Some, like pencil cases, are meant to carry a few specific small items, while others, like handbags, carry a wider range of small items. Shopping bags and school bags are designed to carry many things of different shapes and sizes.

Whatever they carry, bags have to be the right size and look good. Many need straps or handles to be useful.

▲ *Can you work out how to change the shape of these simple bags?* ▼

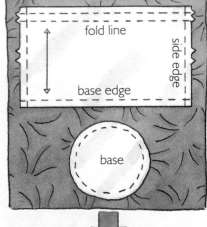

Questions to help you design your bag

1 Starting ideas
Look at existing bags or at pictures from catalogues. You might change a design to suit your requirements. You could produce a style image board to help decide on the fabric or decoration.

2 Who is it for?
Can you find out about what the bag must do and be like?
Is it for you?
If it is for someone else, can you find out what they want?
How will you find out whether they like your suggestions?

3 When or where will it be used?
Is it for everyday or for a special occasion or purpose?
Will it have to match other things?
How will it open and close?
How will it be carried?

4 Shape
What shape and size should it be?
How will you check whether your design is the right shape and size?

5 Fit
What things will be put into it?
If it is designed to contain special things, it must be large enough to fit them in.
How can you check this?
How will you check that the person can carry the bag comfortably?
What personal measurements will you need?

6 Which fibre and fabric?
Performance – Which properties are important? Which fabrics have these properties?
Appearance – What should the fabric look like? Will you decorate it?
Feel – What should the fabric feel like?
Cost – How much can you afford?
Use the Fabrics Chooser Chart on page 118 to help you decide.

Ideas for openings and fastenings

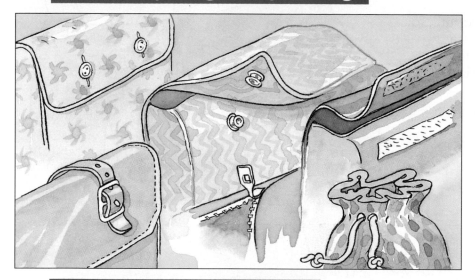

◀ *What other ideas can you think of for openings and fastenings?*

Making bags stiff

You can make a floppy bag stiff by adding a stiffer material to the structure. You can make the base stiffer with a piece of cardboard or thin sheet of plastic in the bottom (like some rucksacks). You can add wadding to make the sides of your bag both thicker and stiffer.

You can add iron-on Vilene to stiffen fabrics. It comes in a range of different weights so you can choose just how stiff to make your bag.

Ideas for straps and handles

▲ *What other ideas can you think of for straps and handles?*

Making bags waterproof

Bags may need to be waterproof both on the outside and on the inside.

If the fabric you are using is not waterproof, you could add a waterproofing spray or coating. These are sold in sports and outdoor shops. Or you could add a second layer of fabric that is waterproof, either on the outside or the inside.

Making the insides look good

Bags need to look good both on the inside and the outside. You need to sew them together very carefully. Use edging techniques (see page 127) to stop the fabric from fraying and to make the seam allowance neat.

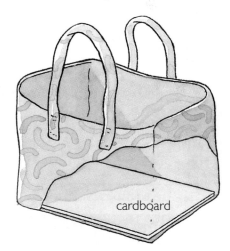

cardboard

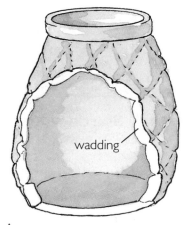

wadding

▲ *Ways to increase stiffness.*

Resource Tasks
TRT 7, 8

Designing shorts

People wear shorts for sleeping, for beachwear, as underwear, for casual wear. They have to look good, fit comfortably and last well.

▲ *Shorts made using the basic pattern below.*

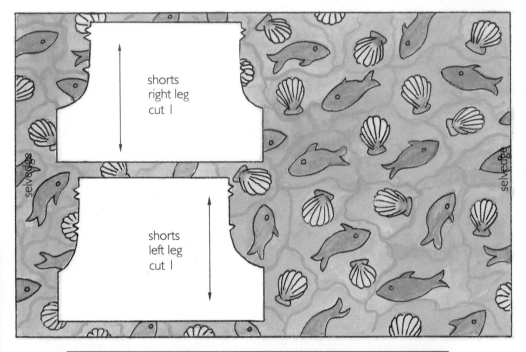

shorts
right leg
cut 1

shorts
left leg
cut 1

selvedge

selvedge

◄ *A basic shorts pattern. There is a Resource Task to help you to alter it to suit your own design ideas.*

Questions to help you design your shorts

Q

1 Starting ideas
Look at existing shorts or pictures from fashion magazines. You could produce a style image board to help decide on the fabric or decoration.

2 Who will wear it?
Is it for you?
If it is for someone else, can you find out what they want?
Can you find out whether they like your suggestions?

3 When or where will they be worn?
Are they for day or night, ordinary or special occasions, sports or leisure?
Do they need to look good with other clothes?

4 Shape
How long should they be?
Are they short, medium length, knee length or longer?
How baggy or tight should they be?
Should they fit close to the body?

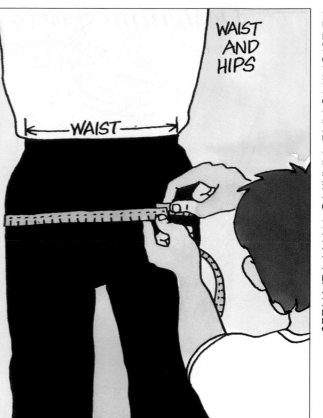

 5 Fit
Should they have elastic at the waist or a cord to keep them up?

Shorts fit between your legs and round your bottom, so they should be loose enough to allow you to sit and move comfortably.

To check the fit, measure round the hips, at the widest point, and the crotch depth. The basic pattern in the Resource Task fits:

hips 900 mm
crotch depth 260 mm

It can be altered to fit hips and bodies of different sizes.

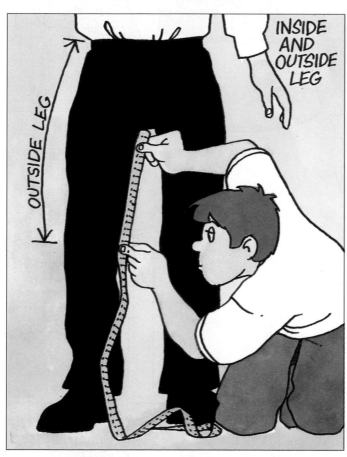

◀ *Taking measurements to check the fit.* ▲
▼

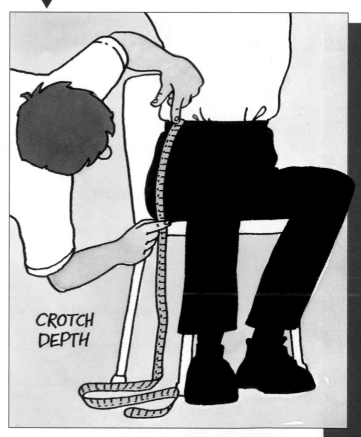

 6 Which fibre and fabric?
Performance – Which properties are important? Which fabrics have these properties? What care will the shorts need after they are made?
Appearance – What should the fabric look like? Should it be plain or patterned? Will you decorate it or will you buy patterned fabric?
Feel – What should the fabric feel like?
Cost – How much can you afford?
Use the Fabrics Chooser Chart on page 118 to help you decide.

Resource Task

TRT 9

Designing T-shirt tops

People wear T-shirts for sleeping, as underwear, for casual wear. A T-shirt should look right, fit comfortably and last well.

▲ *This T-shirt style top is made using the basic pattern.*

Questions to help you

 1 Starting ideas
Look at existing shorts or pictures from fashion magazines. Try improving on an existing design. You could produce a style image board to help decide on the fabric or fabric decoration.

2 Who will wear it?
Is it for you?
If it is for someone else, can you find out what they want?
Can you find out whether they like your suggestions?

3 When or where will it be worn?
Is it for ordinary wear or special occasions?
Are you designing a top to go with other clothes?
How can you check that the outfit 'works'?

4 Shape
How long should it be? Will the neck opening be round or V-necked? How long should the sleeves be?

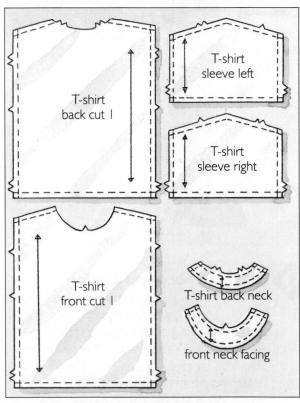

▲ *A basic T-shirt pattern. There is a Resource Task which explains how to draft this pattern and alter it to suit your design idea.*

5 Fit
The neck opening must be big enough to let the wearer's head through. Some fabrics stretch enough for this. How will you check the size?

The T-shirt should be loose enough for you to put it on and take it off comfortably. To check the fit, measure round the chest and the length from the shoulder point. The basic pattern in the Resource Task fits:
chest 900 mm
length from back neck to hem 600 mm
sleeve length 150 mm

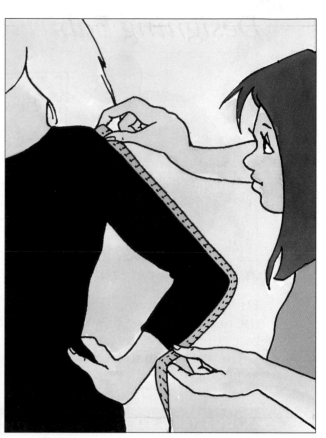

◀ *Taking measurements to check or* ▲
alter the basic pattern. ▼

6 Which fibre and fabric?
Performance – Which properties are important? Which fabrics have these? What care will the T-shirt need after it is made?
Appearance – What should the fabric look like? Should it be plain or patterned? Will you decorate it or buy it as you want it?
Feel – What should the fabric feel like?
Cost – How much can you afford?
Use the Fabrics Chooser Chart on page 118 to help you decide.

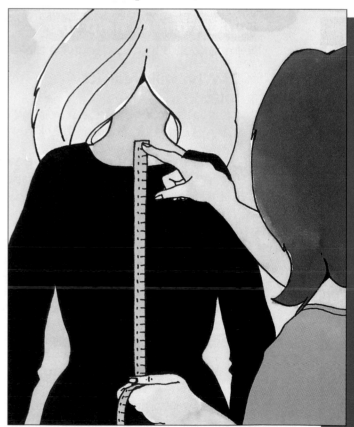

Resource Task

TRT 10

139

Designing hats

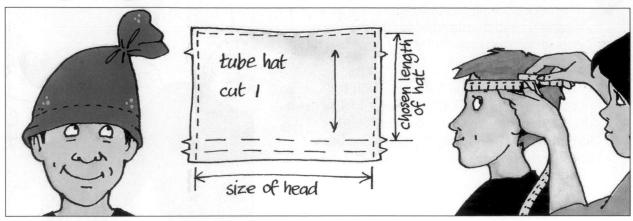

▲ *A simple one-piece hat can be shaped to make it pointed at the top.*

Hats come in many shapes and sizes. They have to fit the head of the person wearing them. Some are adjustable so they can be worn by people with different-sized heads.

They are worn to keep warm, to keep dry, to look good, to make a statement.

Questions to help you design your hat

 1 Starting ideas
Look at existing hats or pictures from fashion magazines. Books on fashion history will give you ideas for shape. You could produce a style image board to help decide on the fabric or decoration.

2 Who will wear it?
Is it for you?
If it is for someone else, can you find out what they want?
Can you find out whether they like your suggestions?

3 When or where will it be worn?
Is it for everyday or for special occasions?
Is it to protect the wearer from the weather?
Which is more important – that it does a good job or that it looks good?

4 Shape
What shape and size should it be?
How will you check whether it is the right shape and size?

5 Fit
What measurements will you need to make sure that it fits?
How can you check that it will fit?

6 Which fibre and fabric?
Performance – Which properties are important? Which fabrics have these? Will you need to make the fabric stiffer or waterproof?
Appearance – What should the fabric look like? Will you decorate it?
Feel – What should the fabric feel like?
Cost – How much can you afford?
Use the Fabrics Chooser Chart on page 118 to help you decide.

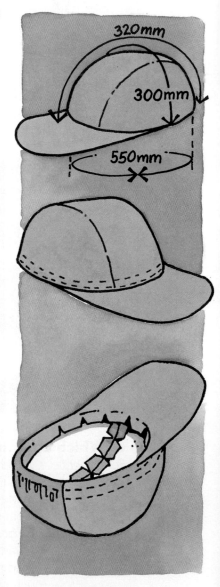

▲ *A baseball type hat can be adjusted to fit any head.*

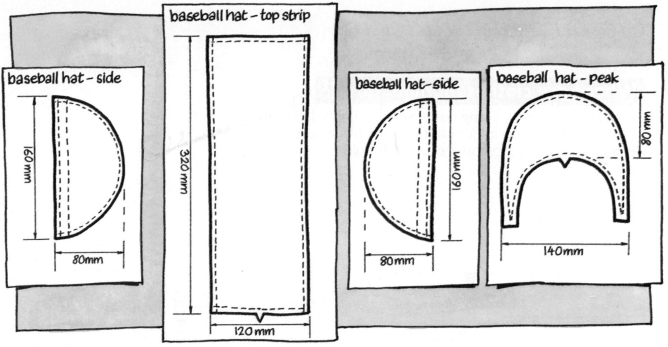

baseball hat – side

160mm

80mm

baseball hat – top strip

320mm

120 mm

baseball hat–side

160mm

80 mm

baseball hat – peak

80 mm

140mm

▲ *You can work out how to change this pattern to make the peak a different size.*

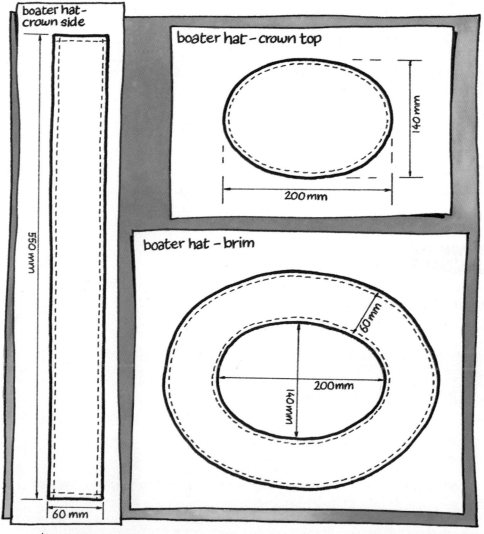

boater hat– crown side

550mm

60 mm

boater hat – crown top

140 mm

200 mm

boater hat – brim

60 mm

200mm

140mm

▲ *You can work out how to change this pattern to make the brim a different shape.*

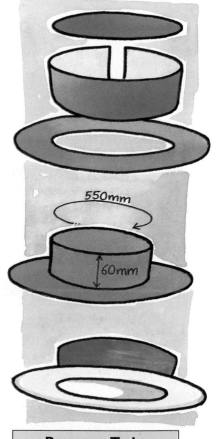

◀ *You can change the height of the crown of this hat as well as the size of the brim.*

550mm

60mm

Resource Tasks
TRT 11–12

Clothing manufacture

Where are clothes manufactured?

The jacket you are wearing could very well have been produced on a global scale. The map below shows the places where it has been designed, manufactured and eventually sold.

Key:

① designed in Scotland

② fabric bought and dyed in Italy

③ lining and padding manufactured in China

④ garment roughly completed in Northern Ireland

⑤ garment finished in London

⑥ garment sold in Liverpool

▲ *Garments are produced on a global scale.*

The UK textiles industry

Considering how cheap labour costs are around the world, it is remarkable how the UK industry competes. It survives for three reasons as shown in the panel.

Pause for thought

Why the UK textiles industry can be competitive

1 There is a short lead time (i.e. the 'turnaround' of a garment can be as short as three weeks), so the British manufacturer can respond to market demand quickly. When trends happen, the response can be almost instant.

2 The UK concentrates on clothing for the retail market. Again it can respond to market demands from its clients, who themselves are close to their customers.

3 There is so much diversity in the demand for clothing – from Savile Row gentlemen's handsewn suits to overalls for the food industry – that firms can find a 'niche' market for their products.

Research activity

This activity will help you find out about the diversity of the UK textiles industry. You will need to work in a team.

1 Using *Yellow Pages* for reference, list as many types of clothing manufacturers as you can find. Add to this list any more you can find from trade journals/magazines.

2 Each person in the team should write to two manufacturers asking for the following information.

- What do you manufacture?
- What raw materials do you use?
- Where do they come from?
- What methods of production do you use?
- Where is your produce sold?
- What is your annual turnover?

3 Present the information you collect as an illustrated display.

Why are clothes as they are?

The common perception of clothing design is that it is 'style' driven. This is an oversimplification. A much wider range of influences are involved. These are shown in the diagram.

 Copy out the table. Decide how important each influence is for the different types of clothing design. Use a blob score to record your decision: 5 blobs for very important down to no blobs for unimportant.

	Cost	Fabric	Style	Functionality	Ease of manufacture	Colour-fastness and washability
Street style						
Sports						
Haute couture						
Everyday clothes						
Work wear						

Resource Tasks

TRT 4–5

Manufacturability

Manufacturability is a vital consideration when designing garments. Some styles can turn out to be extremely difficult to make in significant volume at acceptable standards of quality. If the seam geometry is too complex or the fabric is inappropriate, then poorly shaped or ill-fitting garments can result. The manufacturability of a design is therefore tested out. At the design studio a sample garment for each design will be produced by highly skilled machinists.

Manufacturing clothing

The stages in garment production are shown below. You will see that this is not very different to the way you make clothes at school or at home.

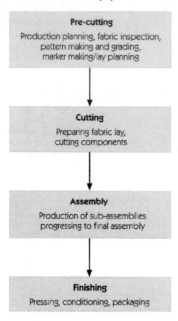

Pre-cutting
Production planning, fabric inspection,
pattern making and grading,
marker making/lay planning

Cutting
Preparing fabric lay,
cutting components

Assembly
Production of sub-assemblies
progressing to final assembly

Finishing
Pressing, conditioning, packaging

Until recently much of the textile industry used craft methods for these processes. But there have been moves to automation and to increase the efficiency of the processes. Two examples are **pattern grading** and **lay planning**. The use of CAD can increase considerably the speed of pattern grading (scaling within the size range). In fact once the details of a pattern are in the computer the software can carry out the scaling automatically. The computer systems that are used to do this have decreased in price greatly over the last 25 years. Lay planning (positioning the pattern on the fabric) is also speeded up by the use of CAD systems.

Assembly

The use of work study to analyse the movements of workers stitching components together revealed that most time is spent positioning the fabric rather than sewing the pieces together. This has led to the redesign of workstations and the introduction of automatic delivery systems. In ideal circumstances measures like these can reduce the time taken for a batch of garments to be produced from three weeks to three days!

Note that the textiles industry has not become as automated as other manufacturing industries because fabric is not easily handled by robots and many garments involve pieces of fabric with complex shapes. The costs of developing alternatives to human workers are still very high and at the moment most automated systems still require highly skilled operators.

Colour and colourways

Fashionable colours

Each season many of the large clothing stores present ranges of clothes that have been designed to a common theme or colour range. How are these colours chosen?

Pause for thought
What are the fashionable colours at the moment? Look at the colours below and list them in order of fashion priority.

Orange   Brown   Green   Purple   Black

Grey   Pink   Yellow

The choice of colour comes about mainly in three ways.

Firstly, an individual designer will often use intuition or personal research for inspiration.

Secondly, there are organizations who predict colour trends and who sell 'forecast' books each year. Before manufacturing large quantities of any design, a small sample batch is made up showing the colourways available. In this way feedback from the client can be incorporated into the final range.

Thirdly, with computer aided design and manufacture (CAD/CAM) designers can work directly on the computer screen to produce large scale colour images. Where colour samples would previously have had to be produced, colours can now be selected quickly using computer print outs. The use of colour fax machines means that designers can receive and relay information quickly between different countries.

▲ *Designer trousers can start a trend.*

Colourways

'Colourways' is the name used to describe the number of coloured versions in which a final product will appear in the shops. For example a white shirt with coloured stripes may be made in four different coloured versions – blue stripes, red stripes, green stripes and black stripes. Before manufacturing large quantities of any design, a small sample batch is made up showing the colourways available. In this way feedback from the garment can be incorporated into the final range. Here is an example:

 Imagine you have to do the colourways for three different sorts of garment:

- a wet-suit (for wind-surfing);
- a jacket for hill-walking;
- a decorative carpet for a busy hotel.

What sort of colours do you think would be appropriate for each?

Brights? Darks? Neutrals?

Resource Task
TRT 3

5 Designing and making with food

The food materials available

An exciting range of food materials is available for designing and making food products. Fruits, vegetables, cereals, meat and fish from all over the world give you a wide choice.

The food that you buy may be raw, processed or pre-cooked.

Sometimes you will use all three types in designing a single food product.

▲ *You can buy potatoes raw, processed or pre-cooked.*

Raw food materials

You can change the appearance of raw food by peeling, chopping or grating.

whole   peeled   chopped   grated

▲ *Raw carrots come in several forms.*

Raw foods have had little or no industrial processing. Some can be eaten without any cooking.

Cooking changes food. ▶

raw   cooked

You can change the colour, texture and taste of raw food by cooking it.

These processed foods can be eaten without cooking.

Processed foods

Processed foods are made by manufacturers from raw foods. Some can be eaten in the form you buy them. Others must be cooked.

Pre-cooked foods

These have already been cooked, like bread or biscuits. You can eat them as they are or use them to make a different food product.

The food industry produces some pre-cooked foods as **convenience foods**. These are complete dishes or meals that only need reheating.

These processed foods must be cooked before you eat them.

▲ *Pre-cooked and convenient!*

The properties and qualities of food

Food materials have properties and qualities that you can control when preparing and cooking. You will need to think about these when you are designing food products. This section will help you to describe the physical properties, taste and appearance of food.

Physical properties of food

Physical properties describe the **state** of the food material – for instance, whether it is liquid or solid, hot or cold.

Below are useful words for describing the physical properties of food:

liquid, solid, foam, gel   hard, soft   pliable, elastic

hot, cold   runny, viscous   crumbly, brittle

smooth, lumpy   heavy, light   absorbent

The examples in the panel will help you understand what they mean.

Foods have different physical properties

Breakfast cereal with milk
The cereal is solid, hard and crumbly. The milk is liquid, smooth and runny. The cereal will absorb the milk and become pliable. If the milk is from the refrigerator it will be cold.

Spaghetti bolognese
The spaghetti is solid, soft and pliable. The sauce is liquid, lumpy and viscous. The sauce sticks to the spaghetti but is not absorbed. Both are hot.

Steamed sponge pudding with custard
The sponge is a solid, light, soft foam. You can see tiny bubbles in it where gas has been trapped in the mixture as it cooked. The custard is liquid, smooth, viscous and hot. It sticks to the sponge and is absorbed by it.

The appearance of food

Food products are designed to be eaten, but most of us judge food first with our eyes! If it looks good, we are more likely to want to eat it.

You can describe the appearance of food in terms of colour, shape and finish as shown in the pictures.

The taste of food

The taste of food is a complex mixture of the smell, flavour and the 'mouth feel' or texture of the food. The taste buds in the tongue can detect four basic **flavours**:

sour

sweet

salt

bitter.

You can add words such as 'strong' or 'weak' to describe the strength of the flavour. You can use words such as 'savoury', 'fruity' or 'fishy' to describe a type of flavour.

The 'mouth feel' – the **texture** of the food in the mouth – can be difficult to describe. You can use these words to describe the texture of the food when you first taste it:

soft, firm, hard

dry, moist

crumbly, crunchy, brittle

thin, creamy, sticky.

As you chew the food it will change in texture as it mixes with the saliva in your mouth. You may need to use these extra words to describe the texture of the food:

tough, tender, chewy, rubbery

gritty, greasy, slimy, gooey.

Describing the appearance of coleslaw salad

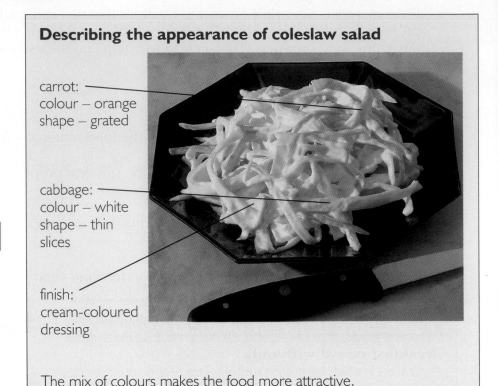

carrot:
colour – orange
shape – grated

cabbage:
colour – white
shape – thin
slices

finish:
cream-coloured
dressing

The mix of colours makes the food more attractive.

Describing the appearance of cakes

shape:
round and
slightly domed

finish:
white icing
with red,
yellow and
blue decoration

colour:
golden brown

Resource Task

FRT 1

Understanding what ingredients do

Colloids

Many of the foods we eat are **colloids**. Colloids muddle up the simple idea of everything being either a solid, a liquid or a gas. A colloid is a mixture of things which usually do not mix but, once they have, can be difficult to separate. A colloid can be a mixture of a solid and a liquid, a liquid and a liquid, a solid and a gas or a liquid and a gas. The two different parts are called phases – one is the **continuous phase**; the other is the **disperse phase**. The continuous phase runs right through the colloid, the disperse phase is in small pockets scattered about in the colloid. Here is a summary table with some examples.

Colloid system	Continuous phase	Disperse phase	Example
Sol	liquid	solid	hot custard
Gel	solid	liquid	jelly
Emulsion	liquid	liquid	mayonnaise
Solid emulsion	solid	liquid	butter
Soft foam	liquid	gas	mousse
Rigid foam	solid	gas	bread

Here are some images to help you imagine what it is like inside different colloids.

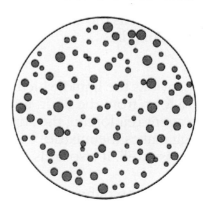

All these different foods are colloids. ▲   ▲ *Inside an emulsion.*

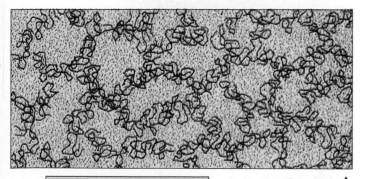

Inside a gel. ▲

Resource Task

FRT 12, 14

The sponge cake

Sponge cake is a solid foam. The gas part of the foam is a mixture of air and carbon dioxide. The solid part of the foam is formed from the carbohydrate and protein in the flour. Whether this has a light texture and pleasant flavour depends on the action of the fat, egg and sugar that are also part of the recipe. Just what each ingredient does is described in the panel below.

This comes from wheat and provides starch (a carbohydrate) and gluten (a protein) which give the cake its structure. It contains baking powder which produces carbon dioxide gas on heating. This makes the cake rise during baking. The gluten is elastic and stretches as the bubbles of gas are formed and expand. It sets firm towards the end of the cooking to give the cake its final form.

▲ *Self raising flour*

This is a fat. It holds air when it is beaten with sugar and gives the cake a tender texture. Too much fat results in a greasy taste; too little fat and the sponge is tough.

▲ *Soft margarine.*

When this is beaten into the fat it causes tiny air bubbles to be trapped. These help the cake rise during baking. It adds sweetness and gives colour to the crust due to dextrinisation. Too much sugar produces sugar crystals in the crust and weakens the structure so the sponge sinks in the middle.

▲ *Caster sugar.*

This provides the liquid which enables the gluten to form from the flour. It acts as a binding agent reinforcing the structure but too much egg makes the mixture too stiff so it does not rise well. It also adds colour.

▲ *Egg.*

Ingredients in the right proportion, blended together well and cooked at the right temperature for the right time.

▲ *Tasty cakes.*

Can you see the even texture of this solid foam? How big are the gas bubbles?

Cream 100 g caster sugar into 100 g soft margarine. Beat in two eggs. Beat in 100 g self-raising flour. If the mixture becomes too stiff, add a small drop of milk. Divide the mixture into 12 baking cases and place on a baking sheet and bake for 20 minutes at gas mark 5 or 190°C.

▲ *Sponge cake.*

Resource Task
FRT 13

Raising agents

Raising agents cause flour mixtures to expand during cooking. They all rely on the production of gases which make the mixture swell. At the same time the heat is also causing changes to the gluten and the starch. The gluten changes from being elastic and stretchy to being stiff and firm (it coagulates). The starch gelatinizes; the granules absorb water and fat and swell becoming soft and tender. If not enough gas is produced the mixture does not rise. If too much gas is produced the mixture rises too much and collapses. If the gluten is not sufficiently elastic the gas cannot make the mixture rise before the gluten sets. If the gluten is too elastic the mixture rises too much and collapses before the gluten can set. If the mixture is not cooked for long enough the gluten may not set and the starch may not be cooked. Recipes using flour have to get everything just right – ingredients, amounts, temperature and time!

▲ *Set in protein!*

There are three sorts of raising agent: mechanical, chemical and biological.

1 Mechanical raising agents work by trapping air into the mixture. Sieving flour increases the air content. Creaming or beating fats results in the formation of a soft foam containing many tiny air bubbles. Beating soft fat with sugar achieves the same result. When these are heated the air bubbles expand. Any water in the mixture will turn into steam and also cause the mixture to rise.

2 Chemical raising agents work by producing carbon dioxide gas which causes the mixture to rise. Baking powder is a mixture of sodium hydrogen carbonate and a weak acid. In the presence of water these react together to produce the carbon dioxide gas.

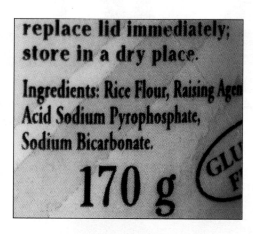

replace lid immediately; store in a dry place.

Ingredients: Rice Flour, Raising Agen Acid Sodium Pyrophosphate, Sodium Bicarbonate.

170 g

You can describe this with a simple word equation:

sodium hydrogen carbonate + weak acid = salt of weak acid + carbon dioxide + water

The salt of the weak acid has very little taste so the flavour of the mixture is not affected.

3 Biological raising agents use yeast, a unicellular plant which, as it grows in the mixture, gives off carbon dioxide. The conditions for this must be just right – the yeast needs food, so some sugar is usually added; moisture prevents the yeast drying out; usually water or milk are used, warmth is necessary: too low a temperature and the yeast does not grow, too high a temperature and the yeast dies. The mixture must be left while the yeast grows. This is called **proving**. Cooking causes the carbon dioxide to expand even further but kills the yeast plant.

Resource Task
FRT 15

Thickening liquids

There are many occasions when you may want to increase the thickness of a liquid. Thick creamy milk shakes are more interesting to drink than ordinary milk. A sauce for pasta needs to be thick enough to cling to and coat the pasta pieces. Some sauces are used to bind ingredients together.

The addition of puréed fruit or vegetables is a very straightforward way to thicken a liquid. The puréed material contains lots of fibre which takes a long time to settle out so stirring this into a thin liquid is a quick way to get a thicker consistency. It will, of course, change the flavour considerably.

▲ *Adding puréed fruit made the difference.*

Another way to thicken a liquid is to use some form of starch – cornflour or arrowroot. This is called gelatinization. You can use this method by following these instructions.

Gelatinization of starch

▲ *Cornflour is blended with a liquid to form a suspension.*

▲ *The mixture is heated and stirred continuously.*

Suspension of starch blended into a liquid before heating ie *a suspension*

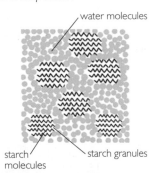

water molecules

starch molecules

starch granules

▲ *The starch granules begin to swell.*

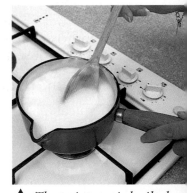

▲ *The mixture is boiled for 1–2 minutes with continuous stirring.*

▲ *The liquid is now thicker – it has become a sol.*

During heating a *sol* is formed (60° – 70° C)

starch molecules escape from granules

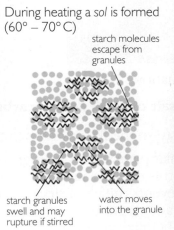

starch granules swell and may rupture if stirred

water moves into the granule

▲ *Inside the sol.*

▲ *As the liquid cools, it becomes thicker and forms a gel.*

A *gel* is formed as the sol cools

water dispersed in network

network of starch

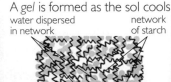

NB The *firmness* of the starch gel depends on

- the amount and type of starch
- the temperature to which the mixture is heated
- the effect of other ingredients ie sugar/acid

▲ *Inside the gel.*

Resource Tasks

FRT 16, 17

Food choices

We eat food because we are hungry and because we enjoy eating. Food is so readily available in Britain that we are unlikely to die of starvation. We are more likely to become unhealthy because we eat too much food or too much of a particular type of food.

This section gives information to help you make a healthy choice of food.

Guidelines for a healthy diet

- Enjoy your food.
- Eat a variety of different foods.
- Eat the right amount to be a healthy weight.
- Eat foods rich in starch and fibre.
- Don't eat too much fat.
- Don't eat sugary foods too often.
- Keep the minerals and vitamins in your foods.
- If you drink alcohol, keep within sensible limits.

The Balance of Good Health

To help us follow these guidelines the 'Balance of Good Health' has been produced. This is a diagram of a plate divided up to show the proportions of groups of foods that a person should eat. By choosing food groups in the approximate proportions shown, and choosing different foods from within each group, a person is more likely to be healthy. Do not be misled by the plate. It is not necessary to eat all these foods in one meal. If the balance is achieved over a day or a week most people will be healthy.

Resource Task

FRT 7

...Food choices

How much do we need?

Nutrients for energy

Carbohydrates, fats and protein provide us with energy. We each have different needs for energy depending on our age and how active we are. So we need different amounts of nutrients to meet our energy requirements.

Our bodies need energy for:

- physical activity like walking, running and jumping;
- bodily processes like the heart beat, breathing and digestion.

The total energy used is called **energy expenditure**. The food we eat should provide enough energy for our expenditure.

> Energy is measured in joules.
> The symbol for joules is J.
>
> 1 kilojoule (1 kJ) = 1000 joules
>
> 1 megajoule (1 MJ) = 1 000 000 joules

Estimated average requirement (EAR) for energy per day		
Age (years)	EAR (MJ/day)	EAR (MJ/day)
7–10	8.24	7.28
11–14	9.27	7.92
15–18	11.51	8.83
19–49	10.60	8.10
50–59	10.60	8.10
60–64	9.93	7.99
65–75	9.71	7.96
75+	8.77	7.61

This person has an energy balance and good health.

This person has an energy imbalance, leading to increase in body fat and poor health.

For an 11–14-year-old, the percentage of EAR supplied by some high-energy foods:

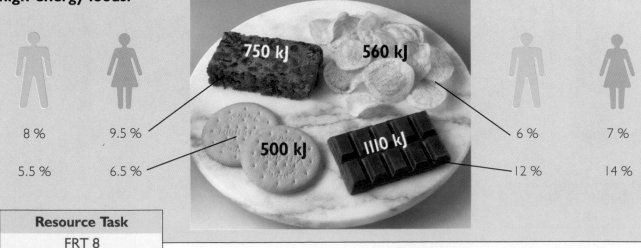

8 %   9.5 %   750 kJ   560 kJ   6 %   7 %

5.5 %   6.5 %   500 kJ   1110 kJ   12 %   14 %

Resource Task

FRT 8

Food choices

We eat food because we are hungry and because we enjoy eating. Food is so readily available in Britain that we are unlikely to die of starvation. We are more likely to become unhealthy because we eat too much food or too much of a particular type of food.

Nutrient	Needs met	Foods
Carbohydrates	energy	
Proteins	growth, repair and energy	
Fats	energy	
Vitamins	protection and maintenance of body processes	
Minerals	structure of body and maintenance of body processes	

The body also needs:
- water for all body cells and body processes;
- dietary fibre to help it get rid of waste products.

Resource Task

FRT 7

Other nutrients

The amount of other nutrients needed in the diet also depends on age: growing children usually need more. The figures in the following table are the **reference nutrient intake** (RNI), which is enough for 97 per cent of the population. You can compare a person's nutrient intake with these figures.

Reference nutrient intake (RNI) per day for different age groups								
Age (years)	Protein (g)		Calcium (mg)		Iron (mg)		Vitamin C (mg)	
7–10	28.3	28.3	550	550	8.7	8.7	30	
11–14	42.1	42.2	1000	800	11.3	14.8	35	
15–18	55.2	45.9	1000	800	11.3	14.8	40	
19–49	55.5	45.0	700	700	8.7	14.8	40	
50+	55.3	46.5	700	700	8.7	8.7	40	

Foods high in protein

Foods high in protein and calcium

Foods high in vitamin C

Foods high in iron

Resource Task

FRT 8

Designing food products

Understanding the market

Thinking about what the consumer needs and likes and the properties of the
food materials will help you write the specification for the product.

The needs and likes of the consumer

Who is it for?

What part will it play in their eating habits?

A luxury item?

A snack?

Part of a main meal?

Fill particular nutritional needs?

Be eaten in a certain way?

People with special diets? e.g. Orthodox Jews cannot eat pork. Hindus cannot eat beef.

HOW TO BE A VEGAN

How much will they pay for it?

£5

This will affect the ingredients you can use.

Health-conscious people

If so, it might need to be low in sugar, fat and salt, but high in dietary fibre.

The food materials

What are the key characteristics of the product?

Flavour?

Shape?

Texture?

What is its shelf life?

Will it keep for a week? For a year?

Does it need to be kept cool?

Can I stop it from going stale?

Will it need further cooking?

Be quick and easy to prepare?

JUST ADD WATER

Microwaveable?

PING

Should it be suitable for home freezing?

✳ ✳ ✳

You may need to consider all these points when you write the
specification.

▲ *Can you tell who will buy these
food products?*

Testing recipes yourself

In developing a food product you might begin by testing an existing recipe. A recipe lists the ingredients used and describes how to combine and cook these to make the food product. Use the ingredients listed and follow the instructions precisely.

Then ask yourself these questions:

The food product itself

● What did I like or dislike about:

the taste and smell?
the texture?
the appearance?

The instructions

● Were they easy to follow?

● Were they always clear?

● Did the ingredients behave in the way described?

▲ *Two ways to find out about recipes.* ▼

The cost

● What does each ingredient cost?

● What is the recipe's total cost?

Your answers to these questions will help you decide whether to use the recipe as it stands in developing a food product or whether it needs modifying.

...Designing food products

Modifying recipes to meet a specification

When you have tested a recipe you may decide to change it. Start by asking yourself:

- Why do I want it to be different?
- What do I want to be different?

This will help you write a specification for the new food product.

Next, think about how you will change the recipe to get the product you want.

Here is an example.

Jamaica Patties

> SPECIFICATION
> What it has to do:
> - taste more spicy
> - use different vegetables
> - be crunchy in the mouth.
> What it has to look like:
> - golden brown
> - a circle folded in half.

1 Jomo wants to change the recipe for Cornish pasties.

Why? Because his family doesn't like them.

What does he want to be different? The vegetables, the flavour, the colour and the texture.

2 He changed the recipe like this: replace half of the white flour with wholemeal flour; add a pinch of curry powder to the pastry wrapping and paprika and curry powder to the filling; use green and red peppers instead of potatoes and carrots; use breadcrumbs to bind the filling; reshape the pattie.

3 Jomo compared his new product, called Jamaica Patties, with his specification.

4 Then he asked his family what they thought.

You can make changes in four areas

Flavour and texture

You can add ingredients to give a different flavour. Adding dried apricots to a scone recipe makes it more fruity and moist.

You can leave out ingredients to get a different flavour. Leaving out chilli powder in a sauce makes it less spicy.

▲ *Extra ingredients give these biscuits more flavour and different textures.*

The way it is cooked

This will affect the final appearance, flavour, nutritional value and texture.

- Boiling instead of baking prevents browning.
- Grilling instead of frying makes food less greasy.
- Stir-frying instead of boiling keeps vegetables crisp and preserves their flavour and vitamin C.

▲ *The results of changing the method of cooking potatoes.*

Shape and finish

This has a major effect on the final appearance. Sponge cake can be presented as small cakes, as a Swiss roll filled with jam or as a party cake decorated to look like a castle.

▲ *It's the same sponge cake, but what a difference in appearance!*

Nutritional qualities

You can change ingredients to suit particular dietary needs. You might use potatoes and parsnips instead of meat to make a stew suitable for a vegetarian.

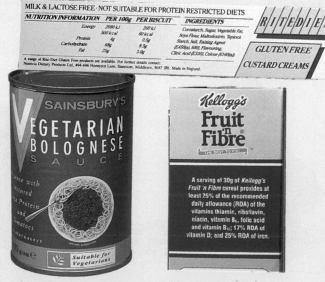

▲ *Packaging sometimes mentions diet.*

You can use **attribute analysis** to help you think up new designs for food products (see page 16).

...Designing food products

Choosing recipes to meet a specification

Choosing recipes for wrappings

Many food products enclose or wrap one sort of food in another. The Food Wrappings Chooser Chart shows how food can be wrapped, and the properties and qualities of each type of wrapping. This will help you choose a wrapping recipe to meet your product's specification.

Handling wrappings

The wrapping needs to be strong enough to hold a filling but not so strong that it is difficult to chew. It should not hide the taste of the filling.

You can spoil a wrapping by the way you handle it when you are making it. Follow this advice to get good wrappings.

Stop it sticking

Put some flour on your hands or the rolling-pin, but not too much or you will unbalance the recipe and make the wrapping dry and brittle.

Avoid bursting

Don't put too much filling in the wrapping.

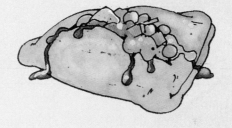

Roll it evenly

Press firmly on the rolling-pin at first and then more gently as you reach the right thickness. Roll it to the shape and size you want.

Avoid splitting open

Seal any joints with water or beaten egg.

Keep the structure

Try to get the shape and thickness right first time. If you handle the mixture too much you can destroy the structure.

Flaky and filo pastry lose their flakiness and shortcrust pastry becomes tough.

Resource Task

FRT 14

Food Wrappings Chooser Chart

Wrapping	Dip-coat 	Wrap-around 	Hold 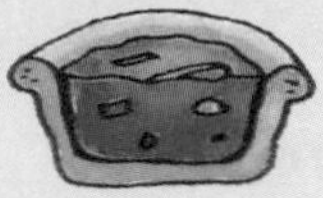	Physical properties	Appearance	Texture
Deep-fried batter 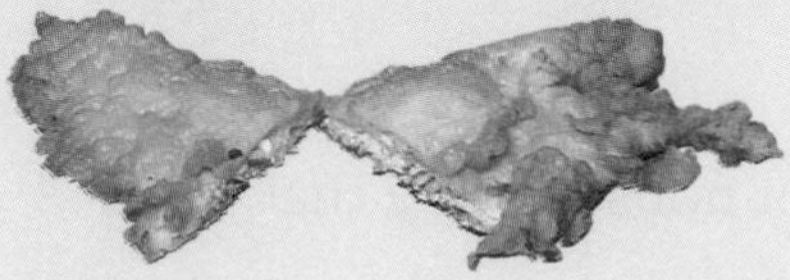	✓	✓	✓	solid and brittle	brown with bubbles on surface; takes shape of food it covers	crisp and crunchy
Shallow-fried batter (pancake) 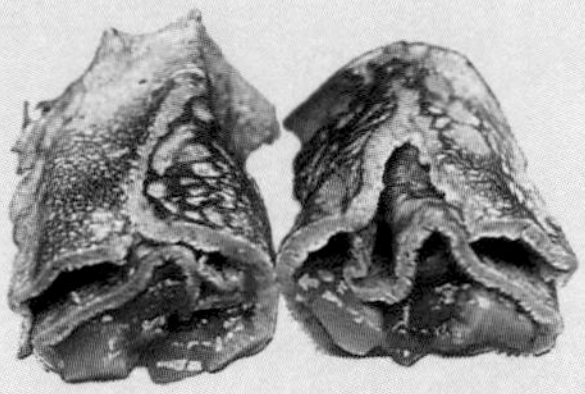		✓		solid, soft and pliable	cream with brown speckles	soft and chewy
Samosa 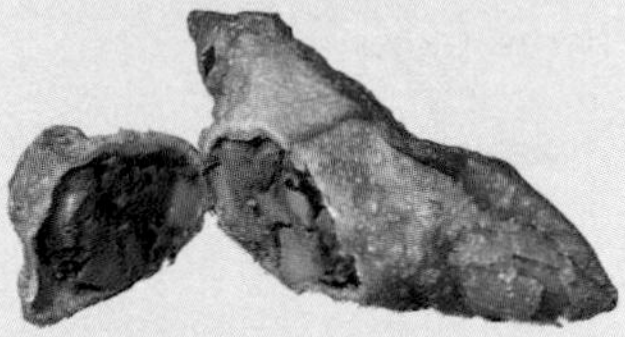		✓		solid, brittle when hot, softer when cold	golden brown, some bubbles on surface	crisp when hot
Shortcrust pastry 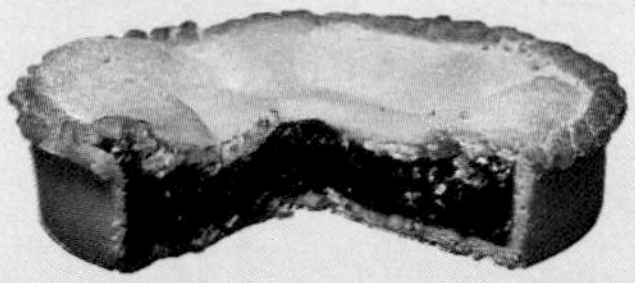		✓	✓	solid, hard and stiff	golden brown and smooth	crumbly, melts in mouth
Flaky pastry 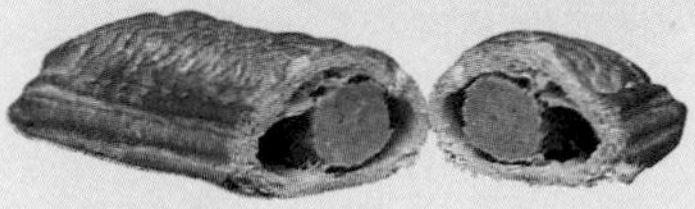		✓	✓	solid in thin layers and stiff	dark brown, shiny, multi-layered	crisp flakes
Filo pastry 		✓	✓	solid in thin layers and brittle	pale brown, darker at edges, multi-layered	crisp flakes

Resource Task

FRT 14

... *Designing food products*

Choosing recipes for fillings

Wrappings do not take long to cook, so fillings should be cooked before wrapping or able to be quickly cooked so that they cook inside the wrapping.

Use small pieces of food in the filling to allow the heat to penetrate more easily. Make small pieces by slicing, chopping, mincing or making a purée (pulp).

▲ *These can be dipped in coating when raw, then deep fried.*

Preparing fillings

Main ingredient	Should I wash it?	Should I cut it up?	Should I pre-cook it?	What other ingredients can I add?
Meat	no	yes	yes	herbs, spices, vegetables, e.g. tomatoes, onions
Fish	yes	yes	yes/no	herbs, spices, vegetables, e.g. mushroom sauce
Cheese	no	yes	no	vegetables, e.g. onions
Fruit	yes	yes	yes/no	sugar, spices
Vegetables	yes	yes/no	yes/no	herbs, spices, sauce

Use egg and milk to hold together or moisten ingredients. Use breadcrumbs to bind together moist or slippery ingredients.

Resource Task
FRT 17

Preparing food ingredients

Measuring the quantities needed

If you are preparing a dish like stir-fried vegetables or stew, the exact amount of each ingredient is not important. The ingredients only have to cook, not to rise or set.

For other dishes, you need precise measurements to make the product work. For example, in a sponge mix the proportions of the ingredients affect the rising of the cake. For these, measure the ingredients to be sure they are in the correct proportions. The two main methods of measuring food ingredients are by weight and by volume.

Weighing
You can use kitchen scales for weighing. Most scales measure weight in grams (g) and kilograms (kg). They are accurate to the nearest gram.

If your recipe is in pounds (lbs) and ounces (oz) you should convert them into grams and kilograms. Most recipes use 25 g to 1 oz and 500 g to 1 lb (16 oz).

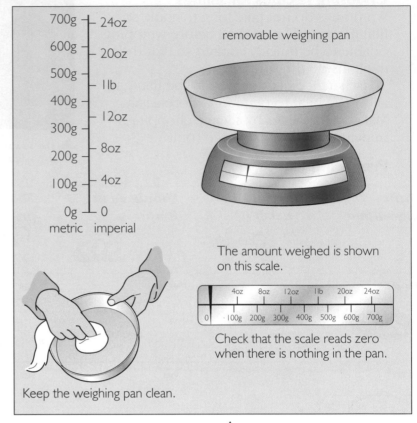

The amount weighed is shown on this scale.

Check that the scale reads zero when there is nothing in the pan.

Keep the weighing pan clean.

▲ *How to use kitchen scales.*

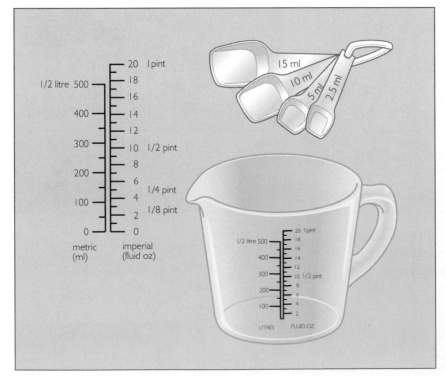

◀ *Ways to measure volume.*

Measuring volume
Use a jug to measure large amounts of liquid. Jugs are usually marked both millilitres (ml) and pints. They are only accurate to the nearest 20 ml. For small amounts of liquid or powdery solids you can use measuring spoons. These come in four sizes: 2.5 ml, 5 ml, 10 ml and 15 ml.

Wipe the spoons after use to avoid contaminating one food ingredient with another.

... *Preparing food ingredients*

Getting the right shapes and sizes

Once you have decided on the shapes and sizes you need you can choose the right tools for the job.

Controlling the shape and size of food materials

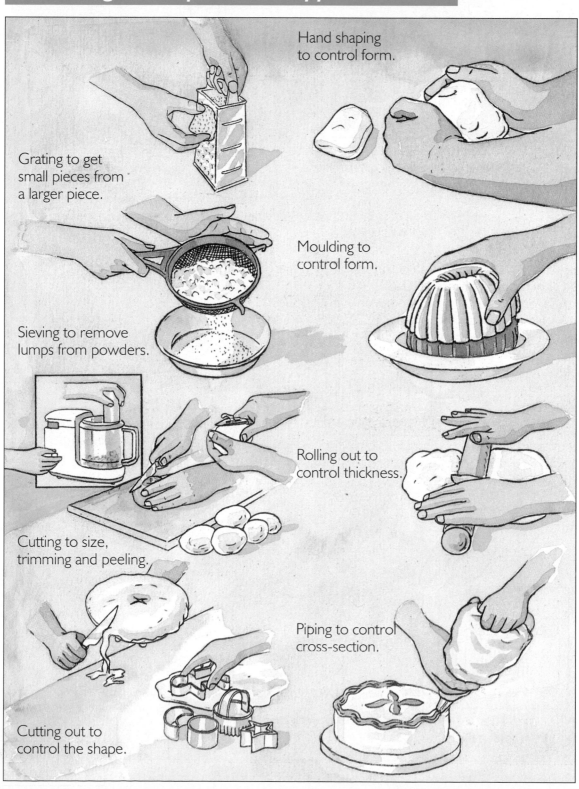

Hand shaping to control form.

Grating to get small pieces from a larger piece.

Moulding to control form.

Sieving to remove lumps from powders.

Rolling out to control thickness.

Cutting to size, trimming and peeling.

Piping to control cross-section.

Cutting out to control the shape.

Combining different food materials

The six main ways of combining food materials are shown in the panel.

Ways to combine food materials

Rubbing in – this introduces air into the mixture and causes the fat to surround flour particles preventing them sticking together.

Beating and creaming – this introduces air into the mixture of fat and sugar; the fat surrounds the tiny air bubbles trapping them in the mixture.

Stirring and blending – combines a mixture quickly with little manipulation or over-handling of the ingredients.

Folding – combines the mixture without beating and developing the gluten in flour.

Whisking – adds air into a mixture quickly, which will often collapse if left to stand.

Kneading – blends ingredients and develops the gluten in flour to make a strong framework.

Resource Task

FRT 18

Cooking the food

Choosing the equipment and method

Cooking always involves the transfer of heat into food materials. There are many different ways of doing this.

Different methods of cooking

> **SAFETY** ⚠
> **Care is required when using boiling water and heating food.**

Steaming
The food is in a container with holes in its base over a saucepan of boiling water. The steam surrounds the food and makes it hot. This is a slow method but helps vegetables keep their flavour and vitamin C. It is also used for puddings.

Using a saucepan
The liquid in the saucepan becomes hot through **convection**. The heat is transferred to the surface of the food and is **conducted** slowly to the centre. Use this method for cooking food in small pieces, like vegetables or pasta. It is also used for stews and sauces, when the liquid becomes part of the food.

Using a hot plate, frying-pan or wok
Heat from the hot plate, pan or wok quickly makes the food surface hot. If the food is too thick the outside is burned by the time the inside is cooked. So this method is best for thinly sliced food.

Use a hot plate or pan for food like bacon or sausages or food that forms shallow pools of liquid like eggs or chapatis. Use a wok for stir-frying food divided into small pieces.

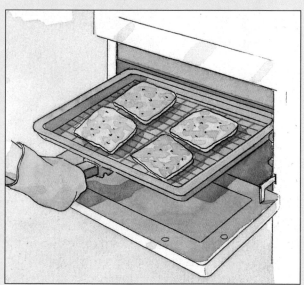

Using the grill or toaster
Radiation makes the food surface hot. This heat is conducted only slowly to the centre of the food. If the food is too thick the outside is burned by the time the inside is cooked. This method is best for food that is in thin slices, such as sausages, bacon or bread.

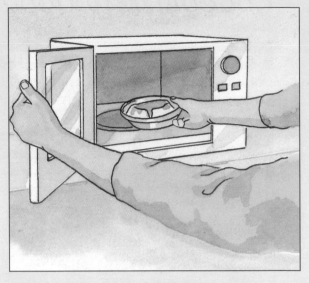

Using a deep-fat fryer

This works like a saucepan. The food is often held in a wire basket so it can be removed and drained easily. Fat gets much hotter than water, so a crisp coating is formed on the outside of the food and it is browned evenly all over. This method can be used for quick-cooking fish, meat, fruit and vegetables in batter, chips and doughnuts.

Using a microwave cooker

Microwave radiation makes water molecules in the food vibrate. This fast movement makes the food hot. Food with a high water content heats up quickly.

The microwaves can only penetrate food up to a depth of about 50 mm and produce heat rapidly from the inside. So food cooked by microwaves is cooler on the surface than in the centre. That is why microwave cooked foods are left to stand for a short time to ensure that the heat generated in the middle of the food is conducted to the surface. This method is particularly useful for defrosting frozen food and heating ready-cooked, convenience food.

Using an oven

The air inside the oven becomes hot through convection. This heat is transferred to the food's surface. It is conducted slowly to the centre of the food. The oven can be set at a temperature to ensure that the outside of the food does not burn while the inside is cooking.

Use this method for roasting joints of meat and poultry, baking mixtures that have to rise and set, like breads and cakes, and cooking casseroles.

Using a pressure cooker

Steam under pressure can reach temperatures of over 100°C. The super-heated steam surrounds the food and makes it hot. This cooks the food much faster than ordinary steaming.

Resource Task

FRT 18

... *Cooking the food*

What happens to food as it is cooked?

When food is cooked, the flavour, texture and colour change. What changes take place depend on the method of cooking and the ingredients.

Many foods change in several ways when cooked. Cake mixtures rise, set and brown. Biscuits brown but remain soft until they are cool.

Changes that take place when food is cooked

Browning
The surfaces of these foods have become brown and crisp during cooking due to dextrinisation caused by the action of dry heat on starch granules in the food.

Rising
These foods have risen during cooking due to the expansion of gases introduced into the mixture by physical means (such as beating) or chemical means (such as the use of self-raising flour or baking powder).

Thickening
This sauce has thickened during cooking due to the swelling of the starch granules in the process of gelatinization.

Setting
These foods have set firm during cooking due to the gelatine absorbing water and the protein molecules forming a 3D network or 'gel'. If the gel is heated above 35°C it returns to a liquid and is called a 'sol'.

Is it ready?

It is easy to spoil food by cooking it too much or not enough. Under-cooked food can be dangerous as well as unpleasant because harmful bacteria have not been destroyed in the cooking process. Over-cooked food is often tough or tastes burned.

To tell whether the food you are preparing is properly cooked, ask yourself these questions:

- Is it as brown and crisp as I would like?
- Is it as soft or tender as I would like?
- Is it as set or firm as I would like?
- Is it as thick as I would like?
- Is it cooked through?

Ways of answering these questions are shown in the panel.

Ways to tell if food is cooked

Test for browning by looking, and for crispness by touching gently with a pointed knife.

Test for thickness by seeing how fast it drips off a spoon. A coating sauce should coat the back of a spoon.

Test for tenderness by seeing if a skewer or sharp knife will push in easily.

Gently push a skewer into a fruit cake. If it comes out clean the cake is cooked.

Test for setting by shaking gently. If it is still liquid you will see ripples in the middle.

Use a cooking thermometer to tell if meat is cooked through.

Finishing touches

The final appearance of a food product is important. It should be attractive to those who are going to buy or eat it. The two main ways to make food products look better are:

● including decoration as part of the design;

● adding decoration as part of the way it is served.

Here are some examples.

Use a glaze to give the product sheen.

Use pastry pieces to decorate pies or flans.

Coat cakes and biscuits with icing.
Shape food so it looks interesting.

Use chocolate pieces, wafers and candied fruit as toppings for ice creams and jellies.

Use coloured ingredients.

Garnish with small vegetables.

Add a salad.

Sensory evaluation tests

What will other people think about your food product? Use at least ten people for any tests that you carry out for a range of opinions.

Preparing for the test

- Draw up an answer sheet for the tasting panel.
- Give each taster a glass of water to sip between samples to take away the taste.
- Use the same type of plate or container for each sample.
- Label the samples of food so that the taster does not learn anything from the label. Symbols are best, such as ▲, ■ , ●, or random numbers such as 369 or 472. Do not use 1, 2, 3 or A, B, C, as they may give tasters the impression that number 1 or letter A is best.
- Hold the tasting session somewhere not affected by cooking smells.
- Tell the tasters not to talk to one another. It is their individual opinions that you want.
- Give each person the same size sample to taste – enough for about two bites or sips.

The three types of test you can use are:
Ranking tests
Preference tests
Difference tests

Ranking tests

This type of test will help evaluate the strength of a particular quality of the food. It is good for decisions on flavour, colour and texture. Here is an example.

Which dried fruit gives the most moist biscuit?

Make three batches of the biscuits, each with the same amount of a different dried fruit. Set up your tasting panel like this:

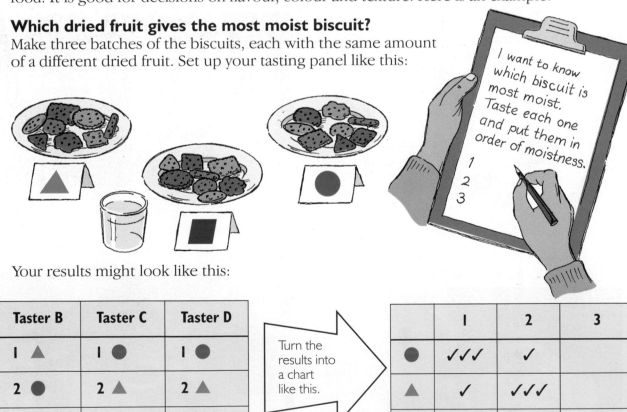

Your results might look like this:

Taster A	Taster B	Taster C	Taster D
1 ●	1 ▲	1 ●	1 ●
2 ▲	2 ●	2 ▲	2 ▲
3 ■	3 ■	3 ■	3 ■

Turn the results into a chart like this.

	1	2	3
●	✓✓✓	✓	
▲	✓	✓✓✓	
■			✓✓✓✓

The ticks tell you the **rank order**. From this small sample, biscuit ● is thought to be the most moist.
   Note: the ranking test does not tell you whether the panel preferred one. For that you need a preference test.

Resource Task
FRT 4

...Sensory evaluation tests

Preference test

This type of test is used to find out how much a person likes or dislikes a food.

Use a five-point scale of descriptive words or faces (for young children), like the one here, to help people describe how much they like a product.

1 Like very much   **2 Like moderately**   **3 Neither like nor dislike**   **4 Dislike moderately**   **5 Dislike very much**

How much do you like the cakes?

Set up a tasting panel like this:

Preference test

1. Taste a sample
2. Circle the number which best describes how much you like or dislike the food
3. Take a drink of water to clean your palate
4. Taste the next sample. Circle the number which best describes how much you like or dislike the food. Do not compare the samples

Repeat this until you have tested all the food samples

	☺	☺	☺	☹	☹
▲■	1	2	3	4	5
	1	2	3	4	5
●		2	3	4	5

With ten tasters your results might look like this:

▲	5	4	5	4	4	2	4	3	5	3
■	3	3	5	4	2	1	3	4	2	5
●	1	1	1	3	2	3	1	2	3	2

	Total score	Average score	Conclusion
▲	39	39/10 = 3. 9	*disliked moderately*
■	32	32/10 = 3. 2	*neither liked nor disliked*
●	19	19/10 = 1. 9	*liked moderately*

Turn the results into a chart like this.

You can draw a conclusion about how much the tasting panel liked each sample as shown in the last column of the table. This type of test is called a **hedonic ranking** test.

Resource Task

FRT 5

Attribute profiling

An attribute profile is a way to describe a food product and present the information visually. It is sometimes called a star diagram. You can use it to evaluate an existing product, a simple recipe that can then be modified, or at the designing stage of a new product. It is particularly useful to show how changes to the design of a food product can affect its sensory characteristics and overall appeal.

Here is an example showing the response of tasters to the attributes of a leek and potato soup.

The average scores are shown here.

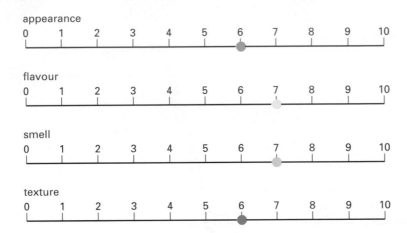

The results are displayed as a star chart like this.

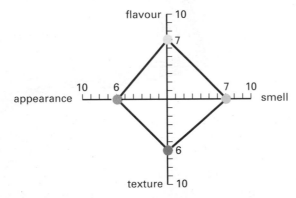

You can use an attribute profile like this to help you to modify the product by changing the ingredients and asking tasters to grade the attributes of the new product. In this case the food product designer decided to add some paprika to give the soup some colour and a slightly hotter taste. You can see from the results that tasters liked the change in colour but not the new taste. So the next step is to find an ingredient that gives the colour change but not the taste change and test again. And so on.

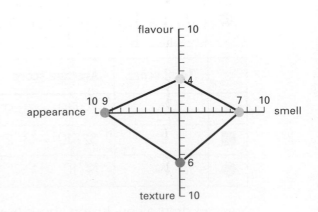

Resource Task
FRT 3

Difference test

This test is useful for finding out whether people can tell the difference between slightly different food products. Here is an example.

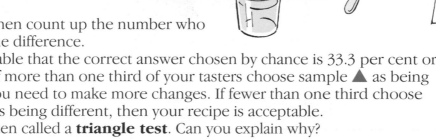

Can people tell the difference between a fruit dessert made with sugar and one made with artificial sweetener?

Make up the two recipes and prepare three samples of food labelled with symbols:

- sample ▲ made with sugar;
- sample ● made with artificial sweetener;
- sample ■ made with artificial sweetener.

Samples ● and ■ are identical.

Give each taster an answer sheet like the one shown.

   You can then count up the number who could tell the difference.

   It is probable that the correct answer chosen by chance is 33.3 per cent or one third. If more than one third of your tasters choose sample ▲ as being different, you need to make more changes. If fewer than one third choose sample ▲ as being different, then your recipe is acceptable.

   This is often called a **triangle test**. Can you explain why?

Being a food product tester

Sometimes you will have to test a food product on your own. You might not be sure that the product is good enough yet to set up a tasting panel. Or, there may not be enough time for a tasting panel. Use your own judgement. Here's how to do it.

Look at it carefully.   Sniff it carefully.   Taste a tiny piece.

What can I do to improve the product?

Chew a small piece.   Keep chewing.

Resource Tasks
FRT 2, 6

Prolonging shelf-life

DAILY MIRROR, Thursday, January 12, 1989

DOUBLE ALERT ON EGG AND CHICKENS PERIL

- Salmonella 'an epidemic'
- Deadly bug hits poultry

By JULIA LANGDON and GORDAN HAY

TOUGH new warnings about the poison perils in eggs and chickens were given last night.

Sir Donald told a Commons committee that the NHS was warned about eggs a month before the public were told.

He said the chances of an egg being infected were small.

But as 200 million were eaten every week, a small proportion could cause a lot of food poisoning.

The committee is probing the salmonella crisis and the Government's response following the resignation of Junior Health Minister Edwina Currie.

She quit after her comment that most eggs were infected caused a storm of protest from producers.

Rampage

Sir Donald, chief medical officer at the Department of Health, was asked about her statement and replied: "Only very few eggs are infected."

The Government knew of the new strain of salmonella enteritidis in 1981 but there was no significant increase in the numbers found until 1986, the committee heard.

The numbers increased again in 1987 and last year.

Dr Joe Smith, director of the Public Health Laboratory Service, said cases had increased 13 fold between 1981 and last year to 13,000 cases — and were still rising.

THE BUG infecting cooked chickens, listeria, is also on the rampage.

Five years ago there were 115 cases. Last year they reached almost 300.

Worried health chiefs have decided to send out leaflets to health centres, supermarkets and doctors giving guidelines on

▲ Rotten food usually looks bad but eggs that cause food poisoning look OK.

Keeping food fresh

You can keep food in good condition by following these rules:

- check the 'use by' or 'best before' dates on the label;
- follow any storage instructions given;
- keep food covered or wrapped to stop it drying out;
- keep foods cool. This slows down the **enzyme** action in raw food that causes it to spoil. It will also slow down the growth of micro-organisms that make food go bad.

USE BY (2)
23 JUN D
£1·23

LIFT HERE TO OPEN

BEST BEFORE 18 JUN
SC2

KEEP REFRIGERATED

dairygate

FRESH PASTEURISED
Semi-Skimmed Milk

Shelf-life is the length of time that a food, if stored correctly, will remain safe to eat and keep its physical properties, appearance and taste. If it is stored for longer than its shelf-life or incorrectly it will spoil.

What makes food go bad?

Micro-organisms are yeasts, moulds and bacteria that grow in foods and make it go bad. Food that has been attacked by micro-organisms often smells 'off' or looks 'mouldy'.

The yeast in fruit-flavoured yoghurt can make the yoghurt **ferment**, producing a gas which pushes the lid up on the yoghurt pot. The yoghurt has an 'off' flavour.

Some bacteria make food look 'slimy'.

Bacteria such as salmonella are particularly dangerous because the food does not look bad. The taste and appearance are not affected but the bacteria cause food poisoning.

Laboratory tests find the cause of food poisoning outbreaks. Salmonella are destroyed by high temperatures during cooking.

Resource Task
FRT 11

Preserving food

People have always tried to preserve food for the winter months when supplies are scarce. Our full supermarket shelves shows how successful we are today in preserving foods.

Food is preserved by killing or preventing the growth of the micro-organisms that spoil it. Micro-organisms need:

- moisture;
- neutral surroundings, neither **acid** nor **alkaline**;
- temperatures of between 5°C and 63°C.

By controlling conditions so that micro-organisms cannot live, you can preserve food. The preservation may alter physical properties, appearance and taste.

Canning and bottling

The high temperatures used in processing food destroy micro-organisms but change its physical properties, appearance and taste.

Drying

This destroys micro-organisms by removing moisture from food but changes its physical properties, appearance and taste.

Irradiation

This destroys the micro-organisms but has little effect on the food's physical properties, appearance and taste.

Pickling

This makes the surroundings of the food **acid**, and changes its physical properties, appearance and taste.

Freezing

This does not destroy micro-organisms but stops them reproducing. It has little effect on the food's physical properties, appearance and taste.

Labelling

(1) Name
The name must describe the food, e.g. 'Chocolate Delight' must also be described as chocolate and cream dessert. Strawberry yoghurt must contain strawberries, but 'strawberry-flavoured' yoghurt need not.

(2) Ingredients
These must be listed in descending order of inclusion by weight. If added water is more than 5% of contents, it must be listed as an ingredient. Additives must be shown by name and E number.

(3) Date mark
Most foods are now date marked. The main exceptions are long-life foods (last more than 18 months). The date marked is the date up to and including which the food will remain at its best if stored correctly. Look for the words 'Best Before' and 'Sell By'.

(4) Storage instructions
The label must give instructions for the best storage methods for the food product.

(5) Name & address
The name and address of the manufacturer, packagers or seller within the EU must be on the label.

(6) Place of origin
If a food has been imported and then packed by a manufacturer in England, it may be misleading if the country of origin is not mentioned on the label.

(7) Preparation
There should be instructions for preparation if necessary (for example, with cake mixes).

(8) Quantity or weight
Most foods are labelled with the weight in grams. An 'e' after the weight means that the manufacturer is complying with the average system of weights and measures which is common throughout the EU.

Special claims
Foods which claim to have special properties, e.g. 'rich in vitamin C', should be labelled with extra information to support this claim.

As well as the information required by law, many people (both consumers and manufacturers) believe that other information is helpful to customers and should be shown on labelling. For example, by law labels do not have to show the amount of fat, sugar or fibre contained in a product but this information is helpful to consumers who wish to eat a healthy diet.

Resource Task
FRT 10

Developing a new product

From the first idea for a new product to its launch, the development process is a team effort in which each member has a special part to play

Businesses grow by identifying new ideas for products and meeting new needs. The superstore chain, Tesco, has 60 product teams developing ideas and working with food suppliers to launch over 1000 new products a year. Each product will have been checked for quality at every stage in its development. Each member of the team has a part to play in making sure that the product is a success.

Pause for thought
Think about all the things that would need to be done to develop a new food product. How big a team would be needed to do this? What might each team member do?

Introducing the team

In the past a single person might have come up with an idea for a product and develop, produce and sell it. Today it is more complicated, and design technologists work in teams. Each team member is an expert in one area and has a specific job to do. Together, the team knows more about the product development process than any individual team member could.

Let's meet the members of a real product team.

- **The product evaluation officer** – 'I work with the other members of the team to develop a product with the right taste, texture and appearance. I need to coordinate the work of the other team members to make sure that the product is acceptable to our customers and of the best possible quality, when it is sold and after it has been stored and then cooked by the customer.'

- **The marketing manager –** 'I make sure that customers will want to buy the new product. Is there a gap in the market? Are there trends in the kinds of food people are buying? Does the new product fit in with our existing products and our marketing strategy?'

- **The buyer –** 'I need to find a supplier who will be able to produce the volume of product we need, as quickly and cheaply as possible without sacrificing quality. I then negotiate terms with them. I will work closely with the food technologist to maintain a good relationship with the supplier.'

- **The food technologist –** 'I work with the supplier to make sure the product is of the right quality. This involves inspecting raw materials and production processes and advising on the problems which often occur when kitchen samples are scaled up for factory production. The product specification is my responsibility.'

- **The design executive –** 'Most people are first attracted to products by their packaging. My job is to produce attractive packaging and to make sure that it shows all the necessary information, such as the ingredients and nutrition information tables.'

- **The microbiologist –** 'People are naturally worried when they read about bacteria such as listeria and salmonella. I check the product to make sure it does not contain bacteria that could make the consumer ill or that would make it go bad before its use-by date.'

- **The chemist –** 'I check the product for two things. Firstly, is it legal? For example, if the product is advertised as 'low fat', I need to test the product to find out the amount of fat in it. Secondly, is it safe? There must be no trace of dangerous chemicals.'

1 Read through the roles of each member of the team. Discuss and then write down the particular skills and knowledge that each team member needs.

2 What advantages can you see in this type of team?

3 What problems might there be for the team? How might these problems be solved?

Now we are going to see how the team goes about developing a new product.

The product development process

Each new food product passes through several stages from initial idea to launch. This process is designed to make sure that only successful products reach the superstore shelves. No one can guarantee success, but evaluating the product at every stage greatly reduces the risk of failure.

Pause for thought
What might happen if an unsuccessful product is launched? How might it influence the customers? What might be the consequences for the retailer?

▲ *All these products started as ideas.*

The initial idea

Initial ideas for new food products come from various sources. Consumer research might have shown a gap in the market for a higher quality version of a basic product or a cheaper version of an expensive product. Competitors might have launched a new product which is doing well. There may be a consumer trend, for example towards buying healthier products.

A brainstorming session produces a list of possible new products. These ideas might be good or bad. The next part of the process is to examine the potential of each idea.

1 Think about the products you can buy in a large superstore. List any new products which have appeared on the shelves.

2 Do you notice any trends in these new products? For example, are there trends in the type of food, its packaging or its intended market?

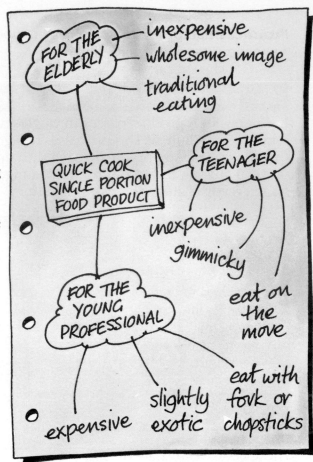

▲ *Ideas for new food products from a brainstorming session.*

Concept screening

Each idea needs to be looked at in detail.

- Will the product be popular with the customers?
- Does it match the company's quality image?
- Will it reduce the sales of other goods in the store?
- Can it be made in bulk?
- Does it look attractive?
- Can it be produced at the right cost?
- Is it the right time of year to launch this product?

If the answer to any one of these questions is 'no' then the idea is rejected. If all the answers are 'yes' the product idea passes on to the next stage.

3 All design technologists need to screen new ideas before developing them. You will be developing many new ideas throughout your design and technology course. Look at the list of questions above.

a Write down those which you could use to screen your own ideas.
b Which do not apply?
c Can you think of any others to add to the list?

▲ *The checklist used to screen an idea for a new product.*

Product development

A supplier has to be found to make the product. The supplier must have a good reputation. The factory is inspected to check that it is clean, that the ingredients and products are kept at the right temperature and that the necessary quality control checks are in place. All the supplier's staff must have been properly trained.

The supplier is given a brief describing the product and is asked to produce some samples. The product team will taste these samples and suggest improvements. Samples are also sent to the labs for chemical and microbiological testing. The supplier modifies the recipe until the best product is made which all the team agree is suitable to bear the company's brand name.

Now the product needs to be tested on the consumers.

Product testing

Tesco has six Consumer Advice Centres in superstores in different parts of the country. These centres are staffed by home economists who advise the public and organize consumer-tastings of new products. Customers in the store are asked if they are willing to take part in the market research. It is important to ask the right people: you wouldn't ask pensioners to taste a product aimed at young children.

The people who agree to take part are given samples to taste, usually one of the new product and one of an existing similar product. They are not told which is which. This is called a 'blind' tasting. The customers fill in a questionnaire. They are asked to compare the two products in a variety of ways. One hundred customers in two different stores are asked for their opinions and the results of the survey are fed into a computer. If the new product scores highly in the testing it goes on to the next stage. If the product fails the consumer test the product team and supplier start the product development stage again.

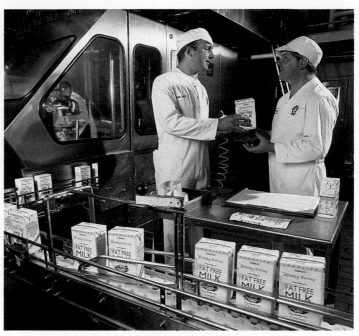

▲ *Inspecting the factory and products of a possible supplier.*

Pause for thought
What things are people looking for when inspecting a food factory?

▲ *Customers try out a new product.*

Pause for thought
Why are customers usually asked to compare two products? Why are they not told which is which? Why is research carried out at two different stores?

185

Pack design

The new product needs to be packaged. A sample of the product is tested to find out all the nutritional information needed for the pack. Photographs of the product are taken and artwork produced. Cooking instructions are written along with suggested ways of serving the product.

Meanwhile the supplier is preparing to make the product in bulk.

The first production run

The supplier now needs to convince the team that they are ready to go into full production. Up to now the samples used in the tests may have been produced in special kitchens at the suppliers. The final product will be produced on a production line. Under supervision, the supplier organizes a first production run of the product. This will last half a day, which is long enough to show that the product can be produced consistently to a high standard.

The launch

The product is now ready to be launched, but this is not the end of the story. The team will be looking at the product regularly to check its quality, to see whether people are buying it and whether it could be developed further.

▲ *Attractive, informative and effective packaging is very important to the success of a product.*

▲ *A new product on the production line.*

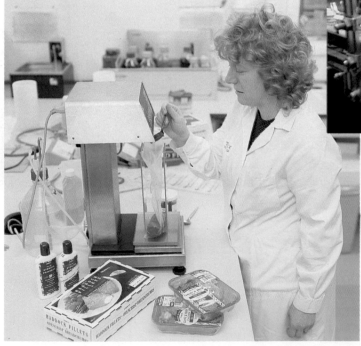

▲ *A new product's quality being checked.*

1 Look back at the roles of the team members. Which team members are involved at each stage of the product development process?

2 Make a chart showing what each team member does at each stage of the process.

Being safe in designing and making

Introducing some important words

A **hazard** is anything which might cause harm or damage. A kitchen knife is a hazard. It is very sharp and there is a chance that you could cut yourself with it. This chance is called the **risk**. You can work out how big the risk is by thinking about whether the harm or damage is likely to happen. This is called **assessing** the risk. This is not always easy.

If a chef uses a sharp knife then the risk of an accident is low. If a small child uses the knife then the risk is high.

Risk control is the action taken to ensure that the harm or damage is less likely to happen. The chef has been trained to use the knife and he is always careful. This training and his way of working control the risk. The child is prevented from using the knife and this controls the risk.

Both the chef and the child are in safe situations because the risk has been controlled, so the chance of harm or damage is small.

Designing products that are safe to use

When you design a product, think about the hazards there might be in the way it is used. Your design should try to control any risk by making the risk as small as possible. Here are some products being used with questions to help you assess the hazards.

Q

1 Who is likely to get hurt here?

2 Can designers help people to use their products carefully?

3 What are the risks here?
4 What can be done to prevent them?

 5 What are the risks from using these wrappers?
6 Who is most likely to be in danger?

 7 How can you tell that the iron is on and hot?
8 What are the risks in this situation?

9 What are the risks here?
10 Would you want to make roller skating completely safe?

Designing products that are safe to make

When you design a product think about the hazards there might be in the way it is made. Your design should try to control these risks by choosing materials and methods of manufacture that are as safe as possible.

Here are some products being made with questions to help you assess the hazards.

How many of the following hazards can you spot?

- being cut
- becoming deaf
- getting strained
- getting blinded
- being burned
- being poisoned
- getting bruised

 1 What are the risks here?
2 How would you control them?

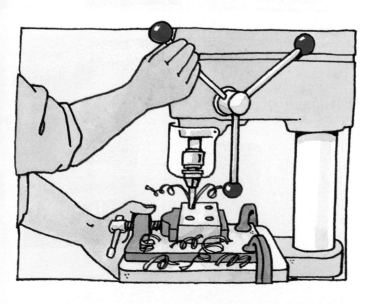

 5 What are the risks here?
6 How would you control them?

 3 What are the risks here?
4 How would you control them?

 7 What are the risks here?
8 How would you control them?

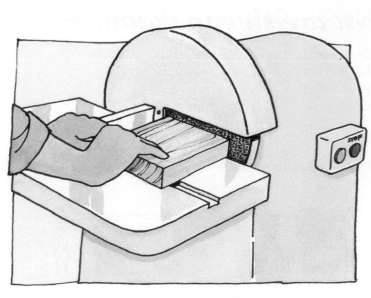

Effects over time

Some hazards are not very dangerous in small amounts but with regular exposure over a period of time they cause serious damage to health. For example, it is important to wear a mask to prevent breathing in fibres and dust. It is important that any liquid or process that gives off fumes is used in a well-ventilated area or fume cupboard.

9 What are the risks here?
10 How would you control them?

Sources of information

Where should you look for information to help you with risk assessment? A useful place to start is with your teachers. They are responsible for showing you safe ways to use tools and equipment, so they can give you guidance. Instructions that come with a product are important. To use a product safely you should follow the instructions carefully. This applies particularly to food, cosmetics and medicines.

Safety standards are the government-agreed regulations for the design of a wide range of products. Consumer magazines often contain articles about the product safety. Ask your teacher to help you use these published materials.

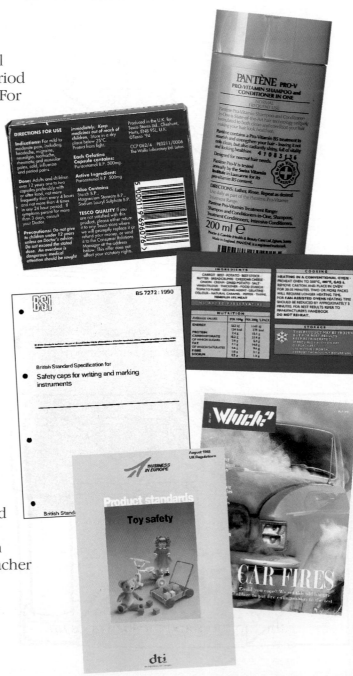

Resource Tasks
HSRT 1–4

7 Designing and making with mechanisms

What can mechanisms do?

Change the type of movement

At the supermarket check-out your shopping is moved forward by a belt and pulley. The motor makes the pulleys *rotate*, but the belt and the shopping on it move in a *straight line*.

You can describe movement in four ways and give each type of movement a symbol.

Linear movement
Movement in a straight line (a car moving along a road, or a ski lift up a mountain).

Rotary movement
Movement in a complete circle (a wheel turning).

Oscillating movement
Movement backwards and forwards in part of a circle (a pendulum).

Reciprocating movement
Movement backwards and forwards in a straight line (a saw sawing).

Change the direction of movement

When you pull *down* on the rope of the hoist, the pulley at the top turns and the load goes *up*.

Resource Tasks
MCRT 1, 2

191

...What can mechanisms do?

Turn the axis of rotation through an angle

The axis of the gear wheel that drives the hand-whisk is at right angles to the axis of the blades.

This arrangement turns the movement through 90°.

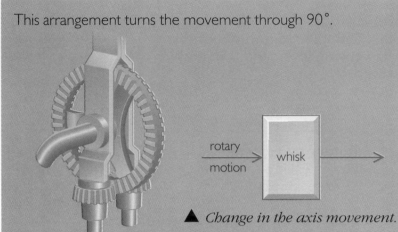

rotary motion → whisk →

▲ *Change in the axis movement.*

Increase output speed and decrease force

This clockwork mouse uses a gear box to turn the wheels much faster than the drive axle from the motor.

The toy must be light because the moving force provided by the wheels is much less than that applied to the gears by the motor.

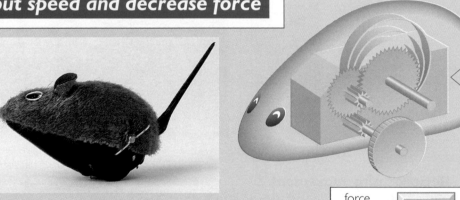

force → gear box → smaller force

speed → → higher speed

▲ *Increasing speed, decreasing force.*

Increase output force and decrease speed

The handles on these pruners act as levers. They are much longer than the blades.

So the cutting force that the blades exert on the branch is much greater than the force applied to the handles.

Decreasing speed, ▶ force → pruners → larger force
increasing force.

speed → → lower speed

Resource Tasks
MCRT 2, 3

Apply and maintain a force

The clothes peg – a spring and two levers – exerts two equal and opposite forces which hold the clothes tightly against the washing line.

▲ *Applied and maintained force.*

Transmit movement and force

Mechanisms that transmit force or movement from one place to another are often called **transmission mechanisms**.

In this muck-spreader the linking shaft transmits a turning force from the tractor to the spreader.

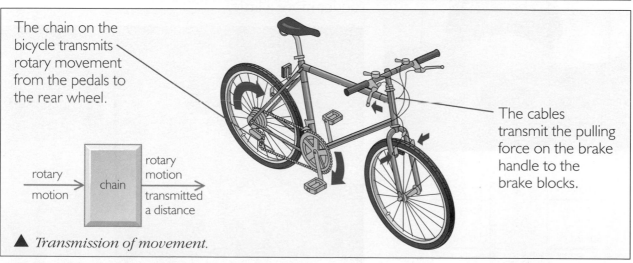

The chain on the bicycle transmits rotary movement from the pedals to the rear wheel.

The cables transmit the pulling force on the brake handle to the brake blocks.

rotary motion → | chain | → rotary motion transmitted a distance

▲ *Transmission of movement.*

Using wheels and axles

Wheels are usually *fixed* to axles so the wheel and axle turn together.

But sometimes, as in a supermarket trolley, they can spin freely on their axles. Here there are usually bearings between the wheel and the axle to reduce friction (see page 103).

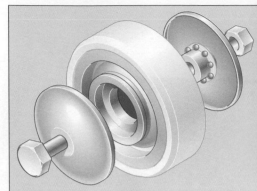

To change the type of movement

The wheels on the wheelchair rotate but the wheelchair moves forward in a straight line. *Rotary* movement has been converted into *linear* movement.

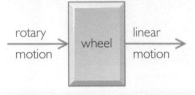

▲ *Changing the type of movement.*

To reduce friction between sliding surfaces

Wheels or rollers are often used to reduce friction. The roller-way enables the lifeboat to be launched easily.

To increase force and decrease speed

The large diameter of the ship's helm means that the helmsman only has to use a small effort to turn the rudder. His hands move a long way to make the rudder move a little.

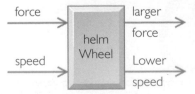

▲ *Decreasing speed, increasing force.*

Using shafts, bearings and couplings

A **shaft** is a rod which transmits rotary movement along its length. There are usually **bearings** between the rotating shaft and its support to reduce friction.

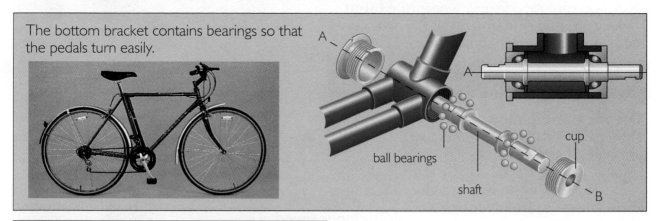

The bottom bracket contains bearings so that the pedals turn easily.

ball bearings

shaft

cup

To transmit movement and force

The shaft connecting the pedal crank to the chain wheel in a bicycle transmits movement and force.

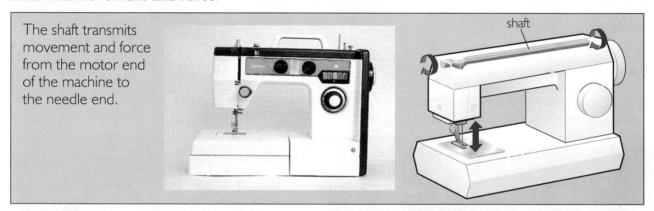

The shaft transmits movement and force from the motor end of the machine to the needle end.

shaft

Couplings connect shafts and transmit movement from one shaft to another.

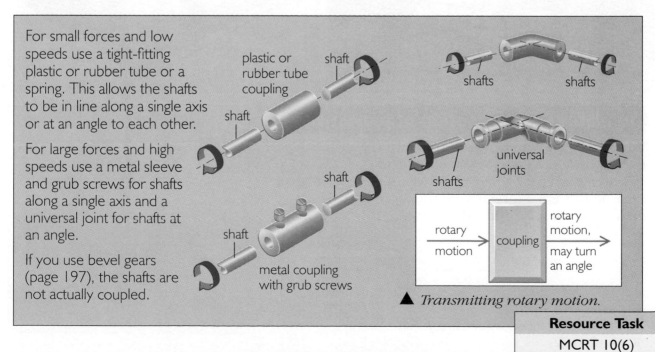

For small forces and low speeds use a tight-fitting plastic or rubber tube or a spring. This allows the shafts to be in line along a single axis or at an angle to each other.

For large forces and high speeds use a metal sleeve and grub screws for shafts along a single axis and a universal joint for shafts at an angle.

If you use bevel gears (page 197), the shafts are not actually coupled.

plastic or rubber tube coupling

shaft

shaft

shafts

shafts

shaft

shafts

universal joints

shaft

metal coupling with grub screws

shaft

rotary motion → coupling → rotary motion, may turn an angle

▲ *Transmitting rotary motion.*

Resource Task
MCRT 10(6)

Using gears

A gear is a wheel with teeth. It can be fixed to a shaft so that it turns at the same speed as the shaft. You can use one gear wheel (the **input**) to drive another (the **output**) if the two sets of teeth mesh together (a **gear train**).

To change the type of movement

The rack and pinion

This changes *rotary* movement to *linear* movement. The pinion is fixed on a shaft. When the pinion turns it makes the rack move in a straight line. Pulling or pushing the rack makes the pinion turn.

▲ *Gears come in many different shapes and sizes.*

This rack moves 40 mm for every turn of the pinion.

The **input speed** of the pinion is 20 revolutions per minute (**r.p.m.**) so the rack moves at a speed of 20 x 40 mm per minute = 800 mm per minute. This is the **output speed**.

input: 20 r.p.m.   pinion gear with 20 teeth

rack with 5 teeth per 10 mm

output: rack moves at 800 mm a minute

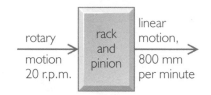

rotary motion 20 r.p.m. → | rack and pinion | → linear motion, 800 mm per minute

▲ *Changing the type of motion.*

A rack and pinion is used to move the drawer of this CD player in and out. ▼

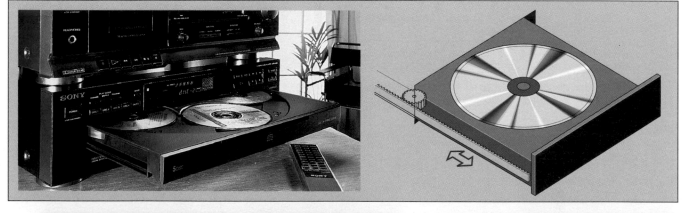

To change the direction of movement

When two gear wheels mesh the output gear turns in the *opposite* direction to the input gear.

With a third gear wheel in between, the output gear turns in the *same* direction as the input gear. The middle gear is called an **idler gear**.

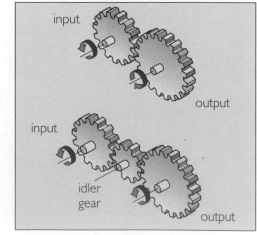

input

output

input

idler gear

output

rotary motion → | gear train | → transmitted rotary motion, direction and speed of may change rotation

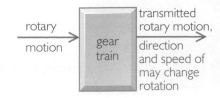

Resource Tasks
MCRT 10(1), (2)

To turn the axis of rotation through an angle

Bevel gears

Bevel gears have sloping sides so they can be used for driving shafts that are at an angle to one another.

The bevel gears in a hand drill turn the driving force through 90°. Why does the drill bit rotate much faster than the handle?

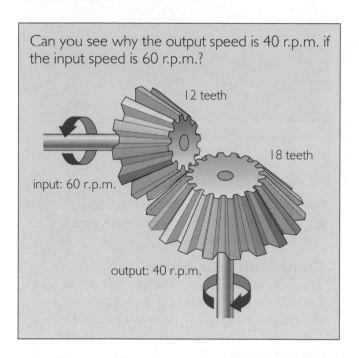

Can you see why the output speed is 40 r.p.m. if the input speed is 60 r.p.m.?

12 teeth

18 teeth

input: 60 r.p.m.

output: 40 r.p.m.

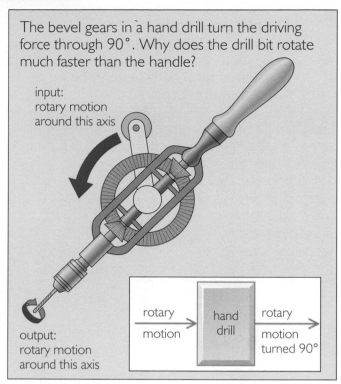

input:
rotary motion
around this axis

output:
rotary motion
around this axis

| rotary motion | → | hand drill | → | rotary motion turned 90° |

▲ *Changing the axis and speed of rotation with bevel gears.*

To increase output force and reduce speed

The worm and gear wheel

When this worm gear turns once the gear wheel is 'moved on' by one tooth. The input shaft must turn 22 times to turn the output shaft once. This is **gearing down**.

A worm and gear wheel are used to tighten tennis nets. A small force used to turn the crank handle produces a large force to stretch the net.

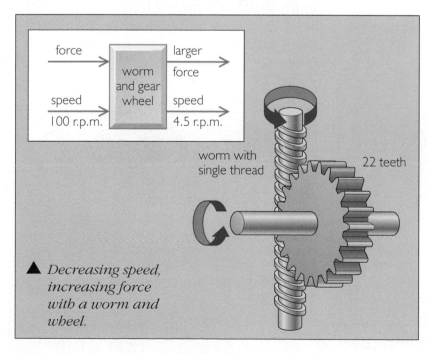

| force | → | worm and gear wheel | → | larger force |
| speed 100 r.p.m. | → | | → | speed 4.5 r.p.m. |

worm with single thread

22 teeth

▲ *Decreasing speed, increasing force with a worm and wheel.*

It is a good way of obtaining large increases in force and large decreases in speed. A *small* force turning the worm is turned into a *large* force turning the gear wheel.

...Using gears

Simple gear trains

These **gear down** if the output gear has more teeth than the input gear. The output shaft turns more slowly than the input shaft but with more force.

There are three times as many teeth on this output gear as on the input gear. So the input shaft turns three times to make the output shaft turn once. The output shaft turns at one-third the speed of the input shaft, but with greater force.

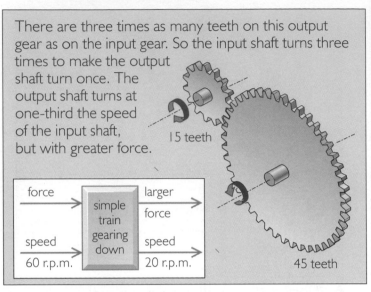

15 teeth

45 teeth

force	simple train gearing down	larger force
speed		speed
60 r.p.m.		20 r.p.m.

▲ *Decreasing speed, increasing force with a simple gear train.*

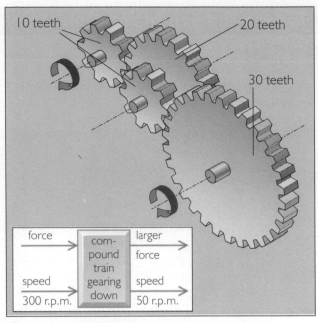

10 teeth   20 teeth

30 teeth

force	compound train gearing down	larger force
speed		speed
300 r.p.m.		50 r.p.m.

▲ *Decreasing speed, increasing force with a compound gear train.*

Compound gear trains

These produce large changes in speed and force. In a compound gear two different-sized gear wheels are fixed to one axle. A compound gear train can contain many pairs of gears.

To decrease output force and increase speed

Simple gear trains

These **gear up** if the output gear has fewer teeth than the input gear. The output shaft turns faster than the input shaft but with less force.

There are three times as many teeth on the input gear as on the output gear. When the input shaft turns once, the output shaft turns three times. The output shaft turns at three times the speed of the input but with less force.

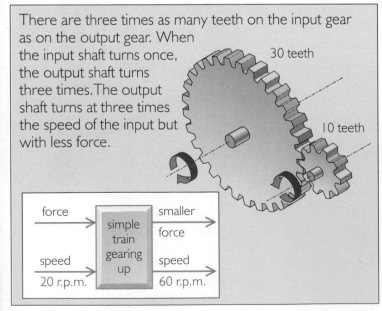

30 teeth

10 teeth

force	simple train gearing up	smaller force
speed		speed
20 r.p.m.		60 r.p.m.

▲ *Increasing speed, decreasing force with a simple gear chain.*

Compound gear trains

Each meshing pair of gears acts in the same way as a simple gear train. When gearing up, the output shaft will turn faster than the input shaft but with less force.

The salad is spun dry by high-speed rotation from a low-speed input.

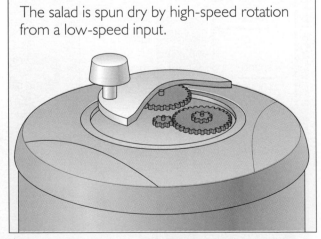

▲ *Salad spinners use compound gear trains to gear up.*

Resource Tasks
MCRT 5, 10(1)

Using pulleys and sprockets

A **pulley** is a wheel used with a **belt** that grips onto it. There may be a groove in the pulley to help the belt grip.

A **sprocket** is a gear wheel used with a **chain** wrapped around it. The teeth on the sprocket fit into the gaps in the chain.

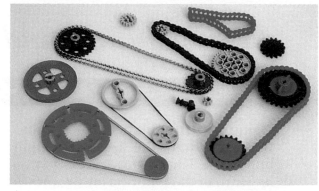

▲ *Belts and pulleys, chains and sprockets.*

To change the type of movement

Belts and pulleys and chains and sprockets change *rotary* movement to *linear* movement. In conveyor belts and escalators a motor provides the input (rotary movement). The output is the belt or steps moving along in a straight line (linear movement).

To change the direction of movement

You can use pulleys to change the direction of movement.

A pulley system changes a *downward* pull on the cord of this blind into *upward* movement of the blind.

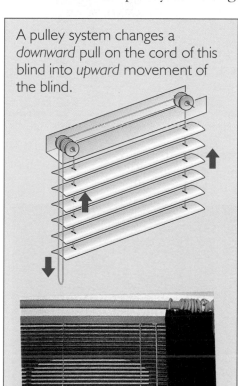

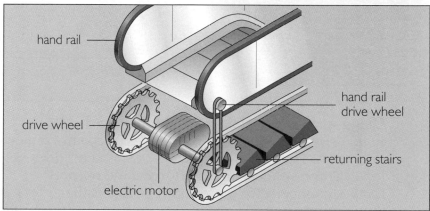

hand rail

drive wheel

electric motor

hand rail drive wheel

returning stairs

▲ *This escalator is a large chain and sprocket system. The steps are fixed to the chain.*

To turn the axis of rotation through an angle

You can turn the axis of rotation by using a twisted belt.

In this vacuum cleaner the axis of the motor is at right angles to the axis of the rotating brush. They are connected by a twisted belt.

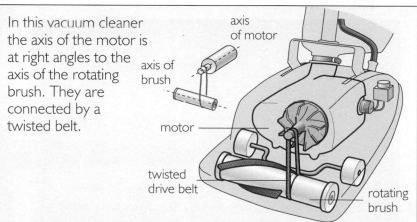

axis of motor

axis of brush

motor

twisted drive belt

rotating brush

...*Using pulleys and sprockets*

To increase output force and decrease speed

Using continuous belts or chains
In these systems the sizes of the input and output pulleys or sprockets are important. The output force is increased if the output pulley or sprocket is larger than the input pulley or sprocket. This is the same as 'gearing down' with gear systems.

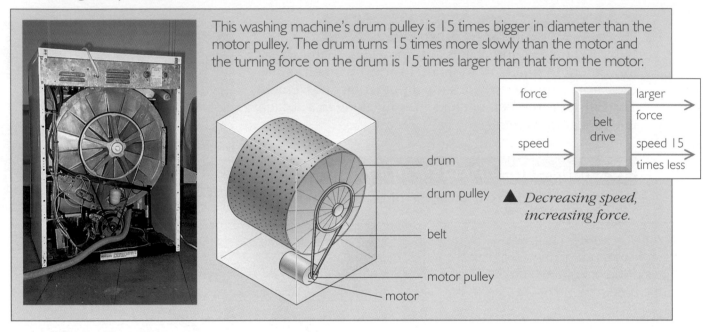

This washing machine's drum pulley is 15 times bigger in diameter than the motor pulley. The drum turns 15 times more slowly than the motor and the turning force on the drum is 15 times larger than that from the motor.

drum

drum pulley

belt

motor pulley

motor

▲ *Decreasing speed, increasing force.*

Using a rope or chain with a loose end
In these systems the number of ropes or chains connected to the output are important. The size of the pulleys or sprockets does not affect the speed or force. These systems increase force if the output force is connected to more ropes or chains than the input force.

Railway engineers use a pulley system to keep overhead cables tight. The input force is provided by iron masses hanging from one rope. The output force holding the overhead cable tight is supplied by three ropes. So it is three times larger than the input force.

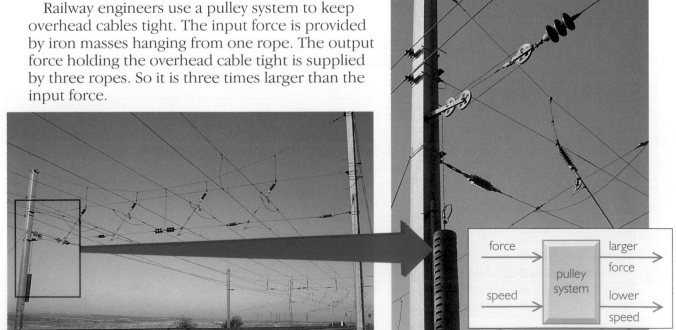

To increase output speed and decrease force

Use continuous belts or chains to do this. The speed is increased if the output pulley or sprocket is smaller than the input pulley or sprocket, as with 'gearing up' with gear trains.

Here the pulley and sprocket make the cutting blades turn faster than the rollers.

The pulley or sprocket connected to the roller (input) is five times larger than that connected to the blades (output). So the blades turn five times more quickly than the roller.

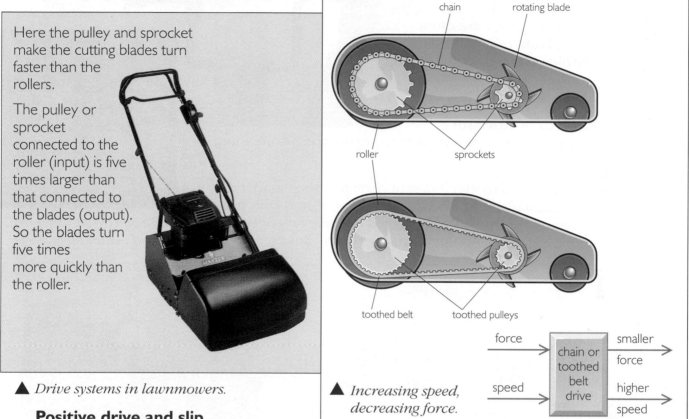

▲ *Drive systems in lawnmowers.*

▲ *Increasing speed, decreasing force.*

Positive drive and slip

The drive system of a lawnmower must transmit a large force without slipping. This is called **positive drive**. Both the toothed belt and pulley and the chain and sprocket can do this.

Positive drive is also useful when something needs to be located precisely, such as paper feeding into a computer printer, or when slip would be dangerous, as when riding a bicycle.

Sometimes slip can reduce damage or danger if output is likely to jam occasionally, as with a pillar drill. In these cases belts without teeth are used.

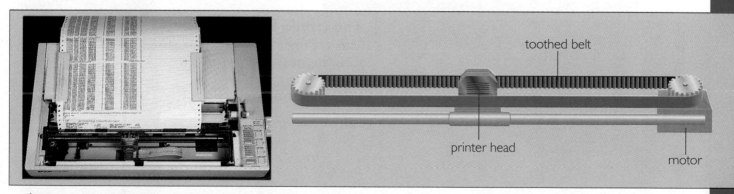

▲ *Precise control of this computer printer head is provided by a toothed belt.*

To transmit movement and force

In the lawnmower and washing machine, movement and force are transmitted with belts and pulleys or chains and sprockets.

Resource Tasks
MRT 10(3), (4)

Using cranks, levers and linkages

Cranks

Cranks are stiff arms fixed to a shaft, so when the shaft rotates, the arm rotates too. They are often attached to handles and used to make turning and tightening easier.

Levers

Levers are bars or rods that move about a **pivot** or **fulcrum**. Sometimes they are made in pairs to grip or crush something.

Linkages

Linkages are used to join different parts together so that they move in a particular way. They are often connected with **pin joints**. You can use **parallel linkages** to make two or more parts move together and/or stay parallel as the linkage moves.

▲ *These cranks make drilling and pedalling easier.*

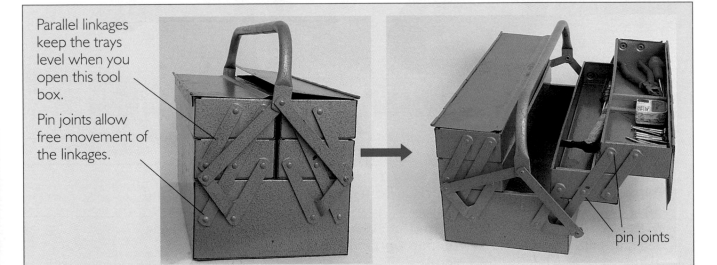

Parallel linkages keep the trays level when you open this tool box.

Pin joints allow free movement of the linkages.

pin joints

To change the type of movement

The small 'crank arm' rotates. It is connected by a link to a lever which oscillates (rocks to and fro). This is often called a **rocking arm**. The fourth link is the base, which does not move.

drive shaft

crank arm

rocking arm

connecting link

base

The crank, link and lever

This changes *rotary* movement to *oscillating* movement, called a **four-bar linkage**.

The to-and-fro movement of this electric fan is controlled by a four-bar linkage. ▶

rotary motion → crank link and lever → oscillating motion

▲ *Changing the type of movement.*

The crank, link and slider

This changes *rotary* movement to *reciprocating* movement (or the reverse). It is similar to the crank, link and lever but has a **slider** instead of a rocking arm. The rotating crank arm makes the slider move backwards and forwards in a straight line.

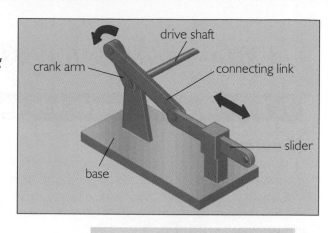

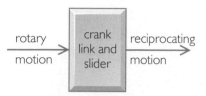

▲ *Changing the type of movement.*

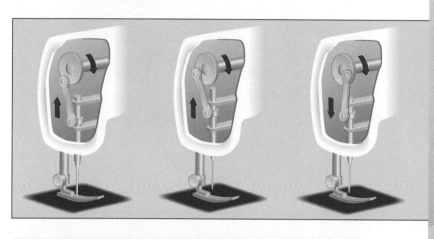

To change the direction of movement

Reversing direction

You can use levers that have the fulcrum between the input and output to reverse the direction of movement.

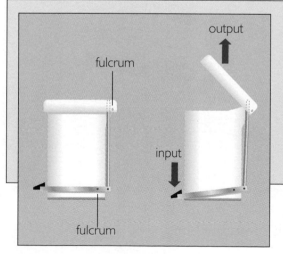

▲ *The movement of the sewing machine needle is controlled by a crank, link and slider mechanism.*

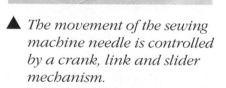

The output movement is opposite to the input movement in this pedal bin. Moving your foot *downwards* makes the lid open *upwards*.

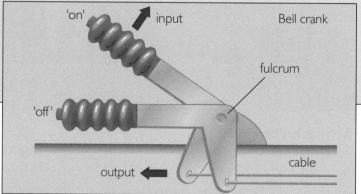

Changing direction through 90°

You can use a right-angled lever called a **bell crank** to change the direction of linear movement.

...Using cranks, levers and linkages

To increase output force and decrease speed

Using cranks

The twisting effect of a crank depends on both the force applied (measured in newtons, N) and the length of the crank arm (measured in metres, m). The crank multiplies your effort. The longer the crank arm, the more the effort is multiplied.

Tightening a wheel nut
The small force you apply to the crank handle becomes a large force on the nut.

force → crank handle → larger force
speed → crank handle → lower speed

50 N
0.2 m

▲ *Decreasing speed, increasing force.*

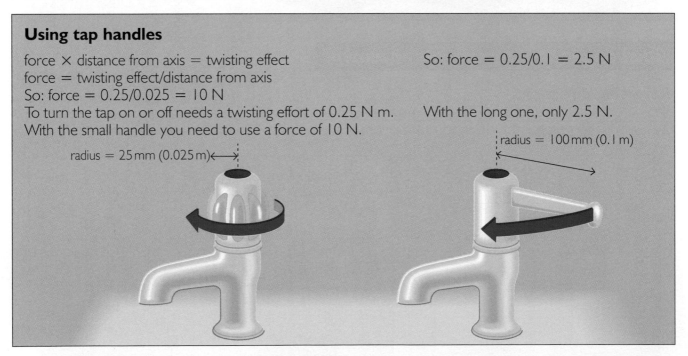

Using tap handles

force × distance from axis = twisting effect
force = twisting effect/distance from axis
So: force = 0.25/0.025 = 10 N
To turn the tap on or off needs a twisting effort of 0.25 N m.
With the small handle you need to use a force of 10 N.

radius = 25 mm (0.025 m)

So: force = 0.25/0.1 = 2.5 N

With the long one, only 2.5 N.

radius = 100 mm (0.1 m)

Using levers

The output force you can exert with a lever depends on three things:

- input force (effort), measured in newtons (N);
- distance of the effort from the fulcrum (metres);
- distance of the output force (load) from the fulcrum (metres).

These balance out like this:
input force × distance from fulcrum = output force × distance from fulcrum.

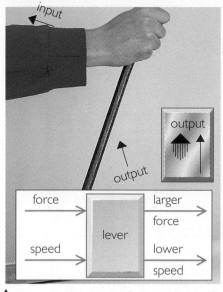

▲ *Decreasing speed, increasing force.*

▲ *Both these levers increase the output force.*

To increase output speed and decrease force

Using levers

In some levers, such as tweezers, you apply the effort between the load and the fulcrum. The tips grip with much less force than the user's fingers, helping prevent damage to delicate objects.

Nail clippers contain this sort of lever. But you would find it impossible to cut nails if this were the only lever. Can you explain why?

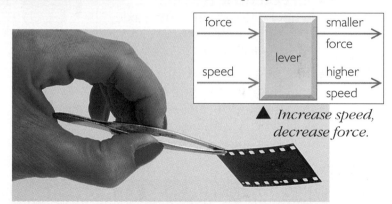

▲ *Tweezers can grip delicately.*

▲ *Increase speed, decrease force.*

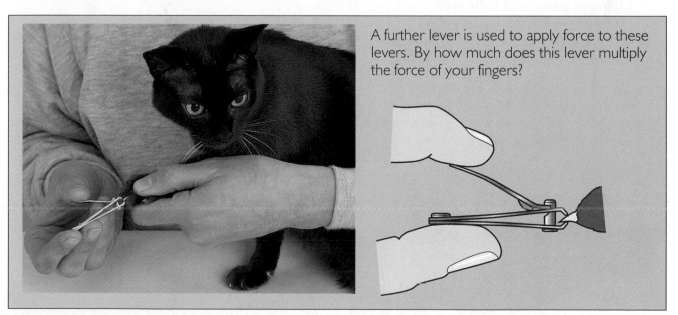

A further lever is used to apply force to these levers. By how much does this lever multiply the force of your fingers?

▲ *Nail clippers need to make large forces.*

To transmit movement and force

Linkages are often used to transmit movement and force. The linkage in a pedal bin transmits movement and force from the pedal to the lid.

Resource Tasks
MRT 5, 10(5)

205

Using cams, eccentrics, pegs and slots

All these mechanisms have two parts:

- the input (cam, eccentric, peg);
- the output (follower, slot).

They come in different forms:

- A **cam** is often a non-circular wheel that rotates. As it turns, it pushes a **follower** that moves according to the shape of the cam. The follower is usually a slider or a lever. It is held against the cam by a spring or by gravity.

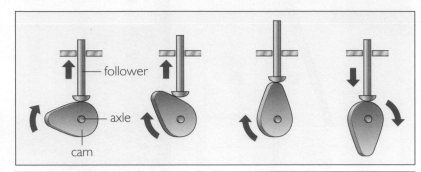

- An **eccentric** is a circular wheel with an off-centre axle. The edge of the wheel can move a follower.

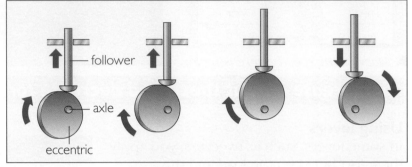

- In a **peg and slot** mechanism, the peg is sometimes fixed to a rotating input. The peg fits into a slot in the follower. As the peg moves in a circle the follower moves backwards and forwards.

To change the type of movement

Using a cam and follower

Cams change *rotary* movement to *reciprocating* or *oscillating* movement.

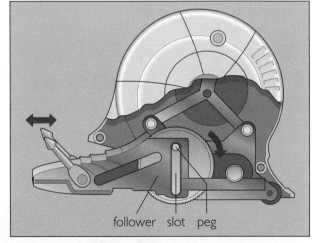

The heart-shaped cam (the input) moves the thread-guide of a sewing machine (the output) backwards and forwards along the reel.

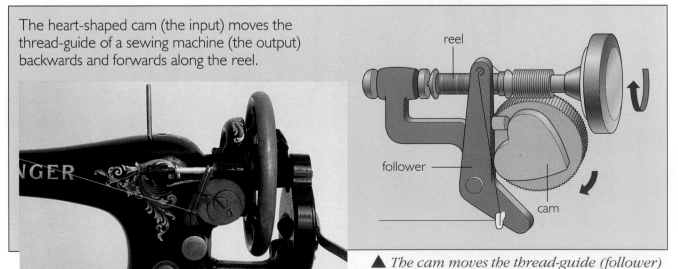

▲ *The cam moves the thread-guide (follower) to ensure that the thread is wound evenly along the reel.*

Resource Task
MCRT 8

Using an eccentric wheel

You can use this mechanism to change *rotary* to *reciprocating* movement.

This toy fire engine has an eccentric wheel inside fixed to the front axle. When the engine is pulled the eccentric wheel turns, making the driver resting on it bob up and down.

Using a peg and slot

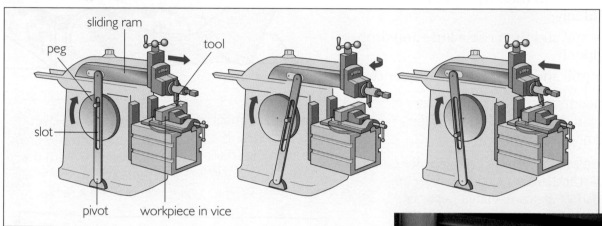

This industrial shaping machine controls a 'quick-return mechanism' with a peg and slot. It turns rotary movement into reciprocating movement. The peg revolving on a wheel moves a slotted lever slowly forwards and quickly backwards. This mechanism is called a crank and slotted lever.

To apply and maintain a force

Using cams

The cams in the **cleat** let a sailor pull a rope in one direction. If she stops pulling, the cams grip, preventing the rope from slipping back.

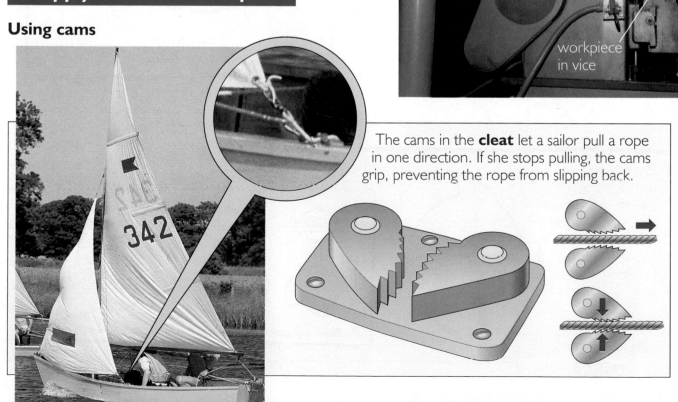

...Using cams, eccentrics, pegs and slots

Designing cams

Jo had designed a toy band and wanted to use a cam to get a cymbal to go up and down. She wanted the cymbal to move like this:

- rise a lot slowly and then drop suddenly;
- stay still and then rise a little and drop suddenly;
- stay still and then rise a little and drop suddenly;
- stay still and then start the sequence again.

1 Jo wrote this on a sector diagram, adding how far the cymbal had to rise.

2 Then she placed a piece of tracing paper over the diagram and drew a circle to show the smallest part of the cam, with a radius of 30 mm.

3 As the maximum rise of the cam was 20 mm, she drew a concentric circle with a radius of 50 mm.

4 To make the cymbal rise slowly she drew in a curve from the small circle to the large circle over three sectors.

5 To make the cymbal drop suddenly she drew a straight line from the large circle to the small circle along a radius.

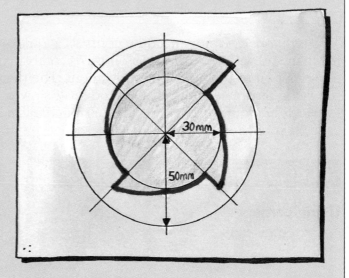

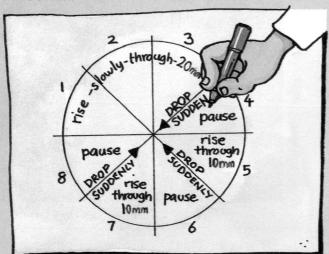

6 Jo completed her shape like this. Can you see how she gets the smaller rises?

7 To make the cymbal stay still she drew a curve along the small circle for one sector.

8 Finally, Jo cut out the cam shape and stuck it onto a piece of plywood. She cut carefully round the shape to produce the cam.

Action of cam through half a revolution (180°)

Resource Task

MCRT 8

▲ *This is how Jo's cam worked.*

Using screw threads

Screw threads come in many shapes and sizes. Which sort you choose will depend on what you want it to do.

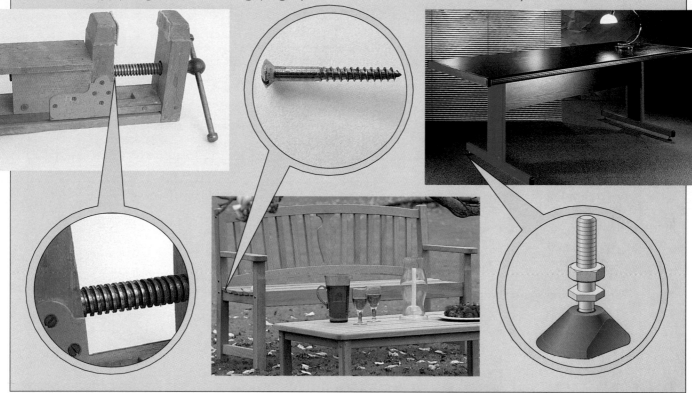

The screw thread in this woodworking vice is big: it can be used to apply large forces.

This screw thread is sharp: it can get between wood fibres and grip tightly.

This screw thread is fine: it can be used to level the desk top accurately.

To change the type of movement

The vice and the levelling foot use a screw thread to change *rotary* to *linear* movement. In the spinning top a screw thread is used to turn *linear* into *rotary* motion.

▲ *This screw thread makes the top spin.*

To apply and maintain a force

The screw threads on the jar and lid grip tightly after you have stopped turning the lid.

◀ *Friction keeps the lid on tight.*

Resource Task
MCRT 7

Mechanisms Chooser Chart

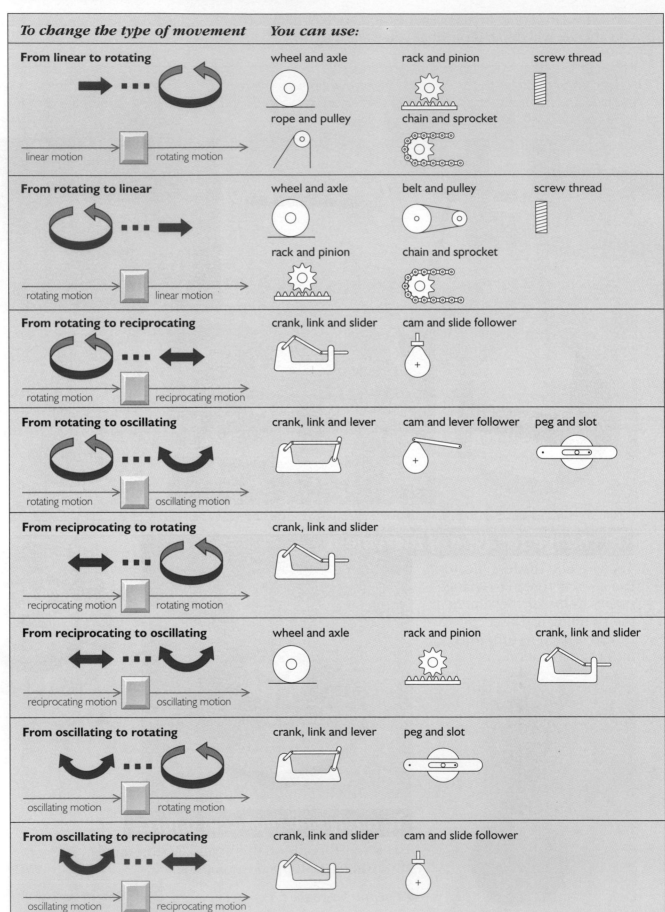

To change the type of movement	You can use:

From linear to rotating

linear motion → rotating motion

wheel and axle · rack and pinion · screw thread

rope and pulley · chain and sprocket

From rotating to linear

rotating motion → linear motion

wheel and axle · belt and pulley · screw thread

rack and pinion · chain and sprocket

From rotating to reciprocating

rotating motion → reciprocating motion

crank, link and slider · cam and slide follower

From rotating to oscillating

rotating motion → oscillating motion

crank, link and lever · cam and lever follower · peg and slot

From reciprocating to rotating

reciprocating motion → rotating motion

crank, link and slider

From reciprocating to oscillating

reciprocating motion → oscillating motion

wheel and axle · rack and pinion · crank, link and slider

From oscillating to rotating

oscillating motion → rotating motion

crank, link and lever · peg and slot

From oscillating to reciprocating

oscillating motion → reciprocating motion

crank, link and slider · cam and slide follower

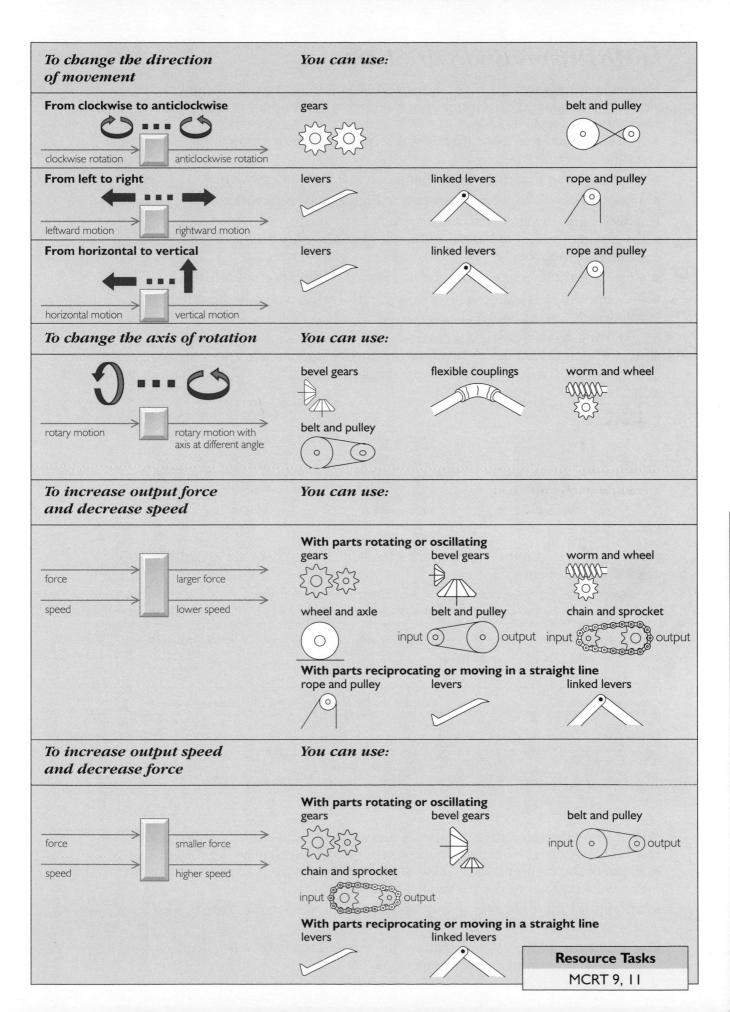

To change the direction of movement

You can use:

From clockwise to anticlockwise

clockwise rotation → anticlockwise rotation

gears

belt and pulley

From left to right

leftward motion → rightward motion

levers

linked levers

rope and pulley

From horizontal to vertical

horizontal motion → vertical motion

levers

linked levers

rope and pulley

To change the axis of rotation

You can use:

rotary motion → rotary motion with axis at different angle

bevel gears

flexible couplings

worm and wheel

belt and pulley

To increase output force and decrease speed

You can use:

force → larger force

speed → lower speed

With parts rotating or oscillating

gears

bevel gears

worm and wheel

wheel and axle

belt and pulley

input — output

chain and sprocket

input — output

With parts reciprocating or moving in a straight line

rope and pulley

levers

linked levers

To increase output speed and decrease force

You can use:

force → smaller force

speed → higher speed

With parts rotating or oscillating

gears

bevel gears

belt and pulley

input — output

chain and sprocket

input — output

With parts reciprocating or moving in a straight line

levers

linked levers

Resource Tasks

MCRT 9, 11

Complex mechanisms

Harsha is designing a wooden toy for a small child. The toy will be pulled along by a string and do a number of interesting and intriguing things as the toy is pulled. These include:

- a rabbit's head that pops up and down out of a hole (reciprocating motion);
- a waving hand that makes a slapping noise (oscillating motion);
- a horizontal colour wheel that spins at high speed (rotary motion).

Harsha's other design constraints are that:

- the driving motion of her toy is going to be the rotary motion from the turning of the wheels;
- she wants the mechanisms to be on show and brightly coloured;
- only one effect is going to be driven directly by the wheels – the others will drive each other in a chain.

As a starting point, Harsha decides to have the effects in the order written above: wheels drive rabbit's head; rabbit drives clapper and clapper drives colour wheel. The system diagram for this looks like:

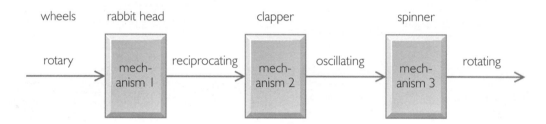

Harsha can now use the Mechanisms Chooser Chart to help her pick three suitable mechanisms.

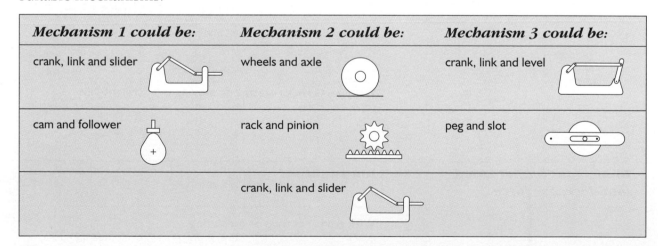

Mechanism 1 could be:	Mechanism 2 could be:	Mechanism 3 could be:
crank, link and slider	wheels and axle	crank, link and level
cam and follower	rack and pinion	peg and slot
	crank, link and slider	

This shows that there are a number of ways that she can realize her design. Harsha now needs to investigate this further with a mechanism kit to see:

- which of the combinations will work (not all mechanisms have an output powerful enough to drive a second mechanism);
- whether a different order of mechanisms would work better (she'll need a new system diagram for this);
- whether any additional mechanisms are needed to change the speed, force or direction of any of the motions.

Using springs

Springs can be used to apply forces and to store and release energy. They come in many shapes and sizes. Which sort you choose will depend on what you want it to do.

To apply and/or maintain a force

This lamp has **tension** springs. When stretched they pull inwards.

Compression springs are in the mattress. When squashed they push outwards.

Torsion springs make the peg work. When opened out they try to close.

Leaf springs provide suspension for this antique car. When bent they try to straighten.

To store energy

You store energy in the spring of the jack-in-the-box when you close the lid and compress the spring. When you lift the lid the energy is released and the clown jumps up.

Resource Task

MCRT 6

Choosing springs

Choose the type of spring that:

- exerts the force you need – push, pull, twist or bend;
- has the stiffness you need – too stiff and it won't change its shape, not stiff enough and it will lose its springiness;
- is the right size to fit the rest of your design.

Remember, compression springs may buckle if they are not supported at the sides or are too long compared with their diameter. Tension springs need a loop or hook at each end to connect to other components.

Using syringes

Syringes are useful for making working parts move and for gripping things. You can connect them together with flexible tubing and use them to send force and movement around bends and corners.

They may contain air or water. Air in a syringe will compress if the output movement is resisted. Water will not compress easily but may leak.

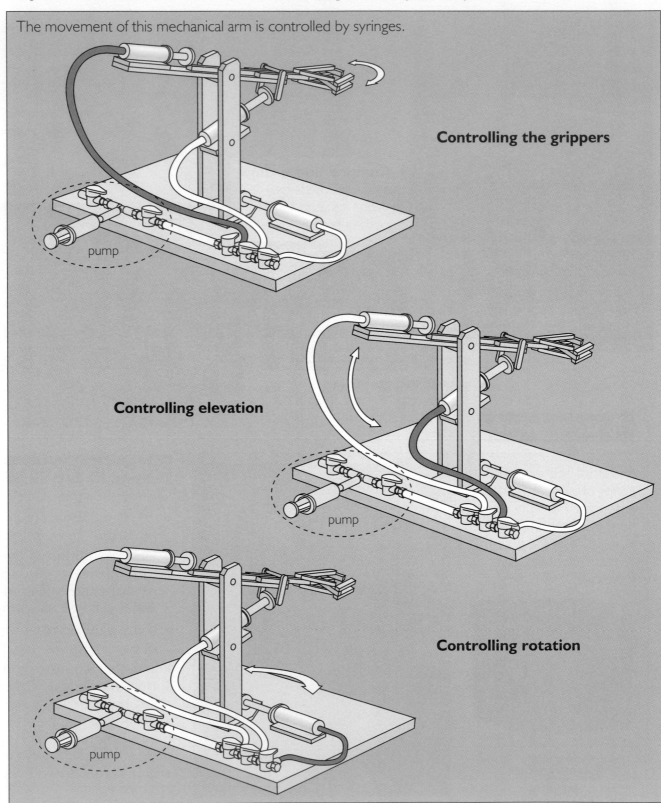

The movement of this mechanical arm is controlled by syringes.

Controlling the grippers

pump

Controlling elevation

pump

Controlling rotation

pump

To change the direction of movement

The tubes connecting the syringes are flexible. They can go round corners, so it is easy to change the direction or angle of linear movement.

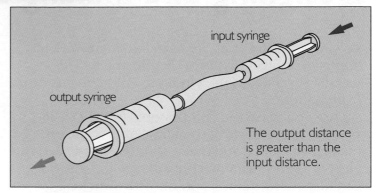

input syringe

output syringe

The output distance is greater than the input distance.

To decrease speed

If the output syringe has a bigger diameter than the input syringe, the output distance is less than the input distance. This should also increase force, but friction in the syringe usually prevents it.

To increase speed

If the output syringe has a smaller diameter than the input syringe, the output distance is greater than the input distance.

To apply and maintain a force

You can use a non-return valve to let water or air into an output syringe and stop it coming out again. The output syringe will exert a force even if you let go of the input syringe.

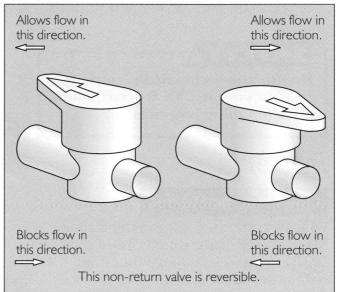

Allows flow in this direction.

Allows flow in this direction.

Blocks flow in this direction.

Blocks flow in this direction.

This non-return valve is reversible.

▲ *This non-return valve is reversible.*

To transmit movement and force

Syringes filled with water transmit force and movement well. If you try to move a heavy object with an air-filled syringe you will find that the air in the syringe gets compressed instead of the object moving.

Use non-return valves to overcome this. You use the input syringe as a pump and increase the pressure of air in the output syringe so it is harder to compress.

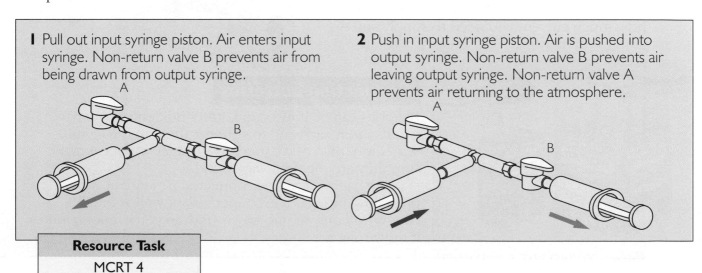

1 Pull out input syringe piston. Air enters input syringe. Non-return valve B prevents air from being drawn from output syringe.

A

B

2 Push in input syringe piston. Air is pushed into output syringe. Non-return valve B prevents air leaving output syringe. Non-return valve A prevents air returning to the atmosphere.

A

B

Resource Task

MCRT 4

8 Designing and making electric circuits

Products using electricity to make them work all contain circuits to control the electricity. This is usually supplied to the circuit from the mains or from batteries.

Depending on the components in the circuit, you can use electricity to make lights come on, make parts move and make sounds. The size of the electric current can be controlled with resistors. Circuits are turned on and off with switches.

This chapter tells you about these components and how to use them.

SAFETY ⚠

Do not connect mains electricity to your circuits. Wash your hands after handling batteries.

circuit symbol
|⊢---⊣|

Batteries

Choosing batteries

When you choose a battery, think about:

Size – A large battery holds more energy than a small one. It will last longer but it will cost more. There must be enough room for it in your design.

Voltage – The bigger the voltage, the harder the battery 'pushes' the electricity around the circuit. If the voltage is too large, the components get hot and 'burn out'. If it is too low, they do not work properly. The common voltages available are: 1.5 V, 3 V, 4.5 V, 6 V and 9 V.

Type – Rechargeable batteries are expensive. The three types of non-rechargeable battery shown here are readily available. Your choice will depend on how much current you need to supply and the amount of daily use.

◀ *Providing 4.5 V from three 1.5 V batteries.*

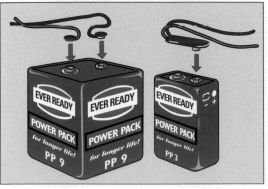

▲ *Easy connection is important.*

Connecting batteries

Batteries can be housed in battery holders, which have metal tags at each end to connect them to the circuit. With more than one battery in a holder you must make sure they are the right way round.

Some batteries can be connected to a circuit with press-stud fittings. The connector shown for the PP3 battery will only fit one way round, so you cannot connect it the wrong way.

Resource Task

ECRT I

Making connections

Join components together in a circuit with plastic-coated copper wire. Remove the plastic insulation where the join is made. Use solder or special connecting components for the join.

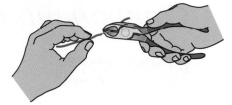

Using solder

Soldering is quick and effective. Good soldering is essential: a badly soldered joint can stop a circuit from working and make fault-finding difficult. It is easy if you follow these rules.

SAFETY△

Take care not to rest the hot tip of the soldering iron on the electric cable. Make sure that there is plenty of fresh air where you are working.

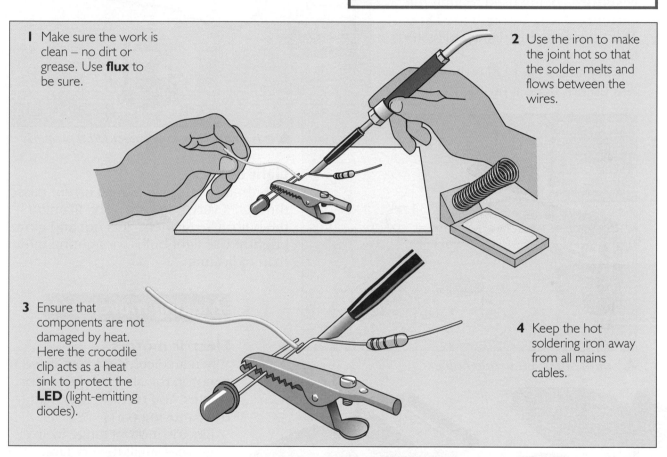

1 Make sure the work is clean – no dirt or grease. Use **flux** to be sure.

2 Use the iron to make the joint hot so that the solder melts and flows between the wires.

3 Ensure that components are not damaged by heat. Here the crocodile clip acts as a heat sink to protect the **LED** (light-emitting diodes).

4 Keep the hot soldering iron away from all mains cables.

Using connectors

You can also make connections using crocodile clips, jack-plugs and connection blocks. These are useful for making temporary connections when you are testing a circuit to see if it works.

You can make temporary circuits on breadboards for testing before you make a more permanent circuit using soldered joints. Batteries often have press-stud connectors.

Resource Tasks
ECRT 2, 3, 9

▲ *Other ways of connecting components.*

Components to make things happen

Making light

Light-emitting diodes (LEDs)

LEDs light up when current passes through them. They are often used as **indicators** in control panels because they do not get hot and only use a small current.

In the circuit shown here a **resistor** is being used to limit the current passing through the LED. This stops it being damaged by too large a current.

You can also get LEDs that flash, and do not need a protecting resistor.

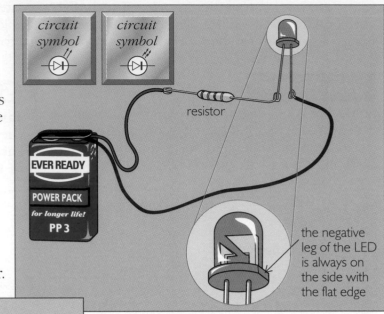

circuit symbol

circuit symbol

resistor

EVER READY
POWER PACK
for longer life!
PP 3

the negative leg of the LED is always on the side with the flat edge

▲ *It is important to connect LEDs properly.*

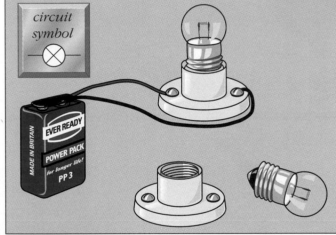

circuit symbol

EVER READY
MADE IN BRITAIN
POWER PACK
for longer life!
PP 3

▲ *Small bulbs screw into holders.*

Light bulbs

Light bulbs light up when a current passes through a very thin wire – the filament – of the bulb. The filament gets hot and glows brightly. Use light bulbs for lighting rather than indicating.

Making movement

Electric motors

When an electric current is fed to a motor, the shaft of the motor rotates. You can use this shaft to drive moving parts.

Electric motors range in size from very small to very large. The shafts of small motors often rotate quickly, but produce little useful twisting effect.

You can use gears to decrease the rotational speed and increase the twisting effect.

circuit symbol

electric motor

◀ *The electric motor inside a cassette player is very small.*

Making sounds

Use bells and buzzers as sounds for alarm and warning systems. Buzzers must be connected the right way round.

Protecting components

Resistors control the size of an electric current. They restrict the flow of a current by providing a **resistance** to it.

The value of the resistance is measured in ohms (Ω).

You can use resistors to protect other components in your circuit, like LEDs and transistors (see pages 163–6), from too large an electric current.

The resistor colour code

Four coloured bands on the resistor show the value of the resistance provided. The first three bands give the value; the fourth, usually silver or gold, gives the accuracy to which it has been made (the tolerance).

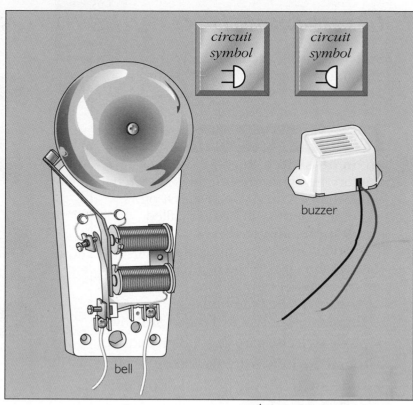

▲ *Electric noise makers.*

buzzer

bell

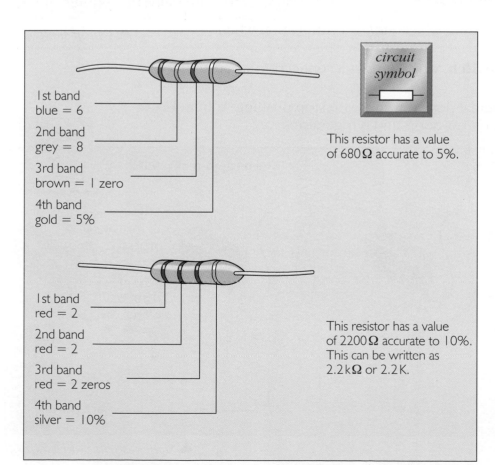

1st band
blue = 6

2nd band
grey = 8

3rd band
brown = 1 zero

4th band
gold = 5%

This resistor has a value of 680 Ω accurate to 5%.

1st band
red = 2

2nd band
red = 2

3rd band
red = 2 zeros

4th band
silver = 10%

This resistor has a value of 2200 Ω accurate to 10%. This can be written as 2.2 kΩ or 2.2 K.

RESISTOR COLOUR CODE

Colour	Value	
Black		0
Brown		1
Red		2
Orange		3
Yellow		4
Green		5
Blue		6
Violet		7
Grey		8
White		9

◀ *Calculating resistor values.*

Resource Task
ECRT 6, 7

Using switches

Switches turn a circuit on or off by 'making' or 'breaking' connections. There are several types of switch.

For setting on or off

An **on/off switch**, such as a light switch stays in the off position until you switch it on. It stays on until you switch it off.

Simple on/off switches are called **single-pole, single-throw** switches. The **poles** are the number of circuits that the switch makes or breaks. The **throws** are the number of positions to which each pole can be switched.

There are four types of on/off switches:

- **push switches** are pushed on and off;
- **toggle switches** are flicked on or off;
- **slide switches** are pushed or pulled;
- **rocker switches** are usually pressed.

For holding on or off

Two types are available:

- the **push-to-make switch**, which *makes* a connection when pushed;
- the **push-to-break switch**, which *breaks* a connection when pushed.

Both return to their original position when you stop pushing. You find push-to-break switches on car doors and refrigerators.

circuit symbol

push switch

toggle switch

slide switch

rocker switch

Whichever type of on/off switch you choose in this circuit the light remains off until you switch it on. Then it stays on until you switch it off.

▲ On/off switches.

circuit symbol

The push-to-break switch

circuit symbol

The push-to-make switch

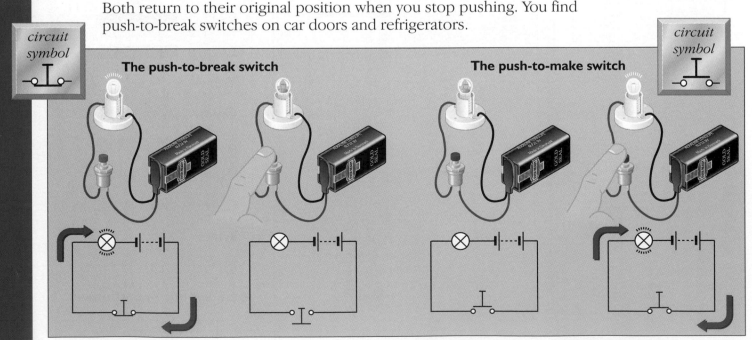

▲ Switches you hold on or off.

For turning on and off at the same time

These are called **change-over switches**. The circuit diagrams show a **single-pole, double-throw** change-over switch turning off one light bulb while turning on another. This could be a slide, toggle or rocker switch, or a **micro-switch**, which needs only a very light touch to operate.

A **double-pole, double-throw** change-over switch, which could be a slide, toggle or rocker type, is used to reverse the direction of an electric motor. They are used for the rewind in cassette tape players.

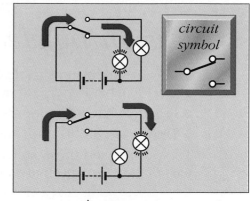

▲ *Change-over switching.*

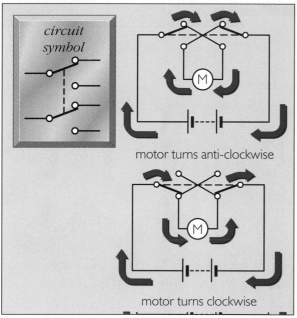

motor turns anti-clockwise

motor turns clockwise

▲ *Reversing a motor.*

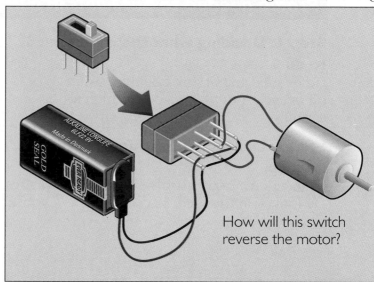

How will this switch reverse the motor?

▲ *Wiring a reversing switch.*

Special switches

Tilt switches
These contain a blob of mercury that moves when the switch is tilted. Electricity can flow through mercury, so when the blob covers both connections, the circuit is made and electricity flows.

Tilt switches are useful in security systems to detect things being moved.

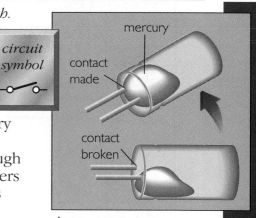

▲ *The tilt switch.*

Reed switches
These are controlled by a magnet. When the magnet is close to the switch the contacts are held together and the circuit is made, allowing current to flow. When the magnet is removed the contacts separate and the circuit is broken.

Reed switches are useful in security systems to detect intruders opening doors or windows.

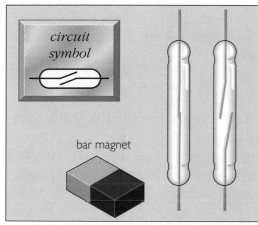

▲ *The reed switch.*

Bimetallic strip
Use this sensor to detect changes in temperature. The **bimetallic** strip changes shape by curling up as it gets hot.

Resource Tasks
ECRT 3–5

Designing electric circuits

There are three steps to designing an electric circuit:
1 Decide what the circuit needs to do – the specification.
2 Decide what components are needed.
3 Draw a circuit diagram and try it out.

Two pupils used these steps to design electric circuits for part of a design and make task.

Pradip needed to put lights in a model house

Step 1: Deciding what the circuit needs to do

He needed a light that could be switched on and off in each room – the specification for his circuit.

Step 2: Deciding what components are needed

He needed a power source, lights and switches. He looked at the Electric Components Chooser Chart for help.

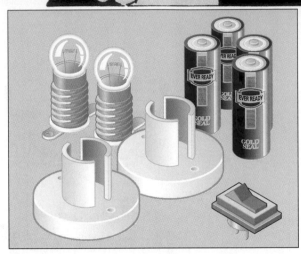

▲ *The components Pradip needed.*

For the lights he chose two 6 V bulbs with bulb holders.

For the power source he chose four 1.5 V batteries providing 6 V (to match the bulbs) of zinc chloride type for medium current and regular use.

For the switches he chose a small rocker switch to set the lights on or off.

Step 3: Drawing a circuit diagram and trying it out

He drew a circuit diagram and made it up on a breadboard with just one bulb to try it out. When he added another in series to the circuit the bulbs did not shine as brightly. As he added extra bulbs they all gave less light. Also, he could only switch them all on or off together.

By connecting the bulbs in parallel he realized he could use a separate switch for each bulb. Trying this out on the breadboard he saw that the bulbs did not get dimmer when more than one was switched on. He drew the circuit diagram for this new circuit.

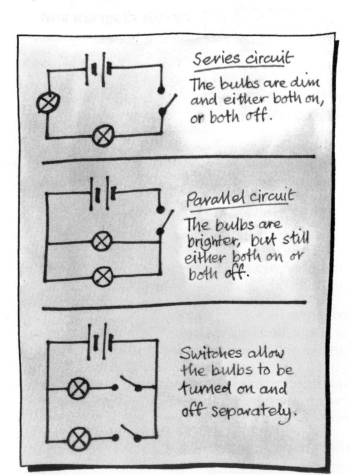

Series circuit
The bulbs are dim and either both on, or both off.

Parallel circuit
The bulbs are brighter, but still either both on or both off.

Switches allow the bulbs to be turned on and off separately.

▲ *How Pradip's ideas changed.*

Resource Tasks

ECRT 6, 7

Sally needed to power a model buggy

Step 1: Deciding what the circuit needs to do

She wanted the buggy to go forwards and backwards. This was the specification for her circuit.

Step 2: Deciding what components are needed

She needed a power source and a means to make the wheels go round in either direction. She used the Electric Components Chooser Chart to help her choose the right components:

- for rotational movement she chose a small electric motor that worked on 6–12 V;
- for the power source she chose a 9 V battery (to match the motor) of alkaline type for high current and heavy use;
- for a way to reverse the current she chose a double-pole, double-throw switch, in the form of a toggle switch because this is easy to operate.

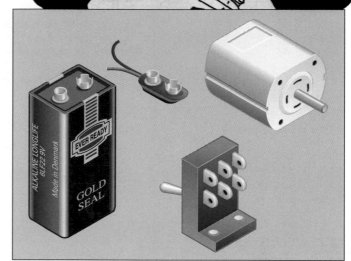

▲ Sally's components.

Step 3: Drawing a circuit diagram and trying it out

Sally drew the circuit diagram for a reversing circuit (see page 221) and made up the circuit using leads and crocodile clips. A friend suggested that an improvement would be to add a warning signal when the buggy went backwards.

She used the Chooser Chart on page 224 to decide on a buzzer. She drew the new circuit diagram and tried it out. It worked, so now she could make the permanent circuit on the buggy with soldered connections.

Can you see any problem with the new circuit?

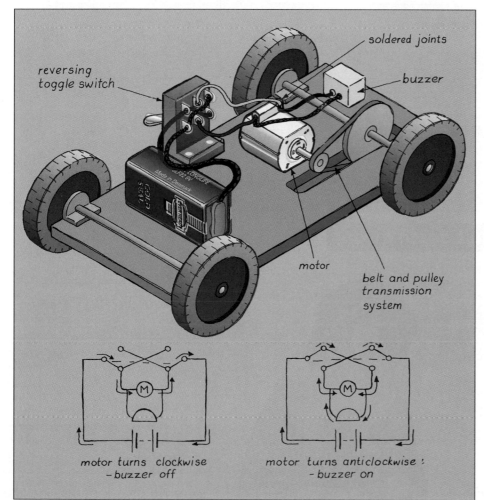

▲ The completed buggy with a warning circuit.

Electric Components Chooser Chart

What the component might need to do	Options	Symbols	Points to check
To provide a power supply	batteries: • zinc carbon for low current, infrequent use • zinc chloride for medium current, regular use • alkaline for high current, heavy use		Make sure voltage of battery is suitable for components in the circuit.
To make light			
To give a signal	a light-emitting diode		Use protecting resistor. Must be correct way round.
	a flashing light-emitting diode		Does not need protecting resistor. Must be correct way round.
To provide illumination	a light bulb		Must match power source.
To give rotary movement	an electric motor		Must match power source. May need 'gearing'.
To make sound	a bell		Must match power source.
	a buzzer		Buzzer must be correct way round.

What to do if your circuit doesn't work

Use this checklist before you ask your teacher.

Must have got something wrong. . . where's that diagram?

Check carefully against your circuit diagram.

Maybe the battery isn't connected properly?

Check to be sure.

Might be a dud battery. . .

Test it with a light bulb that you know works.

Perhaps it's the solder?

Check for any 'dry' solder joints.

Could be a loose connection somewhere. . .

Look carefully to check.

Must be something else not working. . .

Remove components one at a time and test them in a circuit that does work.

What the component might need to do	Options	Symbols	Points to check
To control current size			
By setting at a fixed value	a fixed resistor		Value provides the required current.
To switch			
To hold something on or off	a push-to-make switch a push-to-break switch a reed switch a tilt switch		Two connections to the switch.
To set something on or off	a single-pole, single-throw switch ● push switch ● slide switch ● toggle switch ● rocker switch ● bimetallic strip		Two connections to the switch. Which type will be most suitable for the user?
To turn something on and something else off	a single-pole, double-throw change-over switch ● micro-switch ● slide switch ● toggle switch ● rocker switch		Three connections to the switch. Which type will be most suitable for the user?
To reverse direction	a double-pole, double-throw change-over switch ● slide switch ● toggle switch ● rocker switch		Four connections to the switch. Which type will be most suitable for the user?

Resource Task

ECRT 8

9 Designing and making electronic circuits

Electronic control

You can think about electronic control by using the systems ideas described in Chapter 1, *Strategies*.

Electronic devices have **input** and **output** subsystems so are often called **electronic systems**. The control panel on a car is an example.

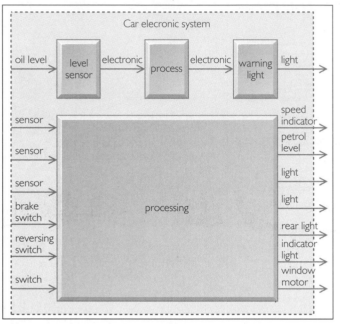

Car eleronic system

oil level → level sensor → electronic → process → electronic → warning light → light

sensor →
sensor →
sensor →
brake switch →
reversing switch →
switch →

processing

→ speed indicator
→ petrol level
→ light
→ light
→ rear light
→ indicator light
→ window motor

▲ *Some of the subsystems and signals in a car's electronics.*

A modern car is able to provide a lot of information to the driver. For example if the oil level gets low this is sensed and an electronic signal is created. This signal is processed by the car's electronic system and used to switch on the oil warning light on the control panel.

This oil warning system is just one of many subsystems which provide information to the driver. Other subsystems do more than provide information, they allow the driver to control a wide range of things from the external lights to opening the window and turning on the radio.

The input signals to an electronic control system are provided by sensors which react to changes in the surroundings, such as temperature, light level, noise level or moisture.

Electronic control in action

Sensors and processors

Sensors

Sensors can be used to turn physical signals into electronic signals. They allow electronic systems to respond to their surroundings. The devices shown below all contain electronic control systems using sensors.

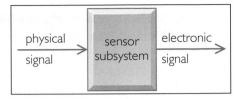

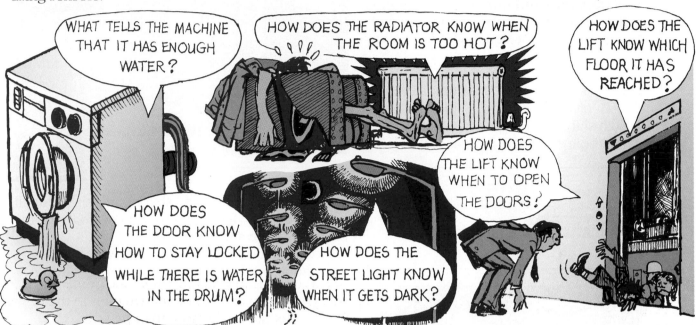

Sensor subsystems

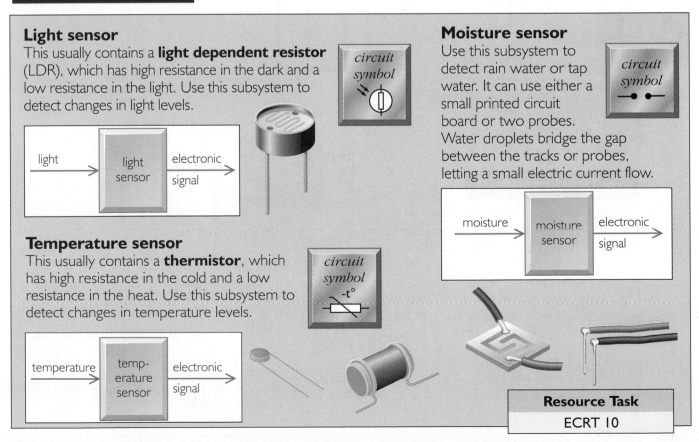

Light sensor
This usually contains a **light dependent resistor** (LDR), which has high resistance in the dark and a low resistance in the light. Use this subsystem to detect changes in light levels.

circuit symbol

Temperature sensor
This usually contains a **thermistor**, which has high resistance in the cold and a low resistance in the heat. Use this subsystem to detect changes in temperature levels.

circuit symbol -t°

Moisture sensor
Use this subsystem to detect rain water or tap water. It can use either a small printed circuit board or two probes. Water droplets bridge the gap between the tracks or probes, letting a small electric current flow.

circuit symbol

Resource Task

ECRT 10

227

...Sensors and processors

Transistor subsystem

The signals from most electronic subsystems are not able to provide enough power for output components such as lamps and motors. To solve this difficulty a 'driver' subsystem is needed that will provide a signal with the power required.

A very common driver subsystem is the transistor driver. This subsystem acts like an electronic switch. When it detects a high signal coming in, it switches the signal going out of it high as well.

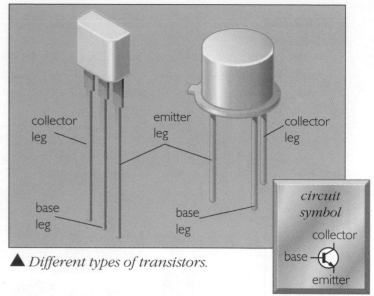

▲ *Different types of transistors.*

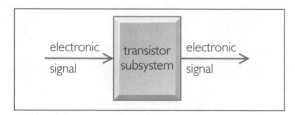

Transistors come in many shapes and sizes but all have three legs. Each leg has a special name – the **emitter, base** and **collector**.

Their positions tell which leg is which. This is important, because if you connect a leg wrongly the circuit will not work and the transistor will be damaged.

Note the positions of the legs on the circuit symbol for a transistor.

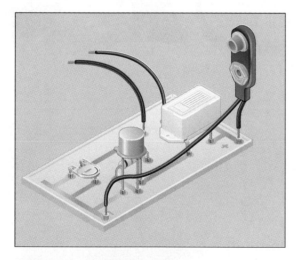

Variable resistors

These allow you to vary the size of the current in a circuit by changing the value of the resistance. You can use them in input subsystems to alter the sensitivity of a sensing system.

Unlike fixed resistors, they have three legs. Usually you connect the middle and one of the outside legs to your circuit.

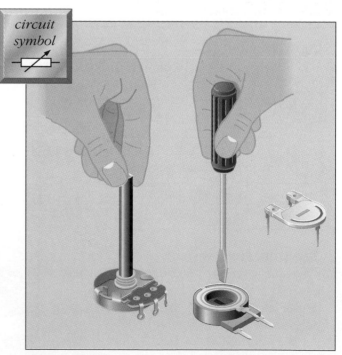

▲ *Variable resistors come in different shapes and sizes. You adjust the resistance by turning a control with your fingers or with a small screwdriver.*

Resource Task

ECRT 9

Combining sensor and transistor subsystems

A lighting control system

This electronic control system detects when the surroundings become dark and lights a bulb. Look at the panel to find out how it works.

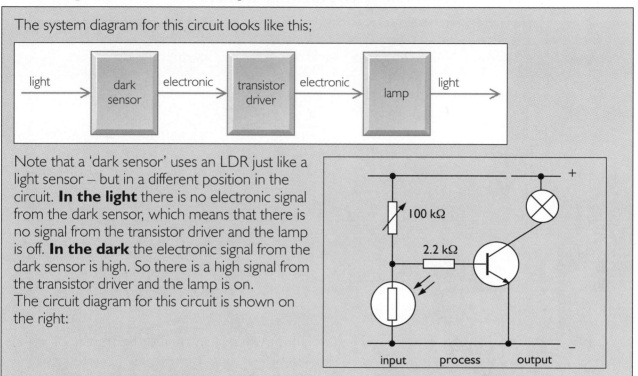

The system diagram for this circuit looks like this;

light → dark sensor → electronic → transistor driver → electronic → lamp → light

Note that a 'dark sensor' uses an LDR just like a light sensor – but in a different position in the circuit. **In the light** there is no electronic signal from the dark sensor, which means that there is no signal from the transistor driver and the lamp is off. **In the dark** the electronic signal from the dark sensor is high. So there is a high signal from the transistor driver and the lamp is on.

The circuit diagram for this circuit is shown on the right:

100 kΩ
2.2 kΩ

input   process   output

On a printed circuit board this circuit looks like this:

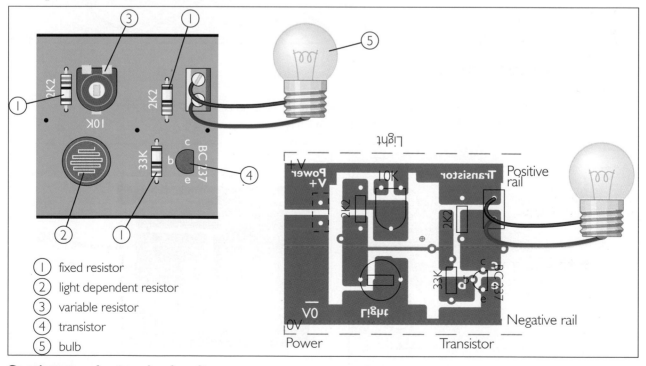

1. fixed resistor
2. light dependent resistor
3. variable resistor
4. transistor
5. bulb

Setting up electronic circuits

Note how the components are connected between a positive and negative rail in electronic circuits. In this way it is easy to connect many different components into a circuit.

Resource Task

ECRT 10

229

...Sensors and processors

What's in a sensing subsystem

Here are some useful sensing arrangements.

These two-resistor arrangements are called **potential dividers**.

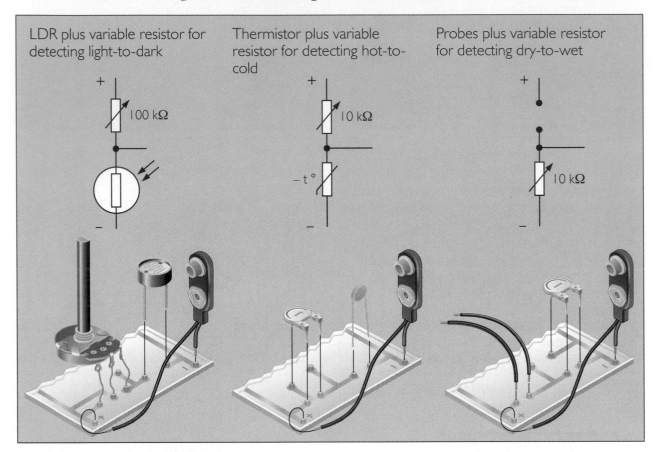

LDR plus variable resistor for detecting light-to-dark

Thermistor plus variable resistor for detecting hot-to-cold

Probes plus variable resistor for detecting dry-to-wet

The Darlington driver

This driver uses two transistors (a 'Darlington pair'). This gives more sensitive and rapid switching than the standard transistor driver.

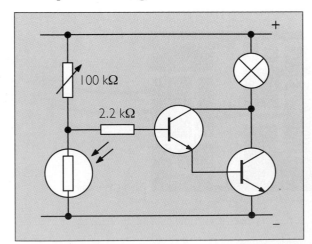

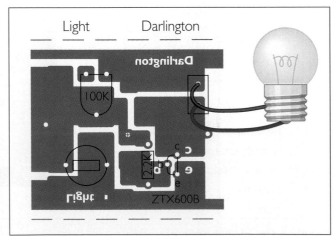

▲ *The circuit diagram and printed circuit board arrangement for detecting changes in light level, using a Darlington pair. Both transistors are contained in a single component.*

Resource Task

ECRT 11

The relay

What it does

The current output from a transistor may not be large enough to drive the output device – an electric motor, perhaps. Here you can use a **relay**.

A relay is made of two parts – an electromagnet and a set of switches. When a small current passes through the electromagnet it is turned on and operates the switches. These are connected to another circuit with a more powerful supply of electricity, which is used to drive the high-current output device.

Protecting the circuit

Always use a **diode** with a relay to prevent the electromagnet from damaging the rest of the circuit.

This is the circuit board arrangement to connect a relay into a circuit.

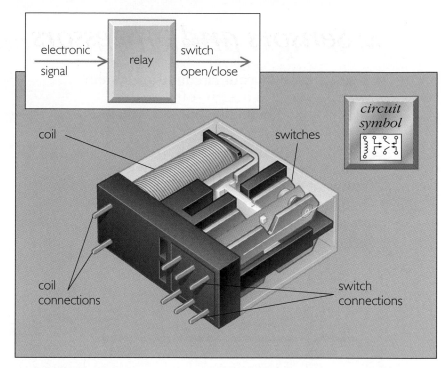

electronic signal → relay → switch open/close

circuit symbol

coil

switches

coil connections

switch connections

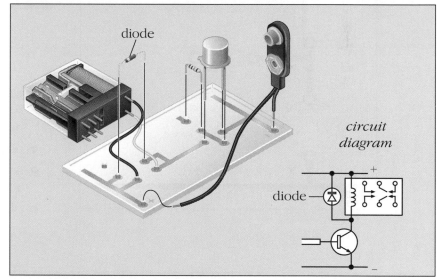

diode

circuit diagram

diode

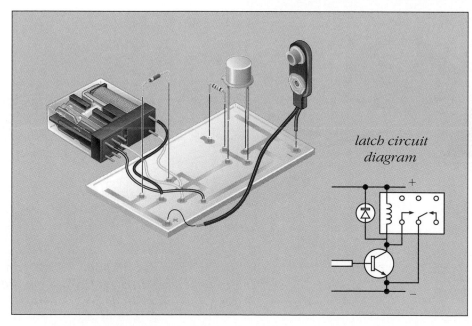

latch circuit diagram

Latching

You can design the circuit so that the output stays on even when the input signal has stopped.

When the relay operates, the switches close and bypass the transistor, so the relay stays on even if the transistor turns off. This is called using a **latch**.

Resource Task

ECRT 12

Making a printed circuit board (PCB)

1 If you modelled your circuit using system boards: use PCB design software that allows you to build up your PCB using system elements.

2 If you modelled your circuit using individual components: use PCB design software to draw out a PCB mask that matches your circuit diagram.

3 Either print your mask directly onto clear acetate sheet, or print onto paper and then photocopy onto acetate.

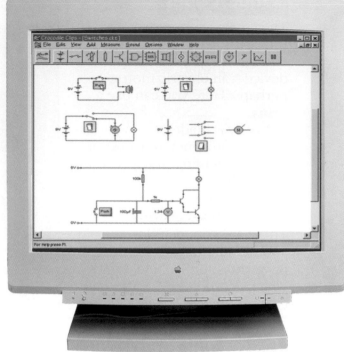

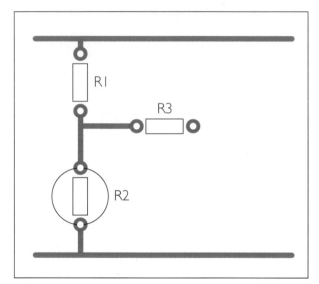

4 Use a **UV** light box and the mask to transfer your layout onto photosensitive board.

- remove the black plastic from the board;
- lay the board face down on top of the acetate mask;
- place in the UV light box.

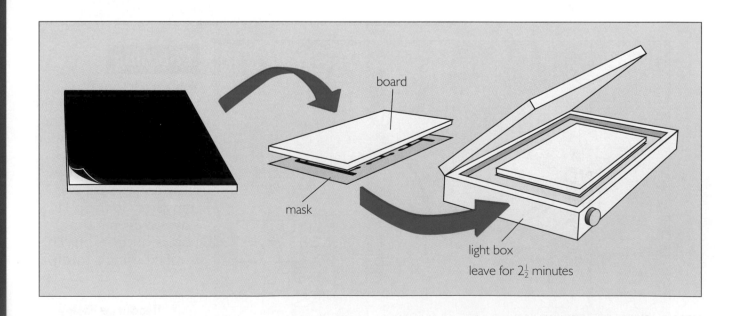

board

mask

light box
leave for $2\frac{1}{2}$ minutes

5 Develop the layout with sodium hydroxide solution. Rinse the board under the tap.

SAFETY △

Take care – sodium hydroxide is toxic and causes burns – wear eye protection and gloves.

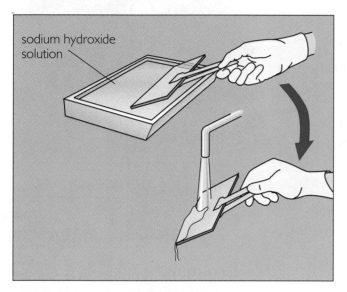

sodium hydroxide solution

6 Etch in ferric chloride solution.

SAFETY △

Take care – ferric chloride is toxic and causes burns and stains – wear eye protection and gloves. Make sure that there is plenty of fresh air in the area where you are working.

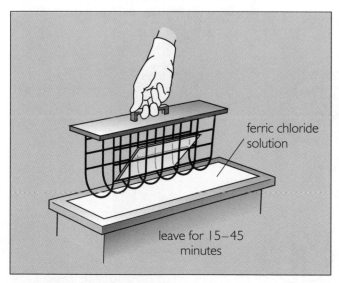

ferric chloride solution

leave for 15–45 minutes

7 Wash the board under the tap and dry it. Clean the track with a PCB eraser.

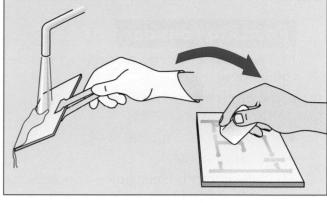

8 Drill holes for **components**.

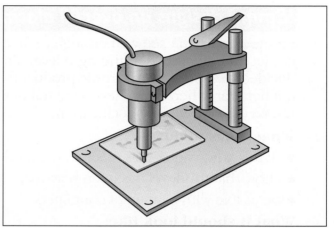

9 Insert components and solder them into place.

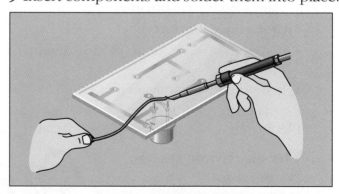

10 The completed circuit.

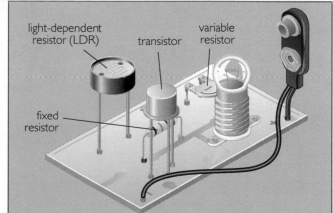

light-dependent resistor (LDR)

transistor

variable resistor

fixed resistor

Designing an electronic product

Points to consider

In designing an electronic product you need to think about:

- the electronic system – the input, processor and output;
- the product casing and style;
- the user interface.

The Sensing with Electronics Chooser Chart on page 172 will help you.

Emma designs an overfill alarm

Emma's gran can't see well enough to fill cups, kettles and saucepans to the right level. Emma decided to design an electronic product that would tell her gran when containers were full of water. Emma developed this specification:

What it has to do:

- detect when liquid has reached the level;
- show that this level has been reached;
- be usable with a range of containers.

What it should look like:

- not be easily noticed (Emma's gran didn't want it to be too obvious).

Other requirements:

- it should be easy for an elderly person to operate;
- it should be easy to keep clean.

Emma used the questions in the Sensing with Electronics Chooser Chart to work out the details.

The electronic system
For the **input**:

> What does it need to detect? .... water level.

> What sensors can I use? ... moisture sensor.

For the **processor**:

> Will the signal from the sensor need to be increased? ..... tap water... poor conductor... so, yes, a transistor driver should do it.

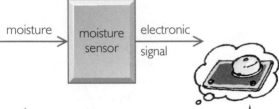

moisture → moisture sensor → electronic signal

For the **output**:

> What does it need to do? ... make a noise ... a buzzer... not too loud.

> Is it a high-current device? no, so I won't need a relay.

> Does the output need to stay on after the input has stopped? ... no, gran will stop pouring as soon as she hears the buzzer.

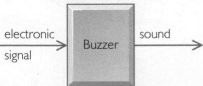

electronic signal → Buzzer → sound

Resource Task

ECRT 10

Emma drew a system diagram of the system and noted the components needed for each subsystem, and their symbols.

She turned the block diagram and circuit symbols into a circuit diagram. From this she worked out the PCB layout diagram.

| inputs | → | processor | → output |

| moisture → | moisture sensor | electronic → | transistor driver | electronic → | Buzzer | sound → |

10 kΩ variable resistor   2.2 kΩ fixed resistor

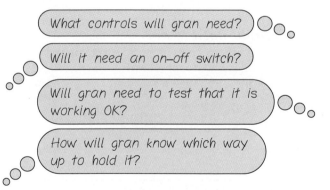

▲ *Emma's final circuit.*

Emma found some tubing that would be easy to hold. She made up several different shaped card developments that seemed stable and good to look at without being too noticeable.

The product casing and style
Emma then thought about how her gran would use the device.

The user interface
She thought through how to make it easy for gran to use.

What controls will gran need?

Will it need an on–off switch?

Will gran need to test that it is working OK?

How will gran know which way up to hold it?

By answering these questions and using the modelling strategies suggested in the Sensing with Electronics Chooser Chart she was able to design a layout that met all her gran's requirements.

Resource Task

ECRT 10

Sensing with Electronics Chooser Chart

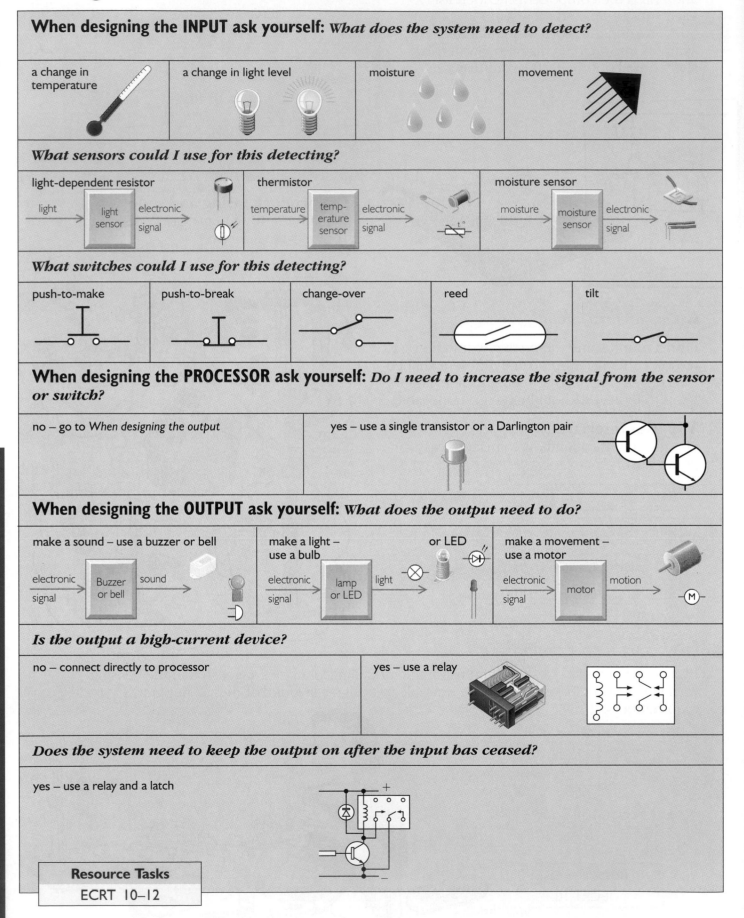

When designing the INPUT ask yourself: *What does the system need to detect?*

| a change in temperature | a change in light level | moisture | movement |

What sensors could I use for this detecting?

light-dependent resistor

light → light sensor → electronic signal

thermistor

temperature → temp-erature sensor → electronic signal

moisture sensor

moisture → moisture sensor → electronic signal

What switches could I use for this detecting?

| push-to-make | push-to-break | change-over | reed | tilt |

When designing the PROCESSOR ask yourself: *Do I need to increase the signal from the sensor or switch?*

no – go to *When designing the output*

yes – use a single transistor or a Darlington pair

When designing the OUTPUT ask yourself: *What does the output need to do?*

make a sound – use a buzzer or bell

electronic signal → Buzzer or bell → sound

make a light – use a bulb   or LED

electronic signal → lamp or LED → light

make a movement – use a motor

electronic signal → motor → motion

Is the output a high-current device?

no – connect directly to processor

yes – use a relay

Does the system need to keep the output on after the input has ceased?

yes – use a relay and a latch

Resource Tasks

ECRT 10–12

When designing the PRODUCT CASING AND STYLE ask yourself:

What overall shape and size would be suitable?	large enough to take the contents but small enough for hand-held use – try modelling for fit
What does the user like?	try using an image board
How can I get an appearance that fits in with where it will be used?	try out some ideas against the image board

When designing the USER INTERFACE ask yourself:

What switches, other controls or indicator lights will the user need?	try an imaginary user trip
How can I make the layout of the controls look easy to understand?	try modelling with a plan
How can I make it clear what each switch or indicator light is for?	try labelling with signs or symbols
How can I position switches and other controls so they are easy to operate?	try ergonomic modelling

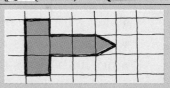

What if it doesn't work?

Ask yourself these questions:

Is the battery working and the right way round?

Check to be sure.

Is everything in the right place?

Check against your layout diagram.

Are all the components the right way round?

Check the transistors, LEDs and diodes.

Are there any loose connections?

Look carefully to check.

Are there any dry joints?

Check carefully.

Are there any cracks in the copper tracks of the PCB?

Look carefully to check.

10 Computer control

Most modern electrical machines are controlled by a complex integrated circuit called a **microprocessor**. It is programmed to work the various electrical devices in the machine.

The car wash

The microprocessor in this car wash controls:

- valves for the spray-jets;
- electric motors for the roller and wheel-scrubbers;
- hot-air blowers to dry the car;
- hydraulic cylinders to move the roller and driers into position.

Information from sensors makes sure that the machine works safely and well.

▲ *The motorist presses a push switch to start the wash sequence. Sensors are used to position the roller and wheel-scrubbers correctly for the size of car being cleaned.*

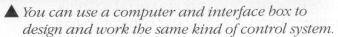

▲ *You can use a computer and interface box to design and work the same kind of control system.*

Computer control systems

The diagram below describes a computer control system.

The signals processed inside a computer are very low voltage and cannot be used directly to power electrical devices.

An interface box has its own electrical power supply. It is used to drive the output devices connected to it. Circuits inside the box allow the tiny signals from the computer to switch this power on and off.

Input signals from switches and sensors are also processed in the interface box before they pass into the computer.

The two kinds of input to a computer control system are:

- **digital input** signals which come from switches that are either on or off.
- **analogue input** signals which come from sensors that sense constantly changing values such as temperature, light or sound levels.

Analogue input signals must be converted into digital form before they can be processed by the computer.

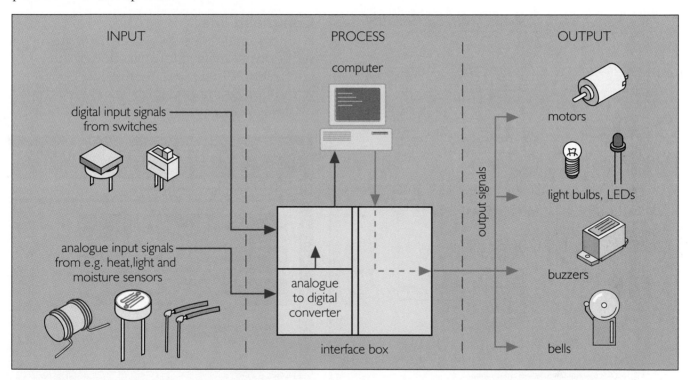

A computer is controlled by a **program**. The program tells the computer exactly what it should do and when to do it; if it goes wrong it is usually because you have written the program badly!

When you are writing a control program you need to think about:

- reading the input signals;
- controlling the output signals;
- the order in which you want things to happen.

Structures and mechanisms

A control system is more than just a control program. You will be controlling something you have designed and made. This means that you will also need to pay just as much attention to designing well-made structures (see pages 106–112) and mechanical systems (see page191–215) as to the design of the control program. You may also need to think about matters such as the user interface (see pages 41 and 237) for your control system.

Programs

Writing programs

There are various ways of writing control programs. The main ones are **flowcharts, system diagrams** and **command line**.

Flowcharts

Flowchart software allows you to draw a flowchart representing your program on the screen. When you run the program the computer highlights the steps in your program as they happen.

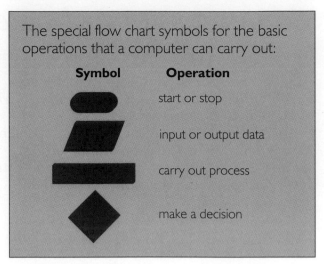

The special flow chart symbols for the basic operations that a computer can carry out:

Symbol	Operation
	start or stop
	input or output data
	carry out process
	make a decision

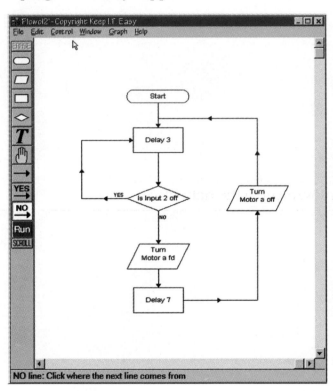

Command line

With command line software you write a sequence of instructions to control the computer. When planning this kind of written programming it is a good idea to plan out your program as a flowchart first.

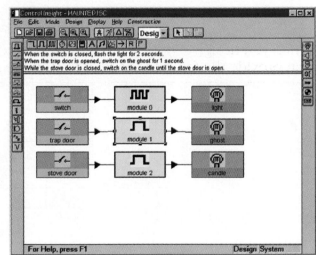

System diagrams

System diagram software allows you to draw a system diagram representing your program on the screen. When you run the program the computer reports the values of the signals as they change.

... *Programs*

A program can be a sequence of actions

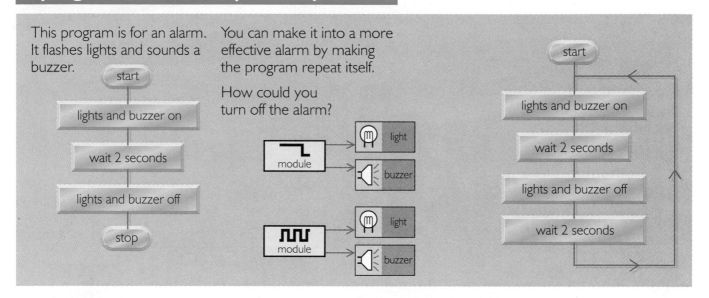

This program is for an alarm. It flashes lights and sounds a buzzer.

You can make it into a more effective alarm by making the program repeat itself.

How could you turn off the alarm?

A program can respond to information from sensors

When you design a system to control movement, it is a good idea to include sensors that provide the feedback needed to stop the movement in the right place.

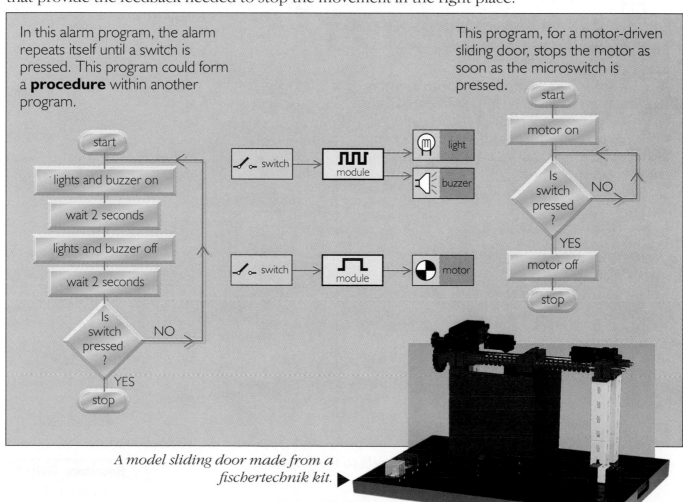

In this alarm program, the alarm repeats itself until a switch is pressed. This program could form a **procedure** within another program.

This program, for a motor-driven sliding door, stops the motor as soon as the microswitch is pressed.

A model sliding door made from a fischertechnik kit. ▶

The switches in these systems provide *digital* input. This system to control automatic blinds in an office block uses an analogue sensor to monitor the light level.

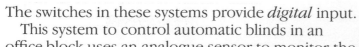

If the light is too bright, the blinds are closed by an electric motor. If it gets too dark, the blinds open.

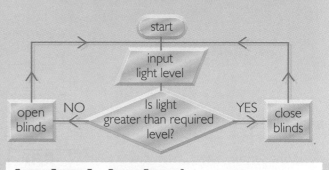

```
module
    When it is lighter than 20, switch on the motor (forwards) until it is darker than 15.
    When it is darker than 10, switch on the motor (backwards) until it is lighter than 15.
```

A program can include a number of procedures

When you design a computer control system, it is helpful to break it down into subsystems and write a separate procedure for each one.

The main program calls up each procedure as needed. This program for a drinks machine shows how this works.

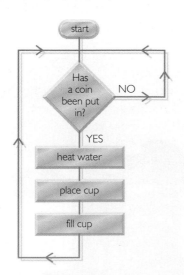

Notice how each procedure responds to feedback from an analogue or digital sensor.

Resource Tasks

CCRT 1–3

Microcontrollers

A microcontroller is a computer on a single integrated circuit (chip). Often these are called PIC (Programmable Interface Controller) chips after one particular and popular make.

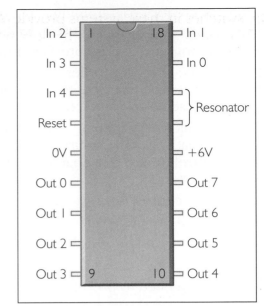

▲ *The connections to a typical microcontroller chip – this chip has five legs for input signals (In0-In4) and eight legs for output signals (Out0-Out7).*

▲ *Mictrocontroller chips. If this ruler is marked in mm, and there are 1000 components on this chip, how big is each component?*

▲ *Modern toys like this Furby use microcontrollers.*

These chips contain:
- the all-important **microprocessor** that runs programs;
- **memory** to both hold and run the programs;
- circuits to read **input signals**;
- circuits to produce **output signals**.

Almost all a circuit needs to work, apart from the microcontroller, is input and output devices. Most importantly these chips are very cheap. Some even cost less than £1. Because they are so compact and cheap it is now possible to embed computer control into the smallest devices.

Working with microcontrollers

Modern programming systems make it possible for you to use microcontrollers. The things you design and make can be given advanced behaviours without you needing to have a computer attached to them.

The procedure for programming a microcontroller typically has the following steps.

1 Develop the program. You use a desktop computer for this.

2 Test the program. Use an interface attached to appropriate input and output devices.

3 Program the microcontroller. A special programmer box connected to the computer is used for this. The microcontroller is placed in a socket in the programmer and the program is sent down the connecting lead by the computer.

4 Place the microcontroller in your control circuit. You might make your own circuit to do this. Alternatively you can use a ready-made circuit board; you place your programmed microcontroller into this board and attach input and output devices and you have a working system.

5 As with any control device you make, you will also need to think about the following:

- how you will package your control system – don't forget you need room for a battery!
- how the input and output devices will be mounted;
- what the user interface will look like;
- whether you need to produce instructions for the user.

Here are some examples of students work which use microcontrollers. Besides producing a microcontroller that works they have thought carefully about all the items listed above.

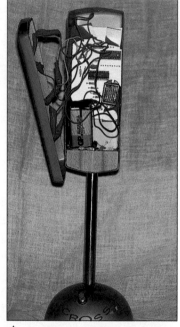

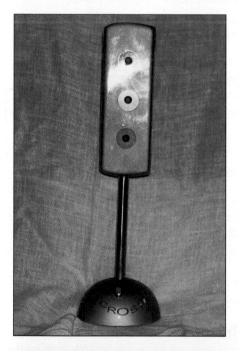

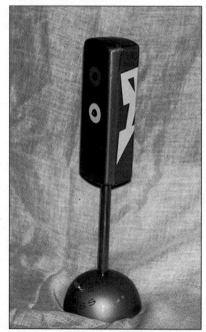

▲ **Safe Cross**, *an aid for teaching young children to cross the road. Press the button and the lights go through the standard sequence and a buzzer beeps when crossing is safe.*

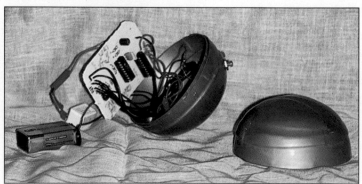

▲ **Time Bomb** *designed to help children count. A buzzer beeps between one and four times and the child presses the appropriate button.*

Real time information for bus passengers

In Birmingham a revolution in public transport has occurred.

It is called Line 33. The transport planners have developed a system that solves the following problems:

- people find the buses difficult to use;
- people don't like waiting at bus stops;
- there are too many cars in the city centre.

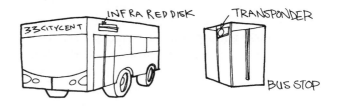

The planners redesigned the bus. It has a special floor that lowers to pavement level, making it easier to get on and off, with special places for push chairs, buggies and wheel chairs.

They designed a communication system that tells people waiting when the next bus is coming. Each bus is fitted with an infra red transmitter and each bus stop is fitted with a transponder. When a bus gets to a stop the transmitter beams a signal to the transponder which sends a radio signal to the central computer letting it know that the bus is at the stop. The central computer then sends signals to all the bus stops along the route telling them how long it will be before the bus gets there. This information is displayed on a screen at the bus stop. The visually impaired have a little key fob transmitter which causes the visual display to read the information out loud. On the bus there is a visual display showing which stop is coming up next and this information is also broadcast as sound.

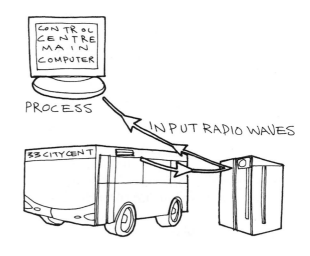

Special bus lanes are controlled by traffic lights operated by the infrared transmitters on the buses. If private cars use the bus lane they are held up by the traffic lights.

The project has cost 3.5 million pounds so far but the use of buses has increased by 25% in 18 months and people are leaving their cars at home and taking the bus instead.

Find out more about Line 33 and other examples of hi-tech design by watching the BBC Schools TV programme 'Digital Design' in the *Techno-Designers* series.

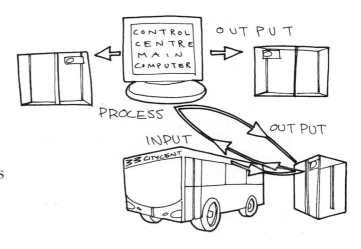

Research

Find out how popular your local bus service is.

245

11 Manufacturing

Batch production

Caterina Fadda designs stylish ceramic table ware. Recently she became interested in moving away from the traditional circle shape for a plate. She had seen a TV programme about amoeba at the Natural History Museum and explored the shape through her sketch book and using a computer to 'mutate' circular shapes.

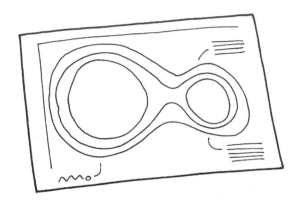

The result was an interesting design for plates. To check that it would work and that it could be manufactured, Caterina made a plaster model which she sent to the factory where they made a mould for slip casting. The slurry of clay is fed into the mould and left overnight. It dries out to the consistency of chocolate. This soft plate is removed and cleaned (fettled) before it is sprayed with glaze and fired in a kiln.

About 100 plates can be fired at one time. Once they have cooled down they are checked, packed and sent to the customer. The new design has been well received and is being used at the Hilton Hotel in London.

Research

Find out more about Caterina, how Marianne Forrest makes small batches of bronze clocks and how Anna Albright designs with wire for her company Wireworks. Watch the BBC Schools TV programme 'Batch Production' in the *Techno-Designers* series.

Mass production

Authentics is a company that mass produces items made from plastic. The managing director of the company is Hansjerg Maier Aichen. He believes that plastics have unique physical properties and aesthetic qualities. He does not design with them as substitutes for other materials but as materials in their own right. His designs for plastic objects have been influenced by traditional designs from the Far East which he says give new cultural directions. The Burmese food container shown here led to the design of a modern storage item with many applications

Most of the items designed by Authentics are produced using injection moulding. This process is explained in the sequence of diagrams below.

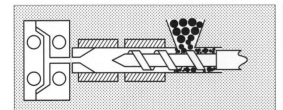

Plastic granules are fed into the hopper and transported by the feed screw

Heaters melt the plastic, which is injected into the mould under pressure

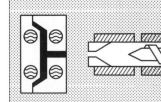

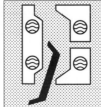

Water coolers solidify the plastic, and the mould opens to eject the product

The manufacturing capacity of an injection moulding machine is considerable. It can produce an item every 40–60 seconds. So when it is producing plastic plates, for example, it can produce 90 per hour, 2 100 per day, 46 000 per month and up to 550 000 per year.

Mass production

Matthew Hilton is a freelance designer who works for Authentic. He has wanted to design an injection moulded chair for some time. He was particularly keen to develop one that has no arm rests. He started by buying a plastic chair with arms and seeing what happened when he cut the arms off.

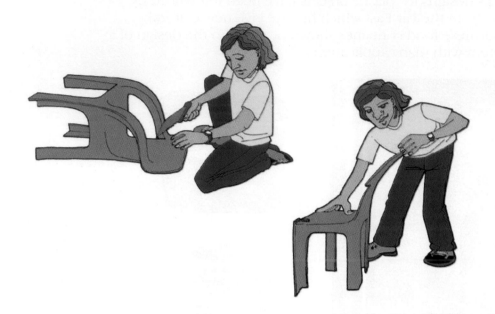

He found that the back of the chair had lost all its stiffness and would give little support. So here was the design problem. To find ways of stiffening a chair back that was not attached to arm rests.

He developed his design on the drawing board and then used CAD to produce an accurate drawing which could be e-mailed to the injection moulding factory in Stutgaart. Here the tool makers looked at the design and suggested adding 'ribs' to stiffen the back. Matthew made these changes and the injection moulding tool was made and a prototype chair produced. This chair was sent to Matthew for testing. The back was still not stiff enough but the inclusion of two more 'ribs' solved the problem.

Research

Find out more about Authentics and mass production by watching the BBC Schools TV programme 'Mass Production' in the *Techno-Designers* series.

Index